AN
OUTSIDE
CHANCE

BOOKS BY THOMAS McGUANE

The Sporting Club
1969

The Bushwhacked Piano
1971

Ninety-Two in the Shade
1973

Panama
1978

An Outside Chance
1980

Nobody's Angel
1982

Something to Be Desired
1984

To Skin a Cat
1986

Keep the Change
1989

An Outside Chance
(Classic & New Essays on Sport)
1990

AN
OUTSIDE
CHANCE

CLASSIC & NEW
ESSAYS ON SPORT

Thomas McGuane

Introduction by Geoffrey Wolff

Houghton Mifflin / Seymour Lawrence
Boston 1990

This book is for my son, Thomas, with love

For information about permission to reproduce selections from
this book, write to Permissions, Houghton Mifflin Company,
2 Park Street, Boston, Massachusetts 02108.

Library of Congress Cataloging-in-Publication Data

McGuane, Thomas.
An outside chance : classic and new essays on sport /
Thomas McGuane ; introduction by Geoffrey Wolff. — New & enl. ed.
p.   cm.
ISBN 0-395-50084-2
1. McGuane, Thomas — Biography.   2. Authors, American — 20th century
— Biography.   3. Sports stories.   I. Title.
PS3563.A31142Z472   1990   90-38562
796 — dc20   CIP

Printed in the United States of America

AGM 10 9 8 7 6 5 4 3 2 1

These essays originally appeared in *The Atlantic Monthly*, *Motor News*, *Outside*,
Quest, *Sports Illustrated*, *The Complete Fisherman's Catalog* (J. B. Lippincott), *Condé
Nast Traveler*, *Montana Spaces* (Nick Lyons Books), *Texas Monthly*, and *Harper's
Magazine*.

Contents

Introduction

GEOFFREY WOLFF

YOU WOULDN'T BE HERE if you hadn't already been hooked and landed by the sport who wrote these essays. Call it overkill, but I'd like to catch you, too, and here's what I'll use for my boss lure: Thomas McGuane's pitch-perfect phrasing. McGuane has a lambent sound as immediately distinguishable as a voiceprint — a compound of passion, wisdom modified by sly unmannered self-deprecation, curiosity, a storyteller's memory tempered by shrewd distrust of nostalgia. His music is lyrical, his essay subjects are the stuff of epics, and his narratives can make you laugh out loud.

Not enough? Let me present range and reach: *An Outside Chance* is about sports the way Joshua Slocum's *Sailing Alone Around the World* is about travel, the way Melville's "Encantadas" are about tropical islands, the way Hemingway's "Big Two-hearted River" is about camping. McGuane's essays are enactments of values, judgments on the behavior of the self alone on a river where no one is watching, which is why critics sometimes and superficially join him at the hip with Hemingway. In fact the two are strikingly distinct: Hemingway's ceremonies are received dogma, rites celebrated without latitude for clumsiness, error, the merely human deviations provoked by unforeseen discovery. Hemingway's hermetic faith excludes *them* from the company of *us*. McGuane's moral vision is generous, inclusive; he is less interested in what he has been given (how to tie a fly, release a caught fish, dress an antelope) than what he is in the act of learning (how *not* to catch fish, how *not* to rope a steer; how *not* to love motorcycling). I mean he is a student and a teacher.

You want more? The vessel of his learning carries a heavy ballast of knowing. Oh, what McGuane knows! Sometimes it pisses me off what he knows. I spend much time on the water, more than a little of that time at the caprice of internal combustion machinery. So perhaps I will be forgiven for bristling at an offhand remark you'll find in "The Longest Silence": "The engine hadn't been running right for a week, and I was afraid of getting stranded or having to sleep out on some buggy flat or, worse, being swept to Galveston on an offshore wind. I tore the engine down and found the main bearing seal shot and in need of replacement." I'm not claiming for this passage the sweetest music in this gorgeous sweet collection, but really! McGuane knows how to do things: he has made it his existential business to learn what's what, how it works, why it works that way, how it might be made to do his (and your) pleasure, which of its essential mysteries is better left unmolested.

Until "Close to the Bone" I didn't know a bonefish from a trouser trout. Now I'm cranked to get myself down to the shoal Key West flats an hour into flood tide and make myself miserable trying to calculate a collision between one alien (bonefish live in deep water but sometimes gourmet-tour in the shallows) and another (yours truly). McGuane's enthusiasms are infectious. It isn't as though he promises you a fun time: In the unlikely chance that you tempt a bonefish to your fly, even if you hook him or her, get "tight to the fish" (in McGuane's locution), and play him/her right, and net that boy (or girl), what then? "When you return to the skiff, it is high and dry; the tide has dropped from under it. You've got a six-hour wait before you can budge the skiff. You pace up and down the flat like an angry executive."

McGuane is a poet of discomfort. Not that he evangelizes the virtues of hardship, plugs the durability of a hair shirt — bad luck makes a good story is all, and a good story is plenty, a laugh is. Let me commend in this context "Angling Versus Acts of God," a most pleasurable account of a most awful fishing adventure in British Columbia. McGuane had his tackle mashed by one airline, was food-poisoned by a prawn, was flown into a wilderness by a bankrupt airline, got rained on relentlessly, was ignored by the fish he and his friend had come all that way to kill, and caught a junkfish squawfish so cold and wet it didn't care if it ate or got et. McGuane, also cold and wet, fell in romantic love with a wood-burning stove. To top things off, he had his luggage lost going home on an unbankrupt airline. I'm glad he made the trip.

McGuane has music, and McGuane can see twenty-twenty. He chooses to write of the hunt rather than the trophy. To his stories of the fierce concentration he invested in unriddling the ways of surf and turf he brings a more distanced point of view, as though — through the optic of essay — he can now see himself this way and that, sometimes ruefully, often ironically, can see now how he looked then, looking with squinty, obsessive, narrow focus. In the wider field of vision of his narratives, he now sees all around the subject under review. "Tarpon Hunting," for instance, takes its eye off the immediate prey to indulge Key West with a bravura description, as languidly loving as it is keen.

McGuane has an ongoing uneasy relationship with his past. "Molly" is a tribute to a beloved and feckless hunting dog, and disclosing her blunders he also confesses to having, as a boy, witlessly set fire to the stock of his father's treasured Winchester Model 12. "But why go over that? It's morbid to think that the past lays its dead hand on all our days." McGuane's compulsion to divulge rubs counter to his distrust of memory's value, and this friction creates a benign heat, the energy of a storyteller recollecting, assaying the value of his recollection, scrapping the junk, giving us the good goods.

You'll find the goods in "Wading the Hazards," an unsweet-ened account of an adolescent outlaw loose on a patricians' golf course. McGuane was once a caddie. Knowing now the fine acuity of his social vision, how would you like to have had him as your caddie? It makes you wonder. If only Dexter Green, Fitzgerald's snubbed caddie in "Winter Dreams," had swiped members' golf balls and sold other members the water-logged Spalding Dots he had fished from the hazards, the miserable social climber might have had a healthier contempt for decorum, not to mention a bit of fun.

Cowboy, sailor, fisherman, hunter, screenwriter, story writer, novelist, essayist, father — Thomas McGuane has squeezed life to the pips. People say you only live once; he won't, for sure, have lived less than once. In "The Heart of the Game," a meditation about hunting and killing game, he puts his hands in the buck antelope right up to his elbows. There it is, like it or not, he does not stint.

My own favorite of these essays (but don't hold me to this) is "Sakonnet," a loving and lovely account of McGuane's re-turn to a childhood haunt near here, where he used to fish and fishes again from surf-pounded rocks for striped bass and for memories. It is a funny and tender remembrance that directly confronts the drag of memory, and confronting it this honest writer yields to its pull, surrendering the comfort of irony. "Sakonnet" rises to a high pitch of wonder, letting go to magic with a reconciliation that has nothing in common with compromise.

Jamestown, Rhode Island

THE
LONGEST
SILENCE

WHAT IS EMPHATIC in angling is made so by the long silences — the unproductive periods. For the ardent fisherman, progress is toward the kinds of fishing that are never productive in the sense of the blood riots of the hunting-and-fishing periodicals. Their illusions of continuous action evoke for him, finally, a condition of utter, mortuary boredom. Such an angler will always be inclined to find the gunnysack artists of the heavy kill rather cretinoid, their stringerloads of gaping fish appalling.

No form of fishing offers such elaborate silences as fly-fishing for permit. The most successful permit fly-fisherman in the world has very few catches to describe to you. Yet there is considerable agreement that taking a permit on a fly is the extreme experience of the sport. Even the guides allow enthusiasm to shine through their cool, professional personas. I once asked one who specialized in permit if he liked fishing for them. "Yes, I do," he said reservedly, "but about the third time the customer asks, 'Is they good to eat?' I begin losing interest."

The recognition factor is low when you catch a permit. If you wake up your neighbor in the middle of the night to tell him of your success, shaking him by the lapels of his Dr. Dentons and shouting to be heard over his million-BTU air conditioner, he may well ask you what a permit is, and you will tell him it is like a pompano, and rolling over, he will tell you he cherishes pompano like he had it at Joe's Stone Crab in Miami Beach, with key lime pie afterward. If you have one mounted, you'll always be explaining what it is to people who thought you were talking about your fishing license in the first place. In the end you take the fish off the conspicuous wall and put it upstairs, where you can see it when Mom sends you to your room. It's private.

I came to it through bonefishing. The two fish share the same marine habitat, the negotiation of which in a skiff can be somewhat hazardous. It takes getting used to, to run wide open at thirty knots over a close bottom, with sponges, sea fans, crawfish traps, conchs, and starfish racing under the hull with awful clarity. The backcountry of the Florida Keys is full of hummocks, narrow, winding waterways and channels that open with complete arbitrariness to basins, and, on every side, the flats that preoccupy the fisherman. The process of learning to fish this region is one of learning the particularities of each of these flats. The narrow channel flats with crunchy staghorn-coral bottoms, the bare sand flats, and the turtle-grass flats are all of varying utility to the fisherman, and depending upon tide, these values are in a constant condition of change. The principal boat wreckers are the yellow cap-rock flats and the more mysterious coral heads. I was personally plagued by a picture of one of these enormities coming through the hull of my skiff and catching me on the point of the jaw. I had the usual coast guard safety equipment, not excluding floating cushions emblazoned FROST-FREE KEY WEST and a futile plastic whistle. I added a navy flare gun. As I learned the country, guides would run by me in their big skiffs and hundred-horse engines. I knew they never hit coral heads and had, besides, CB radios with which they might call for help. I dwelled on that and sent for radio catalogues.

One day when I was running to Content Pass on the edge of the Gulf of Mexico, I ran aground wide open in the backcountry. Unable for the moment to examine the lower unit of my engine, I got out of the boat, waiting for the tide to float it, and strolled around in four inches of water. It was an absolutely windless day. The mangrove islands stood elliptically in their perfect reflections. The birds were everywhere — terns, gulls, wintering ducks, skimmers, all the wading birds, and, crying down from their tall shafts of air, more ospreys than I had ever seen. The gloomy bonanza of the Overseas Highway with its idiot billboard montages seemed very far away.

On the western edge of that flat I saw my first permit, tailing in two feet of water. I had heard all about permit but had been convinced I'd never see one. So, looking at what was plainly a permit, I did not know what it was. That evening, talking to my friend Woody Sexton, a permit expert, I reconstructed the fish and had it identified for me. I grew retroactively excited, and Woody apprised me of some of the difficulties associated with catching one of them on a fly. A prompt, immobilizing humility came over me forthwith.

After that, over a long period of time, I saw a good number of them. Always, full of hope, I would cast. The fly was anathema to them. One look and they were gone. I cast to a few hundred. It seemed futile, all wrong, like trying to bait a tiger with watermelons. The fish would see the fly, light out or ignore it, sometimes flare at it, but never, never touch it. I went to my tying vise and made flies that looked like whatever you could name, flies that were praiseworthy from anything but a practical point of view. The permit weren't interested, and I no longer even caught bonefish. I went back to my old fly, a rather ordinary bucktail, and was relieved to be catching bonefish again. I thought I had lost what there was of my touch.

*

One Sunday morning I decided to conduct services in the skiff, taking the usual battery of rods for the permit pursuit. More and more the fish had become a simple abstraction, even though they had made one ghostly midwater appearance, poised silver as moons near my skiff, and had departed without movement, like a light going out. But I wondered if I had actually seen them. I must have. The outline and movement remained in my head — the dark fins, the pale gold of the ventral surface, and the steep, oversized scimitar tails. I dreamed about them.

This fell during the first set of April's spring tides — exaggerated tides associated with the full moon. I had haunted a long, elbow-shaped flat on the Atlantic side of the keys, and by Sunday there was a large movement of tide and reciprocal tide. A twenty-knot wind complicated my still unsophisticated poling, and I went down the upper end of the flat yawing from one edge to the other and at times raging as the boat tried to swap ends against my will. I looked around, furtively concerned with whether I could be seen by any of the professionals. At the corner of the flat I turned downwind and proceeded less than forty yards when I spotted, on the southern perimeter of the flat, a large stingray making a strenuous mud. When I looked closely it seemed there was something else swimming in the disturbance. I poled toward it for a better look. The other fish was a very large permit. The ray had evidently stirred up a crab and was trying to cover it to prevent the permit from getting it. The permit, meanwhile, was whirling around the ray, nipping its fins to make it move off the crab.

Now my problem was to set the skiff up above the fish, get rid of the push pole, drift down, and make a cast. I quietly poled upwind, wondering why I had not been spotted. I was losing my breath with excitement; the little expanse of skin beneath my sternum throbbed like a frog's throat. I acquired a fantastic lack of coordination. Turning in the wind, I beat the boat with the push pole, like a gong. I conducted what a friend has described as a Chinese fire drill. After five minutes of the direst possible clownage I got into position and could still see the permit's fins breaking the surface of the ray's mud. I laid the push pole down, picked up my fly rod, and, to my intense irritation, saw that the ray had given up and was swimming, not seeing me, straight to the skiff. The closing rate was ruinous. I couldn't get a cast off in time to do anything. About twenty feet from the boat the ray sensed my presence and veered fifteen feet off my starboard gunwale, leaving the permit swimming close to the ray but on my side. As soon as I could see the permit perfectly, it started to flush, but instead just crossed to the opposite side of the ray. Taking the only chance offered me, I cast over the ray, hoping my line would not spook it and, in turn, the permit. The fly fell with lucky, agonizing perfection, three feet in front of the permit on its exact line of travel. There was no hesitation; the fish darted forward and took — the one-in-a-thousand shot. I lifted the rod, feeling the rigid bulk of the still unalarmed fish, and set the hook. He shimmered away, my loose line jumping off the deck. And then the rod suddenly doubled and my leader broke. A loop of line had tightened itself around the handle of the reel.

I was ready for the rubber room. I had been encouraged to feel it might be five years before I hooked another. I tried to see all that was good in other kinds of fishing. I thought of various life-enhancing things I could do at home. I could turn to the ennobling volumes of world literature on my shelves. I might do some oils, slap out a gouache or two. But I could not distract myself from the mental image of my lovingly assembled fly rushing from my hands on the lip of a big permit.

I had to work out a routine that would not depend on such exceptional events for success. One technique, finally, almost guaranteed me shots at permit, and that was to stake out my skiff on the narrow channel flats that are covered with a crunchy layer of blue-green staghorn coral. Permit visit these in succession, according to tide and a hierarchy of flat values known mainly to them but intuited by certain strenuous fishermen. I liked to be on these flats at the early incoming tide — the young flood, as it is called — and fish to the middle incoming or, often, to the slack high. The key was to be able to stand for six hours and watch an acre of bottom for any sign of life at all. The body would give out in the following sequence: arches, back, hips. Various dehydration problems developed. I carried ice and drank quinine water until my ears rang. Pushups and deep knee bends on the casting deck helped. And, like anyone else who uses this method, I became an active fantasizer. The time was punctuated by the appearances of oceanic wildlife, fish and turtles that frequented the area as well as many that did not. With any luck at all the permit came, sometimes in a squadron and in a hurry, sometimes alone with their tails in the air, rooting along the hard edge of the flat. The cast would be made, the line and leader would straighten and the fly fall. On a normal day the fly only made the permit uncomfortable, and it would turn and gravely depart. On another the fly so horrified the fish that it turned tail and bolted. On very few days it sprinted at the fly, stopped a few inches short, ran in a circle when the fly was gently worked, returned and flared at it, flashed at it, saw the boat, and flushed.

On very hot days when the cumulus clouds stacked in a circle around the horizon, a silky sheen of light lay on the water, so that the vision had to be forced through until the head ached. Patience was strained from the first, and water seemed to stream from the skin. At such times I was counting on an early sighting of fish to keep my attention. And when this did not happen I succumbed to an inviting delusion. I imagined the best place to fish was somewhere very far away, and it would be necessary to run the country.

I reeled up my line and put the rod in its holder. I took the push pole out of the bottom and secured it in its chocks on the gunwale. Then I let the wind carry me off the flat. I started the engine and put it in forward, suffering exquisitely a moment more, then ran the throttle as far as it would go. The bow lifted, then lowered on plane, the stern came up, and the engine whined satisfactorily. Already the perspiration was drying, and I felt cool and slaked by the spray. Once on top, standing and steering, running wide open, I projected on my mind what was remembered of a suitable chart to get to this imaginary place where the fish were thick enough to walk on. I looked up and was reproved by the vapor trail of a navy Phantom interceptor. I ran up the channels, under the bridge, using all the cheap tricks I thought I could get away with, short-cutting flats when I thought I had enough water, looking back to see if I made a mud trail, running the banks to get around basins because the coral heads wouldn't grow along a bank, running tight to the keys in a foot and a half of water when I was trying to beat the wind, and finally shutting down on some bank or flat or along some tidal pass not unlike the one I just ran from. It was still as hot as it could be, and I still could not see. The sweat was running onto my Polaroids, and I was hungry and thinking I'd call it a day. When I got home I rather abashedly noted that I had burned a lot of fuel and hadn't made a cast.

The engine hadn't been running right for a week, and I was afraid of getting stranded or having to sleep out on some buggy flat or, worse, being swept to Galveston on an offshore wind. I tore the engine down and found the main bearing seal shot and in need of replacement. I drove to Big Pine to get parts and arrived about the time the guides, who center there, were coming in for the day. I walked to the dock, where the big skiffs with their excessive engines were nosed to the breakwater. Guides mopped decks and needled each other. Customers, happy and not, debarked with armloads of tackle, sun hats, oil, thermoses, and picnic baskets. A few of these sporty dogs were plastered. One fragile lady, owlish with sunburn, tottered from the casting deck of a guide's skiff and drew herself up on the dock. "Do you know what the whole trouble was?" she inquired of her companion, perhaps her husband, a man very much younger than herself.

"No, what?" he said. She smiled and pitied him.

"Well, *think* about it." The two put their belongings into the trunk of some kind of minicar and drove off too fast down the Overseas Highway. Four hours would put them in Miami.

It seemed to have been a good day. A number of men went up the dock with fish to be mounted. One man went by with a bonefish that might have gone ten pounds. Woody Sexton was on the dock. I wanted to ask how he had done but knew that ground rules forbid the asking of this question around the boats. It embarrasses guides who have had bad days, on the one hand, and on the other, it risks passing good fishing information promiscuously. Meanwhile, as we talked, the mopping and needling continued along the dock. The larger hostilities are reserved for the fishing grounds themselves, where various complex snubbings may be performed from the semi-anonymity of the powerful skiffs. The air can be electric with accounts of who cut off whom, who ran the bank on whom, and so on. The antagonism among the skiff guides, the off-shore guides, the pompano fishermen, the crawfishermen, the shrimpers, produces tales of shootings, of disputes settled with gaffs, of barbed wire strung in guts and channels to wreck props and drive shafts. Some of the tales are true. Woody and I made a plan to fish when he got a day off. I found my engine parts and went home.

I worked out two or three bonefish patterns for the inside bank of Loggerhead Key. The best of these was a turnoff point where the bonefish that were contouring the bank hit a small ridge and turned up onto the flat itself. By positioning myself at this turning point, I would be able to get casts off to passing fish and be able to see a good piece of the bank, downlight, until noon.

One day I went out and staked the boat during the middle-incoming water of another set of new-moon tides. I caught one bonefish early in the tide, a lively fish that went a hundred yards on his first run and doggedly resisted me for a length of time that was all out of proportion to his weight. I released him after giving him a short revival session and then just sat and looked at the water. I could see Woody fishing with a customer, working the outside of the bank for tarpon.

It was a queer day to begin with. The vital light flashed on and off around the scudding clouds, and there were slight foam lines on the water from the wind. The basin that shelved off from my bank was active with diving birds, particularly great brown pelicans, whose wings sounded like luffing sails and who ate with submerged heads while blackheaded gulls tried to rob them. The birds were drawn to the basin by a school of mullet that was making an immense mud slick hundreds of yards across. In the sun the slick glowed a quarter of a mile to the south. I didn't pay it much attention until it began by collective will or chemical sensors to move onto my bank. Inexorably, the huge disturbance progressed and flowed toward me. In the thinner water the mullet school was compressed, and the individual fish became easier targets for predators. Big oceanic barracuda were with them and began slashing and streaking through the school like bolts of lightning. Simultaneously, silver sheets of mullet, sometimes an acre in extent, burst out of the water and rained down again. In time my skiff was in the middle of it; and I could see the opaque water was inch by inch alive.

Some moments later, not far astern of me, perhaps seventy feet, a large blacktip shark swam up onto the bank and began traveling with grave sweeps of its tail through the fish, not as

yet making a move for them. Mullet and smaller fish nevertheless showered out in front of the shark as it coursed through.
Behind the shark I could see another fish flashing unclearly. I
supposed it was a jack crevalle, a pelagic fish, strong for its
size, that often follows sharks. I decided to cast. The distance
was all I could manage. I got off one of my better shots, which
nevertheless fell slightly behind target. I was surprised to see
the fish drop back to the fly, turn and elevate high in the
water, then take. It was a permit.

I set the hook sharply, and the fish started down the flat.
Remembering my last episode, I kept the loose, racing line
well away from the reel handle for the instant the fish took to
consume it. Then the fish was on the reel. I lowered the rod
tip and cinched the hook, and the fish began to accelerate,
staying on top of the flat, so that I could see its wildly extend-
ing wake. Everything was holding together: the hookup was
good, the knots were good. At 150 yards the fish stopped, and
I got back line. I kept at it and got the fish within 80 yards of
the boat. Then suddenly it made a wild, undirected run, not
permitlike at all, and I could see that the blacktip shark was
chasing it. The blacktip struck and missed the permit three or
four times, making explosions in the water that sickened me.
I released the drag, untied the boat, and started the engine.
Woody was poling toward me at the sound of my engine. His
mystified client dragged a line astern.

There was hardly enough water to move in. The prop was
half buried, and at full throttle I could not get up on plane.
The explosions continued, and I could only guess whether or
not I was still connected to the fish. I ran toward the fish, a
vast loop of line trailing, saw the shark once, and ran over
him. I threw the engine into neutral and waited to see what
had happened and tried to regain line. Once more I was tight
to the permit. Then the shark reappeared. He hit the permit
once, killed it, and ate the fish, worrying it like a dog and
bloodying the water.

Then an instant later I had the shark on my line and running. I fought him with irrational care: I now planned to gaff the blacktip and retrieve my permit piece by piece. When the inevitable cutoff came I dropped the rod in the boat and, empty-handed, wondered what I had done to deserve this.

I heard Woody's skiff and looked around. He swung about and coasted alongside. I told him it was a permit, as he had guessed from my starting up on the flat. Woody began to say something when, at that not unceremonial moment, his client broke in to say that it was hooking them that was the main thing. We stared at him until he added, "Or is it?"

Often afterward we went over the affair and talked about what might have been done differently, as we had with the first permit. One friend carries a carbine on clips under the gunwale to take care of sharks. But I felt that with a gun in the skiff during the excitement of a running fish, I would plug myself or deep-six the boat. Woody knew better than to assure me there would be other chances. Knowing that there might very well not be was one of our conversational assumptions.

One morning we went to look for tarpon. Woody had had a bad night of it. He had awakened in the darkness of his room about three in the morning and watched the shadowy figure of a huge land crab walk across his chest. Endlessly it crept to the wall and then up it. Carefully silhouetting the monster, Woody blasted it with a karate chop. At breakfast he was nursing a bruise on the side of his hand. We were, at 6:00 A.M., having grits and eggs at the Chat and Chew restaurant. A trucker who claimed to have driven from Loxahatchee in three hours flat was yelling for "oss tie." And when the girl asked if he really wanted iced tea this early in the morning he replied, "Dash rat. Oss tie." My breakfast came and I stared at it listlessly. I couldn't wake up in the heat. I was half dreaming and imagined the land crab performing some morbid cadenza on my pile of grits.

We laid out the rods in the skiff. The wind was coming out of the east, that is, over one's casting hand from the point we planned to fish, and it was blowing fairly stiff. But the light was good, and that was more important. We headed out of Big Pine, getting into the calm water along Ramrod Key. We ran in behind Pye Key, through the hole behind Little Money, and out to Southeast Point. The sun was already huge, out of hand, like Shakespeare's "glistering Phaethon." I had whitened my nose and mouth with zinc oxide, and felt, handling the mysterious rods and flies, like a shaman. I still had to rig the leader of my own rod; and as Woody jockeyed the skiff with the pole, I put my leader together. I retained enough of my trout-fishing sensibilities to continue to be intrigued by tarpon leaders with their array of arcane knots: the butt of the leader is nail knotted to the line, blood knotted to monofilament of lighter test; the shock tippet that protects the leader from the rough jaws of tarpon is tied to the leader with a combination Albright Special and Bimini Bend; the shock tippet is attached to the fly either by a perfection loop, a clinch, or a Homer Rhodes Loop; and to choose one is to make a moral choice. You are made to understand that it would not be impossible to fight about it or, at the very least, quibble darkly.

We set up on a tarpon pass point. We had sand spots around us that would help us pick out the dark shapes of traveling tarpon. And we expected tarpon on the falling water, from left to right. I got up on the bow with fifty feet of line coiled on the deck. I was barefoot so I could feel if I stepped on a loop. I made a couple of practice casts — harsh, indecorous, tarpon-style, the opposite of the otherwise appealing dry-fly caper — and scanned for fish.

The first we saw were, from my point of view, spotted from too great a distance. That is, there was a long period of time before they actually broke the circle of my casting range, during which time I could go, quite secretly but completely, to pieces. The sensation for me, in the face of these advancing forms, was as of a gradual ossification of the joints. Moviegoers will recall the early appearances of Frankenstein's monster, his ambulatory motions accompanied by great rigidity of the limbs, almost as though he could stand a good oiling. I was hard put to see how I would manage anything beyond a per-functory flapping of the rod. I once laughed at Woody's sto-ries of customers who sat down and held their feet slightly aloft, treading the air or wobbling their hands from the wrists. I giggled at the story of a Boston chiropractor who fell over on his back and barked like a seal.

"Let them come in now," Woody said.

"I want to nail one, Woody."

"You will. Let them come."

The fish, six of them, were surging toward us in a wedge. They ran from 80 to 110 pounds. "All right, the lead fish, get on him," Woody said. I managed the throw. The fly fell in front of the fish. I let them overtake it before starting my retrieve. The lead fish, big, pulled up behind the fly, trailed, and then made the shoveling, open-jawed uplift of a strike that is not forgotten. When he turned down I set the hook, and he started his run. The critical stage, that of getting rid of loose line piled around one's feet, ensued. You imagine that if you are standing on a coil, you will go to the moon when that coil must follow its predecessors out of the rod. This one went off without a hitch, and it was only my certainty that someone had done it before that kept me from deciding that we had made a big mistake.

The sudden pressure of the line and the direction of its resistance apparently confused the tarpon, and it raced in close-coupled arcs around the boat. Then, when it had seen the boat, felt the line, and isolated a single point of resistance, it cleared out at a perfectly insane rate of acceleration that made water run three feet up my line as it sliced through. The jumps — wild, greyhounding, end over end, rattling — were all crazily blurred as they happened, while I pictured my reel exploding like a racing clutch and filling me with shrapnel.

This fish, the first of six that day, broke off. So did the others, destroying various aspects of my tackle. Of the performances, it is not simple to generalize. The closest thing to a tarpon in the material world is the Steinway piano. The tarpon, of course, is a game fish that runs to extreme sizes, while the Steinway piano is merely an enormous musical instrument, largely wooden and manipulated by a series of keys. However, the tarpon when hooked and running reminds the angler of a piano sliding down a precipitous incline and while jumping makes cavities and explosions in the water not unlike a series of pianos falling from a great height. If the reader, then, can speculate in terms of pianos that herd and pursue mullet and are themselves shaped like exaggerated herrings, he will be a very long way toward seeing what kind of thing a tarpon is. Those who appreciate nature as we find her may rest in the knowledge that no amount of modification can substitute the manmade piano for the real thing — the tarpon. Where was I?

As the sun moved through the day the blind side continually changed, forcing us to adjust position until, by afternoon, we were watching to the north. Somehow, looking uplight, Woody saw four permit coming right in toward us, head-on. I cast my tarpon fly at them, out of my accustomed long-shot routine, and was surprised when one fish moved forward of the pack and followed up the fly rather aggressively. About then they all sensed the skiff and swerved to cross the bow about thirty feet out. They were down close to the bottom now, slightly spooked. I picked up, changed direction, and cast a fairly long interception. When the fly lit, well out ahead, two fish elevated from the group, sprinted forward, and the inside fish took the fly in plain view.

The certainty, the positiveness of the take in the face of an ungodly number of refusals and the long, unproductive time put in, produced immediate tension and pessimism. I waited for something to go haywire.

I hooked the fish quickly. It was only slightly startled and returned to the pack, which by this time had veered away from the shallow flat edge and swung back toward deep water. The critical time of loose line passed slowly. Woody unstaked the skiff and was poised to see which way the runs would take us. When the permit was tight to the reel I cinched him once, and he began running. The deep water kept the fish from making the long, sustained sprints permit make on the flats. This fight was a series of assured jabs at various clean angles from the skiff. We followed, alternately gaining and losing line. Then, in some way, at the end of this blurred episode, the permit was flashing beside the boat, looking nearly circular, and the only visual contradiction to his perfect poise was the intersecting line of leader seemingly inscribed from the tip of my arcing rod to the precise corner of his jaw.

Then we learned that there was no net in the boat. The fish would have to be tailed. I forgave Woody in advance for the permit's escape. Woody was kneeling in the skiff, my line disappearing over his shoulder, the permit no longer in my sight, Woody leaning deep from the gunwale. Then, unbelievably, his arm was up, the black symmetry of tail above his fist, the permit perpendicular to the earth, then horizontal on the floorboards. A pile of loose fly line was strewn in curves that wandered around the bottom of the boat to a gray-and-orange fly that was secured in the permit's mouth. I sat down numb and soaring.

I don't know what this kind of thing indicates beyond the necessary, ecstatic resignation to the moment. With the beginning over and, possibly, nothing learned, I was persuaded that once was not enough.

TWILIGHT ON THE BUFFALO PADDOCK

DAWN: a curious mixture of noises. Birds, ocean, trees soughing in a breeze off the Pacific; then, in the foreground, the steady cropping of buffaloes.

They are massing peacefully, feeding and nuzzling and ignoring the traffic. They are fat, happy, numerous beasts; and all around them are the gentle, primordial hills of Golden Gate Park, San Francisco, U.S.A. It is dawn on the buffalo paddock.

By midmorning in buffalo country things get a little more active at street level. Out of the passing string of health nuts, ordinary pedestrians, policemen, and twenty-first-century transcendental visionaries with electro-frizz hairdos that look more like spiral nebulae than anything out here in Vitalis country — from this passing string, then, a citizen occasionally detaches himself, avoids the buffalo paddock by a few yards, and enters the grounds of the Golden Gate Angling and Casting Club. The club is the successor of an earlier organization, the San Francisco Fly Casting Club, which was founded in 1894. It has been located in Golden Gate Park only since the 1930s, when its facilities were constructed by the City of San Francisco.

The grounds of the club are not so prepossessing as its seventy-six-year history would lead one to expect. The clubhouse and casting pools are on an elevation that is shaped like a small mesa. The clubhouse is a single story, dark and plain, and faces the pools that are surrounded and overhung by immense, fragrant eucalyptus trees. The clubhouse is thoroughly grown in with laurel and rhododendron and — after street-level Golden Gate — the effect is, distinctly, through-the-looking-glass.

Today, as a man rehearses the ancient motions of casting a fly on the elegant green surfaces of the practice pools, he may even hear one of the stern invocations of our century: *"Stick 'em up!"* and be relieved, perhaps even decorously, of his belongings. It wouldn't be the first time. But that would only happen in midweek. On a weekend many of his fellow members will be there. Stickup artists will go to the beach and it will be feasible to watch your backcast instead of the underbrush.

This particular Sunday has been especially well attended. The men are wandering out of the clubhouse, where you can smell bacon, eggs, and pancakes — just as you might in the cook tent of one of the imperial steelhead camps these same anglers frequent in the Northwest. They pick up fly rods and make their way out along the casting pools, false-casting as they walk and trying occasional preliminary throws before really getting down to business. At the middle pool a man is casting with a tournament rod, a real magnum smoke pole, and two or three people watch as he power-casts a 500-grain shooting head 180 feet.

Between him and the clubhouse, casting for accuracy with a conventional dry-fly rod, is a boy of thirteen. At this point he is a lifelong habitué and he tournament-casts as another city boy might fly remote-control airplanes, and he casts with uncommon elegance — a high, slow backcast, perfect timing, and a forecast that straightens with precision. He seems to overpower very slightly so that the line turns over and hangs an instant in the air to let the leader touch first. He regulates the width of the loop in his line to the inch and at will; when a head wind comes up, he tightens the loop into a perfectly formed, almost beveled, little wind cheater. It is quite beautiful.

Standing beside him, an older man supports his chin with one hand, hangs his fist in one discolored pocket of a cardigan, and looks concerned. From time to time he makes a suggestion; the boy listens, nods, and does differently. Like most who offer advice here, the older man has been a world casting champion. When he takes the rod, you see why; the slowness of the backcast approaches mannerism but the bluff is never called; the man's straightening, perfect cast never betrays gravity with a sag.

So the two of them take turns, more or less. The boy does most of the casting, and while one casts facing the pool, the other is turned at right angles to him, watching his style, the angles, loft, timing, and speed of his cast.

At this point the boy is already more accurate than the older man, and from time to time he lets his backcast drop a little so he can fire a tight bow in, and score — the technical proof of his bravura. But the older man has a way of letting the backcast carry and hang that has moment or something like it. Anyway, the boy sees what it is and when the older man goes inside for breakfast the boy will try what the older man has done — even though it crosses him up and brings the cast down around his ears. It embarrasses him. He looks around, clears the line, fires it out with an impetuous roll cast, and goes back to what he knows.

By this time there are a good many people scattered along the sides of the pools. The group is not quite heterogeneous; and though its members seem less inclined to dressing up than many of San Francisco's citizens, they are not the Silent Majority's wall of flannel, either. To be exact, sartorially, there is no shortage of really thick white socks here, sleeveless V-neck sweaters, or brown oxfords. The impression, you suppose, is vaguely upcountry.

My companion is a superb angler — widely known for it. He is not a member of the club and is inclined to bridle around tournament casters. They remind him of something more housebroken than fishing, and he doesn't like it. He thinks their equipment is too good, and of course it is, largely; and when they talk about fly lines and shooting heads, getting fussy over fractions of grains of weight, he instinctively feels they are letting the tail wag the dog. Nevertheless, the fisherman has something to be grateful for. Shooting-head lines, now standard steelhead gear, modern techniques of power casting, and, in fact, much contemporary thinking about rod design — actions and tapers — have arisen at this small, circumscribed anglers' enclave. Still, it is difficult to imagine a tournament caster who would confess to having no interest at all in fishing — though that is exactly the case with some of them. Ritualistically, they continue to refer their activities to practical streamcraft.

My companion typifies something, too, something anti-imperial in style. Frayed lines and throwaway tackle, a reel with a crude painting on the side of it, brutalized from being dropped on riverside rocks. His rod is missing guides and has been reinforced at butt and ferrule with electricians' tape that, in turn, has achieved a greenish corruption of its own. He is a powerful caster whose special effects are all toward fishing in bad wind and weather. He admits few fishermen into his angling pantheon and, without mercy, divides the duffers into "bait soakers," "yucks," and other categories of opprobrium. Good anglers are "red-hots." His solutions to the problems of deteriorating fishing habitat incline toward the clean gestures of the assassin.

I sit on one of the spectators' benches and chat with a steelhead fisherman about the Skeena drainage in British Columbia. He's been all over that country, caught summer-run fish miles inland that were still bright from salt water. The conversation lags. Another member sits on the bench. "Was anybody ever really held up here?" I ask rather warily.

"Sure was," says the man next to me, and turns to the new fellow on the end of the bench. "Who was that?"

"Guy that got stuck up?"

"Yeah, who was that?"

"There were three of them, at different times."

The man next to me turns to me. "It was this guy from Oakland."

The man at the end of the bench isn't interested. The fellow next to me asks him, "Didn't he get pistol-whipped or something?"

"Who's this?"

"The guy from Oakland."

"I don't know. I don't know. I don't know."

The man next to me turns to me again. "I'm not positive," he says with exaggerated care, "but the dry-fly man from Oakland got pistol-whipped unless I've got my signals real crossed."

"Did they take his rod?" I ask somewhat aimlessly.

"No."

"His reel or anything?"

"No," he says, "just glommed the wallet and cleared out. It was pretty crummy."

I excuse myself. I have a new Winston tarpon and billfish fly rod I am anxious to try and I go down to the last pool, where a handful of members are casting. I am a little sleepy from the gigantic breakfast they've given me. The club grounds are on an elevation that drops off abruptly behind this last pool. There is a path going down through the heavy tree roots to a little space that looks like the banks of a streambed. As I strip line from my reel, I notice that there are three people undulating beneath the trees down there. One is a girl wearing Levi's and an Esther Williams total sun-block hat with mirrors hanging from its edges on strings. One of the men seems to be a Lapp; the other is dressed as Buffalo Bill and he is more frenzied than his companions. Occasionally he adjusts his enormous cowboy hat with one hand that moves rather cautiously into the uproar, somehow finding the hat as it goes by on a weird parabolic course of its own. I wonder if he has seen the buffalo paddock.

Presently a girl in ballet costume leads an attractive pony into the clearing, followed by another young man with a light meter and a viewing lens hanging around his neck and an enormous Bolex movie camera. He walks right past the girl and heads for us. I can see the huge coated surface of his telephoto lens, blue even at this distance, the shoulder stock of his camera, and the knurled turrets that seem to be all over it. His approach becomes imposing. He looks put out.

"We're trying to make a movie," he says.

None of us knows what to reply.

"The thing is, we're trying to make a movie."

The man next to me inquires, "Would you like us to get out of the way?"

"That's right. I want you to get out of the way."

All of the casters get out of the way. The director is startled. "This will take a few minutes," he says apologetically, wanting us to spot that smile of his now.

At the end of the pool is The Pit. You can climb down into it and it puts you at chest level to the water. It is a very realistic approximation of the actual situation when you are fishing, and any fancy ideas you might develop about your casting when you are on the platforms can be quickly weeded out here. My new rod is very powerful and after a couple of hundred casts the epidermis of my thumb slips and a watery blister forms.

I return to the bench. One of the club officials is sitting there. I decide to find out if the Golden Gate outfit is merely exclusive. "It's funny," I say disingenuously, "with as many hippies as this city has, that there aren't any in the club. How's that?"

"They don't ask to join."

Inside the clubhouse, I chat with the membership. They're

talking about casting tournaments and fishing — fishing generally and the vanishing fishing of California in particular. They know the problems. These are anglers in an epoch when an American river can be a fire hazard. The older men remember the California fishery when it was the best of them all, the most labyrinthine, the most beautiful. A great river system initiating in the purling high-country streams, the whole thing substantiated by an enormous stable watershed. Now the long, feathery river systems are stubs.

Many of the men standing here today used to haunt the High Sierra and Cascade ranges, overcoming altitude headaches to catch golden trout in the ultraviolet zone. Probably most of them have been primarily steelhead fishermen, though some fish for stripers in San Francisco Bay.

In view of the fact that the movement of people to California in the last few decades may be the biggest population shift in the history of the world, it is amazing the fishery held up so long. But in the last ten years it has gone off fast. Ironically, it is the greatness of the fishing lost that probably accounts for the distinction of the Golden Gate Club — it has bred a school of casters who are without any doubt the finest there has ever been.

Fishing for sport is itself an act of racial memory, and in places like the Golden Gate Club it moves toward the purer symbolism of tournaments. The old river-spawned fish have been replaced by pellet-fed and planted simulacra of themselves. Now even the latter seem to be vanishing in favor of plastic target rings and lines depicting increments of distance. It's very cerebral.

There has begun to be a feeling among the membership that, like music without the dance, casting without fishing lacks a certain something. And so they are fanatically concerned with the dubious California Water Plan and the rodent ethics and activities of the Army Corps of Engineers. The men sit around a table in the lodge and break out a bottle or two.

They seem to be talking about some secret society, and when I listen in I discover they mean those who have bought fishing licenses in the state of California. The men propose to rouse this sleeping giant of two million individuals to keep their ocean rivers from being converted into outdoor water-ski pavilions. But an air of anachronism hovers over them. The Now Generation seems to substantiate the claims of the high-dam builders. It appears to be true that people really would rather go around and around and around behind those Holman-Moody high-torque ski boats with that old drag-strip mushroom-can exhaust whine coming out of tuned headers and the intake whoosh of double four-barrel Rochester carburetors. But maybe some of them will see, way down beneath the polyester gel-coated surfaces of their triple-laminated controlled-catalyst slalom skis, the drowned forests of California, and the long, stony stripes of old riverbeds.

The Now Generation won't be dropping in today at the Golden Gate Club. Handmade split-cane rods and tapered lines seem a trifle dull. The Eel, the Trinity, the Russian, the Klamath, begin to seem, in the conversation of these men, rivers of the mind. The ecology purists imagine the anglers as ghouls who want to hurt the little fish with sharp hooks hidden in chicken feathers. The versions overlap in new permutations of absurdity. In the park I talk with an incipient futurist who wants to know what difference it makes if the fish are lost since we can already synthesize food anyway, and I think of the high-protein gruel rock climbers carry in plastic tubes as our cuisine of tomorrow.

"Well," I tell the futurist, "I don't know what to say!"

The members begin to drift out of the lodge and head for the parking lot.

It's sundown in buffalo country.

If you are casting at the far pool you are inclined to switch your eye from time to time toward the underbrush. Did someone move in there?

Why go into it. This is too agreeable. I put on a sweater in the evening and watch the diehards. The pools have gone silver. The emptiness around the few members who remain seems to make their casting more singular, more eloquent.

The whole place is surrounded by trees. Nobody knows we're in here. I pick up my rod and cast.

MOTOCROSS

THE FASTEST WAY to go from point to point on the face of the earth, assuming that you do not prepare the ground in front of you but take it rough and unimproved, is on a motorcycle. The right bike in the right hands can travel full tilt in bumps, slides, and vaults over ground that would gunnysack Land Rovers and Power Wagons. In the hands of the cyclists who dominate motocross racing, the progress is made with a power and alacrity that make your hair stand on end.

Motocross, almost unknown in this country until recently but gaining familiarity very rapidly, is easily one of the more popular sports in Europe. It is, to attempt a definition, a kind of motorcycle racing that is done on courses that epitomize the rough terrain of enduro or desert racing. The courses are all different; those of Russia are unlike those of Spain, say, or California; and the courses of some regions have notorious problems — the deep sand of Belgium, for instance — that sometimes allow local heroes to upset the established international stars.

At the moment, the Scandinavians dominate the racing; and no one knows why. You could almost narrow it to Laplanders; and that is really where no one knows why: there is scarcely a proliferation of racing machinery as you approach the Arctic Circle.

Motocross is very properly considered a sport. It requires strength, the balance of a slack-wire walker, incredible coordination, and endurance. It requires a lot of training. The paunches and bubble butts of other motor sports are not seen here. A contending motocrosser can expect to play out sooner than a fighter or football player. There is no retirement plan.

But in Europe motocross offers access to daydreams of folk heroism, much as baseball does here. The great Swedish champions, Torsten Hallman and Bengt Aberg, had at one time both entertained dreams of being soccer stars, a parallel route off the farm. Hallman, whose reputation emboldened him to an autobiography, recounts a career that is both picaresque and yet utterly integral to the wishful daydreams of innumerable young Europeans. When you hear of Hallman and a companion driving down from Sweden towing a trailer that carries their racing motorcycles, crossing into Poland and Russia and Czechoslovakia to hit any race going, bringing back trophies or wrecked motorcycles or nothing, you cannot avoid thinking of knights errant. Nor when you see Hallman or Aberg or Christer Hammargren or Ake Jonsson or any one of the northern superriders can you quite think you are watching yet another West Coast internal-combustion lunacy.

It was new to me. I have since made a rather selective picture of motocross in my mind; in effect, a reconstruction whose components are largely drawn from the Inter-Am events at Morgan Hill, California, and at Saddleback Park, near Orange, California. Inter-Am is a sanctioning body, one of the groups fighting over American motocross as it makes its start here. The entrepreneurs are in on it, too; and, in general, the money boys are atwitter.

In the crowd there is something ghoulish. The day is gone, after all, when you could watch a hanging; and there is one part of you that is a spectator at the event because something might happen.

So there is that. There is also a rather comfortable sense of its being merely a sporting crowd; you might bet on the outcome; there are certain expectations; there are those who could admire the good riding. There are families, friends of racers, couples, hippies, kids who have rigged a balloon on the Schwinn to make it roar. Everywhere, it would seem, are the archetypal California females in bathtub-fitted button-up Levi's, Indian moccasins, and loose peasant blouses.

Another ubiquitous California woman is there — a rather unappetizing item in a pantsuit, weirdly dyed as though the material had been on the scene when Krakatoa let go, and possibly silver slippers, owl glasses, and any number of fashion accouterments that could have made Orwell's vision of an un-inhabitable future so much more convincing. The first of these women that I saw, cross my heart, shot through the crowd on a three-wheeled ATV (all-terrain vehicle), spangled Capezios working the aircraft pedals with a certain élan you couldn't ignore, braked up shy of a refreshment stand, and ordered a Diet Pepsi that she consumed, at speed, one arm authoritatively steering the buggy among the legs of the other spectators.

Another I saw wore a jump suit identical to her husband's, both advertising an oil additive called STP in huge letters. Still another wheeled a pair of infants in matching "Sock it to me!" playsuits. Virtually all the rest of the crowd were just regular people — but who wants to talk about just regular people? The hubby of the mommy of the "Sock it to me!" twins caught up with his family and asked the little woman, "What's happening?"

She replied, "Me and the kids is gonna boogie over to the refreshments." I meant to make my way through these . . . *fans* and head for the pits. But on the way I bumped into the lady of the ATV. A man standing over her kept looking down at the machine and saying, "Fyantyastic!"

To which she replied, "Where this really garners kudos is on dunes."

As I say, it was mostly a regular crowd — but who wants to talk about that?

Some of the junior classes had already been run off. The magic of the sport had thus far eluded me. Watching so many riders, I had lost my perspective on speed, and the sight of muddy, grimacing people evidently chained to bits of rushing, smoking, screaming machinery was less exalting than it could have been. But the 500 International class was coming, and I fully understood that this would be quite different. The very greatest riders living would be entered.

During the junior classes I was dogged by a commentator who wanted to narrate the race for me. This consisted chiefly in relating every upset or mishap we saw to what he called "a basic law of physics." Later his disquisition rose to the philosophical: "I mean, what are these guys doing, getting their jollies, or what?" One despairing rider seemed to have blown up his engine in front of us. "He lunched it," noted my commentator. At a start earlier in which there had been a pile-up, he remarked, "Upwards of three unfortunates center-punched at the first bend."

A long, strolling parade wandered among the pit crews in the universal carnival procedure of walking the midway, eating, and looking. Buying a strange, vulcanized hot dog and a wet paper cylinder of Coca-Cola, I joined the throng.

At one end of the pits a member of a Swedish racing team wearing bib-front tool jeans and an orange cap, was lecturing riders about to compete in one of the small-displacemen classes, the "yoonier" division, he called them. These classe are by no means safe and are often contested by green ride with little more than the motorcycle and the price of admi sion. Therefore, this experienced Swede offered advice d signed to keep them from the kind of vivid wipeouts availab to those who race motorcycles.

Some of the riders were already running practice laps, and loops of hornet noise rose and fell among the glens. From time to time an angrier pitch would rise from a bike as it left the ground in a jump. Then, often as not, the silence of the eliminated contestant.

Because I was anxious not to blunt my perceptions, I waited for the big-bore racing, the 500 International. I wanted that shock to fall upon relatively innocent eyes.

There was a different sensation in the pits altogether. To be sure, solemnity was quite nonexistent here as well. But the work was getting done: racing machinery rolled down out of vans as though the vans were giving birth to bright motorcycles, gently received by men in smocks.

With the International to be run soon, it would have been a mistake not to notice the tension. Earlier, the riders had walked the course, looking for tracks that only they could see, looking for the fall lines on the steep drops and those particularly bad spots on the course where a special ability would let one pass another rider who was trying to maintain control. To a great extent the machinery is all fairly matched, so it is hard to pick up advantages on the parts, or "components," of the track where everyone can ride flat out. But if, for instance, there is a place where a sharp crown of hill makes most riders slow down to keep control going over the face, a certain number of hot shoes will pass there by hitting the crown full tilt, going by the other riders in midair, and maybe only touching with the rear wheel sixty or seventy feet down the face of the hill, and not till then easing the front wheel down for stability. It seems unwarranted to use the word "stability" in any connection here, but the fine riders bring to the most elaborate forms of violence a kind of order.

Balance. In the pits a good American rider was climbing around on his motorcycle. Its kickstand was up. In other words, if he got off the bike and let it go, it would fall over, just as a bicycle would. But here he was, the bike at rest, climbing over the front fender and onto the gas tank, standing on the seat with one or two fingers resting on a handlebar. A handful of people watched in awe. A few yards away, two team riders from Sweden watched quietly; they sat on their machines, their hands in their laps. I noticed that nothing held their bikes up either. If you would like to test the difficulty of this, go out for a ride on your bicycle, come gradually to a stop, and when the bicycle has reached a full stop, don't get off and don't put a foot down for support; just sit there until Walter Cronkite arrives.

By now some of the riders were off alone, "concentrating themselves," as one described it. And every few minutes another of the big bikes would crank up and fill the air with its Sten-gun noise, and shut off. Here and there a rider would be putting on the padded pants or the high racing boots or a jersey with a number or emblem: the British flag, the peace symbol, a portrait of Beethoven. A few riders fastened to the crowns of their helmets silk scarves that would stream behind them as they raced. There was already pressure here sufficient to change the minds of those who might have heretofore thought they'd go in for motocross. It was horribly tense.

The adrenaline addicts were getting ready to ride or getting ready to watch: symbiosis. And yet, talking to riders, you quickly saw that a lot of Secret Lives were being led. One was accustomed to meeting a doctor or a lawyer or a college professor wheeling a competition motorcycle down out of a truck. Not that this is the norm. Typically, a motocrosser in this country is a young man with a near-mystical interest in rapid machinery. It is a duelist's game.

Some of the young American riders who were concentrating themselves preferred to concentrate themselves with one of those troubling little California girls at their side. The girls appeared to be concentrating themselves as well, staring out quite blank from between parallel lengths of perfect hair that they had straightened on the ironing board at home. But very soon now one must go fire up the bike and do it. One must put Sherri or Staci to the side and race.

The two-stroke crackle added voice after voice as the riders prepared. There was a general ripple of hard, harsh noise, and every moment or so another motorcycle appeared and jogged down the muddy track between the rows of vans. Some last bit of preparation, the fastening of a chin strap, the pulling down of goggles, was saved for the starting line; but now there were more and more bikes headed that way, riders threading their way through the spectators with friends walking alongside, taking to the riders, who were thinking more than answering.

High on an infield hill a cluster of loudspeakers began talking with mounting excitement of the 500 International, now about to be run off. And the riders streamed from the pits and down along a small muddy creek to the terrifying noise that was the starting area. The spectators, the gawkers, began to desert the pits, and I was hanging back just a little longer watching the mechanics throw tools into the backs of trucks and then themselves start toward the course. Even on the faces of the factory team mechanics some apprehension showed.

Ready to run. This was the varsity, the 500 International. The starting line, funneling maybe fifty riders toward a maniacal bottleneck, was still beyond my vision. I could see the blue pall rising from the fifty or so screaming engines, rising, rising with the shriek, the more than shriek, the downright millennial thunder of high-tune motocross bikes, the prepotent Swedish Husqvarnas, the Czechoslovakian CZs, the German Maicos, the Suzukis among the innumerable Japanese bikes, and the British BSAs. I ran out from among the trucks in the pit with their declarations and marques emblazoned in canted, speed-

ing letters, ran with pit mechanics to the start, got enough
elevation to look down into the little California glen among
newly greening wet hills that gently heaved up a pretty burden
of oak and manzanita. There before me a wandering white
string of egglike racing helmets on determined forward-lean-
ing heads, knobby racing tires thrust out under short, utilitar-
ian fenders, myriad riders in jerseys of every Aquarian color,
Swedish leather pants, the smell of bean oil from the two-
stroke engines, the blue pall beginning to rise against the hills,
and the more than shriek now coming away from any hint of
the harmonic as the starting flag is raised slowly and all the
riders put their weight forward over the handlebars and every
engine is free-revving in something aurally so close to the
utterly berserk that you feel shock waves of sound against your
chest.

And that little bit of white cloth on a stick comes down; and
the string of eggshell helmets wavers and bulges at the center
and breaks up; and uncountable fountains of dirt rooster-tail
behind a peaking string of motorcycles wheel-standing and
fishtailing down toward the God-awful funnel where suddenly
they are packed, a rider is down, cowering perilously next to
his wiped-out motorcycle, then in an instant miraculously
alone in the mud as the race has utterly vanished in a stream
of still-mounted riders posting and leaping over the first hill.
And gone.

Next to you, normal human voices are audible; the cloud of
engine smoke hangs disembodied, by itself. Then the noise,
diminished, rushes back, and you look across a rolling infield
to see, above the greenery, the brilliant jerseys, the vibrating
torsos. And again: gone.

Still farther past where you have just seen this string of
racers, and associated them with the ears' urgent messages,
you see a band of brown rising what seems vertically against a
broad hill face, like a curtain — broad green with a plain,
vertical brown band. Then, instantly, there are riders on this,

too; and it is an assault with at least two riders unable to control acceleration enough to keep from backflipping very nearly in the course of the oncoming blitzkrieg. But no one is hit, and the downed riders coast their bikes toward the bottom to start them, then swirl around and back into the cyclone. And once more: gone.

These pack perspectives don't last very long. There are some places where the whole field rushes under your very feet in a deep, troughlike part of the course, places where what is wrought and bucolic in the landscape becomes, by the magic of the twentieth century, a hellhole. For the short while that there is still this formation, it is quite safe to cross the track if you know that the pack is someplace else; but gradually things break up; the riders string out and you are never sure when one of the iron monsters will leap into some optical eminence and be gone, the jersey a brilliant rectangle, shrinking and vanishing.

Once the pack has strung out, you may do one of two sensible things: try to figure out who is leading or walk around the course looking for particular loci where something you want to see done on a motorcycle actually is done every few seconds. A sophisticated minority carrying walking sticks that open into seats and very possibly even wearing an Aquascutum and an A&F crushable rain hat and around the neck a pair of Leitz Trinovids — a sophisticated minority, I say, will have posted themselves at some discriminating spot where thousands of cubic centimeters of outlandish motorcycle engine displacement and potency will leap and fly as though to their command.

My own favorite was a hill so steep that ten feet behind its crown only an unmarked expanse of California sky was available as a view. You would not go down this hill on your Flexible Flyer with any less conviction of doom than you would have going over Niagara Falls in a herring barrel. And yet the best motocrossers were gassing it as they went down again, lifting the front wheel with acceleration. Everyone had a favorite spot where he thought he was watching the utter ragged edge; this was mine.

It seemed to me that, with the best riders, I was seeing something close to a dream view of man and vehicle. No one watching one of the great Swedish riders come crossed up off the crown of a hill under maximum power and nearly pirouetting in the air to change the bike's alignment so that it would track when it landed could disagree. My own sporting proclivities run more to the contemplative; but to be blind to these racers' feats was to miss something implicit in all of our routine transportation which was apotheosized in such hands.

Not that you have such reflective instincts while you are watching. Mainly you are astounded. The bikes and bright jerseys come in on luminous waves of sound, rushing at you and past, down over hills, pitching and posting over gullies that deepen toward impossibility with the accretion of laps. Riders drop out, exhaust themselves, and make mistakes. Riders jump the bikes and come down on resistant arms and legs to speed away standing on the pegs. Now the attrition of the race begins to show what it has taken out of them: when they jump, the shock of the landing shows all through them, their chests almost striking the handlebars as they come down. But a minority never tire, never seem to; a few sprint through the wearying pack with almost perverse loft and energy; and among these riders are those who will win and place.

All of the racers are right out where you can see them, upon the machines like horsemen; and not merely the impersonal helmets the auto racing fan sees as the monocoque Formula Ones flash past.

The first heat, or "moto," was over with. Visually, aurally, and emotionally exhausted, I wandered back through the pits, among the trucks of the racing teams, the precisely uniformed Japanese mechanics with their exact haircuts, the Americans looking like everything from General Pershing to Saint Francis of Assisi on an off day, and the Scandinavians: bearded woodlanders. The racers were streaming in between the trucks, coasting or chugging in on first gear, weary two-stroke engines crackling like automatic rifles, faces utterly obscured by mud save where goggles left a raccoon white. The bikes poured around me and I kept on, past the Husqvarna pit, where a pretty Czech girl in bell-bottoms offered me a program, past tents, awning pavilions, and chemical field toilets, to the first grass I hit and where I wouldn't for the moment smell or hear an engine. And there was a barn and a big, well-made corral and half a dozen horses nosing into a fresh offering of hay.

I walked on around the barn and up a slope behind it and sat on the heavy exposed roots of an oak that was leaning up to keep itself perpendicular to the cast of hillside. Between me and the barn were two long watering troughs, and as I watched, racers wandered over to them and rinsed their crash helmets. It was a rainy day on the mid-Pacific coast of North America. I was watching a few racers of totally unspecifiable geographic origin dressed in fantasy colors wash crash helmets in stock-watering troughs. Behind them stood an old, powerfully shaped, low-slung California barn. To the right of it I looked upon a cluster of horses, dark and shiny on top where they had been rained on. The barn was big enough that I could not from my position see the racing pits, though I could hear the crackle of combustion, amplified by the expansion-chamber exhaust systems; but an elevation of the eyes showed, for a full circle, lift after lift of new green hills, of mantling oak, of filamentous and gentle fog in troughs and passes.

ME
AND MY BIKE
AND WHY

As with many who buy a motorcycle, there had been for me the problem of getting over the rather harrowing insurance statistics as to just what it is that is liable to happen to you. Two years in California — a familiar prelude to acts of excess — had made of me an active motorcycle spectator. I watched and identified, finally resorting to bikers' magazines; and evolved a series of foundationless prejudices.

Following the war, motorcycling left a peculiar image in the national consciousness: porcine individuals wearing a sort of yachting cap with a white vinyl bill, the decorative braid pulled up over the hat, their motorcycles plated monsters, white rubber mud flaps studded with ruby stars hung from both fenders. Where are those machines now? Surely Andy Warhol didn't buy them all. Not every one of them is a decorative planter in a Michigan truck garden. But wherever they are, it is certain that the ghosts of cretinism collect close around the strenuously baroque plumbing of those inefficient engines and speak to us of an America that has gone.

It was easy for me initially to deplore the big road bikes, the motorcycles of the police and Hell's Angels. But finally even these "hogs" and show bikes had their appeal, and sometimes I had dark fantasies of myself on El Camino Real, hands hung overhead from the big chopper bars, feet in front on weirdly automotive pedals, making all the decent people say: "There goes one."

I did it myself. Heading into San Francisco with my wife, our Land Rover blaring wide open at fifty-two miles per, holding up a quarter mile of good people behind us, people who didn't see why anybody needed four-wheel drive on the Bayshore Freeway, we ourselves would from time to time see a lonesome Angel or Coffin Cheater or Satan's Slave or Gypsy Joker on his big chopper and say (either my wife or myself, together sometimes): "There goes one."

Anyway, it was somewhere along in here that I saw I was not that type, and began to think of sporting machines, even racing machines, big ones, because I had no interest in starting small and working my way up as I had been urged to do. I remember that I told the writer Wallace Stegner what I intended, and he asked, "Why do you people do this when you come to California?"

"It's like skiing," I said, purely on speculation.

"Oh, yeah? What about the noise?"

But no one could stop me.

There was the dire question of money that ruled out many I saw. The English-built Triumph Metisse road racer was out of the question, for example. Some of the classics I found and admired — Ariel Square Fours, Vincent Black Shadows, BSA Gold Stars, Velocette Venoms or Phantom Clubmen, Norton Manxes — had to be eliminated on grounds of cost or outlandish maintenance problems.

Some of the stranger Japanese machinery, two-cycle, rotary-valved engines, I dismissed because they sounded funny. The Kawasaki Samurai actually seemed refined, but I refused to consider it. I had a corrupt Western ideal of a bike's exhaust rap, and the tuned megaphone exhausts of the Japanese motorcycles sounded like something out of the next century, weird loon cries of Oriental speed tuning.

*

There is a blurred moment in my head, a scenario of compulsion. I am in a motorcycle shop that is going out of business. I am writing a check that challenges the contents of my bank account. I am given ownership papers substantiated by the State of California, a crash helmet, and five gallons of fuel. Some minutes later I am standing beside my new motorcycle, sick all over. The man who sold it to me stares palely through the Thermopane window covered with the decals of the noble marques of "performance." He wonders why I have not moved.

I have not moved because I do not know what to do. I wish to advance upon the machine with authority but cannot. He would not believe I could have bought a motorcycle of this power without knowing so much as how to start its engine. Presently he loses interest.

Unwatched, I can really examine the bike. Since I have no notion of how to operate it, it is purely an *objet*. I think of a friend with a road racer on a simple mahogany block in front of his fireplace, except that he rides his very well.

The bike was rather beautiful. I suppose it still is. The designation, which now seems too cryptic for my taste, was "Matchless 500," and it was the motorcycle I believed I had thought up myself. It is a trifle hard to describe the thing to the uninitiated, but, briefly, it had a 500-cc., one-cylinder engine — a "big single" in the patois of bike freaks — and an eloquently simple maroon teardrop-shaped tank that is as much the identifying mark on a Matchless, often otherwise unrecognizable through modification, as the chevron of a redwing blackbird. The front wheel, delicate as a bicycle's, carried a Dunlop K70 tire (said to "cling") and had no fender; a single cable led to the pale machined brake drum. Over the knobby rear wheel curved an extremely brief magnesium fender with, instead of the lush buddy-seat of the fat motorcycles, a minute pillion of leather. The impression was of performance and of complete disregard for comfort. The equivalent in automobiles would be, perhaps, the Morgan, in sailboats the Finn.

I saw all these things at once (remember the magazines I had been reading, the Floyd Clymer books I had checked out of the library), and in that sense my apprehension of the motorcycle was perfectly literary. I still didn't know how to start it.

I didn't want to experiment on El Camino Real, and moreover, it had begun to rain heavily. I had made up my mind to wheel it home, and there to peruse the operation manual, whose infuriating British locutions the Land Rover manual had prepared me for.

I was surprised at the sheer inertial weight of the thing; it leaned toward me and pressed against my hip insistently all the way to the house. I was disturbed that a machine whose place in history seemed so familiar should look utterly foreign at close range. The fact that the last number on the speedometer was 140 seemed irresponsible.

It was dark by the time I got home. I wheeled it through the back gate and down the sidewalk through a yard turned largely to mud. About halfway to the kitchen door, I somehow got the thing tilted away from myself, and it slowly but quite determinedly toppled over in the mud, with me, gnashing, on top of it.

My wife came to the door and peered into the darkness. "Tom?" I refused to vouchsafe an answer. I lay there in the mud, no longer struggling, as the spring rains of the San Francisco peninsula singled me out for special treatment. I was already composing the ad in the *Chronicle* that motorcycle people dream of finding: "Big savings on Matchless 500. Never started by present owner. A real cream puff." My wife threw on the porch light and perceived my discomfiture.

The contretemps had the effect of quickly getting us over the surprise that I had bought the motorcycle, questions of authorization, and so on. I headed for the showers. Scraped and muddy, I had excited a certain amount of pity. "I'll be all right."

No one told me to retard the spark. True enough, it was in the manual, but I had been unable to read that attentively. It had no plot, no characters. So my punishment was this: when I jumped on the kick starter, it backfired and more or less threw me off the bike. I was limping all through the first week from vicious blowbacks. I later learned it was a classic way to get a spiral fracture. I tried jumping lightly on the kick starter and, unfairly, it would blast back as viciously as with a sharp kick. Eventually it started, and sitting on it, I felt the torque tilt the bike under me. I was afraid to take my hands off the handlebars. My wife lowered the helmet onto my head; I compared it to the barber's basin Don Quixote had worn into battle, the Helmet of Mambrino.

I slipped my toe up under the gearshift lever, lifted it into first, released the clutch, and magically glided away and made all my shifts through fourth, at which time I was on Sand Hill Road and going fifty, my shirt in a soft air bubble at my back, my Levi's wrapped tight to my shins, my knuckles whitening under the giddy surge of pure undetained motion as I climbed gently into the foothills toward Los Altos. The road got more and more winding as I ascended, briskly but conservatively. Nothing in the air was lost on me as I passed through zones of smell and temperature as palpable transitions, running through sudden warm spots on the road where a single redwood a hundred feet away had fallen and let in a shaft of sunlight. The road seemed tremendously spacious. The sound was behind me, so that when I came spiraling down out of the mountains and saw some farm boy had walked out to the side of the road to watch me go by, I realized he had heard me coming for a long time. And I wondered a little about the racket.

These rides became habitual and presumably more competent. I often rode up past La Honda for a view of the sea at the far edge of a declining cascade of manzanita-covered hills, empty and foggy. The smell of ocean was so perfectly evocative in a landscape divided among ranches and truck gardens whose pumpkins in the foggy air seemed to have an uncanny brilliance. A Japanese nursery stood along the road in clouds of tended vines on silver redwood lattice. I went past it to the sea and before riding home took a long walk on the ribbed, immense beach.

A fascinating aspect of the pursuit, not in the least bucolic, was the bike shop where one went for mechanical service, and which was a meeting place for the bike people, whose machines were poised out front in carefully conceived rest positions. At first, of course, no one would talk to me, but my motorcycle ideas were theirs; I was not riding one of the silly mechanisms that purred down the highways in a parody of the equipment these people lived for.

One day an admired racing mechanic — "a good wrench" — came out front and gave my admittedly well-cared-for Matchless the once-over. He announced that it was "very sanitary." I was relieved. The fear, of course, is that he will tell you, "The bike is wrong."

"Thank you," I said modestly. He professed himself an admirer of the "Matchbox," saying it was "fairly rapid" and had enough torque to "pull stumps." Ultimately, I was taken in, treated kindly, and given the opportunity to ride some of the machinery that so excited me: the "truly potent" Triumph Metisse, an almost uncontrollable supercharged Norton Atlas from New Mexico, and a couple of road-racing machines with foot pegs way back by the rear sprocket and stubby six-inch handlebars — so that you lie out on the bike and divide a sea of wind with the point of your chin.

One day I "got off on the pavement," that is, crashed. It was not much of a crash. I went into a turn too fast and ran off the shoulder and got a little "road burn" requiring symbolic bandages at knees and elbows. I took the usual needling from the crew at the bike shop, and with secret pleasure accepted the temporary appellation "Crash Cargo." I began taking dawn trips over the mountains to Santa Cruz, sometimes with others, sometimes alone, wearing a wool hunting shirt against the chill and often carrying binoculars and an Audubon field guide.

Then one day I was riding in my own neighborhood when a man made a U-turn in front of me and stopped, blocking the road. It was too late to brake and I had to put the bike down, riding it like a sled as it screeched across the pavement. It ran into the side of the car and I slid halfway under, the seat and knees torn out of my pants, scraped and bruised but without serious injury. I had heard the sharp clicking of my helmet against the pavement and later saw the depressions that might have been in my skull.

The man got out, accusing me of going a hundred miles an hour, accusing me of laying for a chance to create an accident, accusing me of being a Hell's Angel, and finally admitting he had been daydreaming and had not looked up the street before making his illegal maneuver. The motorcycle was a mess. He pleaded with me not to have physical injuries. He said he had very little insurance. And a family. "Have a heart."

"You ask this of a Hell's Angel?"

At the motorcycle shop I was urged to develop nonspecific spinal trouble. A special doctor was named. But I had the motorcycle minimally repaired and sent the man the bill. When the settlement came, his name was at the top of the stationery. He was the owner of the insurance agency.

Perhaps it was the point-blank view from below of rocker panels and shock absorbers and the specious concern of the insurance man for my health that gave my mortality its little twinge. I suddenly did not want to get off on the pavement anymore or bring my road burn to the shop under secret bandages. I no longer cared if my bike was rapid and sanitary. I wanted to sell it, and I wanted to get out of California.

I did both those things, and in that order. But sometimes, in the midst of more tasteful activities, I miss the mournful howl of that big single engine as it came up on the cam, dropped revs, and started over on a new ratio; the long banking turns with the foot pegs sparking against the pavement and the great crocodile's tears the wind caused to trickle out from under my flying glasses. I'm behind a sensible windshield now, and the soaring curve of acceleration does not come up through the seat of my pants. I have an FM radio, and the car doesn't get bad mileage.

CLOSE
TO THE
BONE

ONE IS TEMPTED to think of bonefish as among the wildest of creatures, if a sensory apparatus calculated to separate them continually from man's presence qualifies them as "wild." Yet when the serious angler insinuates himself into the luminous, subaqueous universe of the bonefish and catches one without benefit of accident, he has, in effect, visited another world, a world whose precise cycles and conditions appear so serene to the addled twentieth-century angler that he begins to be consoled for all he has done to afford the trip in the first place. In his imagination he is emphatic about emptiness, space, and silence. He is searching less for recreation than for a kind of stillness.

Only the utterly initiated think the bonefish is handsome. Those new to or stupid about the sport think the fish is silly-looking, but those who know it well consider the bonefish radiant with a nearly celestial beauty. To me, it seems so perfectly made for both its terrain and my needs as a fisherman that it has the specialness of design seen in experimental aircraft. The nose, it is true, has a curious slant, and there is an undershot mouth that we, with our anthropocentrism, associate with lack of character, but after a while you see that the entire head is rather hydrodynamic and handsomely vulpine.

The body is sturdy, often a radiant gray-green above and pure silver on the sides. The tail, like the fins, is frequently a gun-metal gray and is oversized and powerful, as exaggeratedly proportioned to its size as are the fish's speed and power.

A bonefish doesn't jump. From the fish's point of view, the jump is a wasteful and often ruinous enterprise. Tarpon customarily wreck themselves jumping, which is the only thing that permits the large ones to be taken on light tackle at all. So people who like to be photographed with all the spectacle associated with themselves, their fishing paraphernalia, and their catch ought to forget bonefish and concentrate on tarpon. When you hang a tarpon up at the dock, it will suck gawkers off the highway like a vacuum cleaner. A dead bonefish at dockside scarcely draws flies.

It took me a month to catch my first bonefish, and I regret to say that I killed it and put it in the freezer. For a long time, at the drop of a hat, I would take it out, rigid as a fungo bat, to show to my friends. One said it was small. Another noted that the freezer had given it sunken eyes and a morbid demeanor. I asked how you could speak of demeanor in something which had departed this world. It was the last bonefish I kept.

Hard as it may be to believe, the bonefish leads his life in his extensive multiocean range quite without reference to the angler. For example, off the coast of Hawaii he has betaken himself to great depths, where he is of no earthly use to the light-tackle fisherman. His poor manners extend to the African coast, where he reveals himself occasionally to cut-bait anglers of the high surf who smother his fight with pyramid sinkers that a Wyoming wrangler might use to keep the horses handy.

For these transgressions of ordinary decency the human race can best revenge itself upon the bonefish in the shallows of Central America, the Bahamas, and the Florida Keys. From a topographical perspective, the immensely distributed bonefish seems to be all over the place, but the angler will generally settle for one. At any given moment, the angler will resort to low tricks and importuning the diety for a lonesome single. In the back of his mind, he recalls that marine biologists describe the bonefish as "widely distributed." It doesn't help.

The marine shallows where the bonefish spends much of its existence, from the transparent larval stage to maturity, are accessible only to the fisherman or scientist who wades or transports himself in a light skiff over the sand and turtle grass. As much delicacy of approach is required of these observers as there is of the ornithologist. It is this essential condition that makes bonefishing almost generically different from offshore angling.

Unlike almost any other game fish, the bonefish is not sought where he lives. Bonefish live in deep water; they only do some of their feeding on the flats. A trout fisherman, for example, seeking a particular fish, would attempt to ascertain where that fish lived, in which pool or under which log. The bonefisherman never has any idea where a particular fish lives; he attempts to find combinations of tide and place that are used by feeding bonefish. Occasionally, a particular fish will appear with certain regularity, but this is exceptional.

Flats used by feeding bonefish are flooded by tide. They are flooded at unequal rates, depending upon the location of the individual flats relative to the direction of tidal bore and current, and the presence of keys and basins, which draw and deflect the moving water. One flat, for instance, might have rising water at one time, while another flat half a mile away may not get its first incoming water until an hour later. Even this is not constant, since wind can alter the precise times of rising and falling water.

The beginning bonefisherman is often humiliated to learn that the flats he found empty produced bonanzas for anglers who had a better sense of timing than he had. A tide book and a good memory are the first tools of the bonefisherman.

With experience, a pattern begins to emerge — the shape of the life habits of a wild species.

The novice starts with a simple combination — early incoming water in the morning or evening — and gradually, by observation, begins to include the mosaic of tidal information that finally becomes the fabric of his fishing knowledge. Tide in the tropics, where only a foot of water moves on the average, seems rather ethereal to the new bonefisherman. It does not seem reasonable to him that three- or four-tenths of a foot of tidal variation can be the difference between a great and a worthless fishing tide.

There is another way that tide can work: You are poling across a flat in less than a foot of water. A fish tails high on the flat. You begin your approach, closing in deliberately. There is the small sound of staghorn crunching against the skiff's bottom, then the solider sound of sand. You can't go any farther. The bonefish is still tailing, still out of reach. You get out of the skiff and wade to him and make your cast. His tail disappears as he tilts out of his feeding posture, follows your lure or bait, takes, is hooked and running. For ten minutes you live as never before. Then the bonefish, a fine eight-pounder, is released.

When you return to the skiff, it is high and dry; the tide has dropped from under it. You've got a six-hour wait before you can budge the skiff. You pace up and down the flat like an angry executive. If you are a smoker, you smoke more than you have ever smoked before.

Can't someone get me out of this?

Now, if you have gone aground in the morning on a summer's day and have not brought water, you will be truly sorry. If you have gone aground in the afternoon and can't find your way home in the dark, you'll have to sleep in the skiff. Pick a breezy place where the mosquitoes have taxiing problems. A certain number will crash-land on your person anyway, but the breeze will discourage the rank and file. Curl up in your little flats boat, listen to the wave-slap, and, watching the deep tropical night, think upon the verities of your choice. Tantrums, it is to be mentioned, only keep you from getting to sleep.

Tide, that great impersonal pulse of earth which brought you that eight-pounder on a platter, has cooked your goose.

Bonefish are hard to see. You train yourself to see them by a number of subliminal signs which, after you have fished the flats extensively, give you the opportunity to amaze your friends with feats of the eye. "Bonefish right in front of you!" you say as one ghosts past the skiff, visible only by the palest shadow it makes on the bottom.

"Where?" your good friend whom you shouldn't treat this way asks. "My God, where?"

"Right in front of you!" This starts your companion casting, even though he sees nothing.

"Flushed fish," you say, gazing at the horizon.

The difficulty in seeing fish gives the veteran a real opportunity to lord it over the neophyte, gives him a chance to cultivate those small nuances of power that finally reveal him to be the Captain of the Skiff. After that, the veteran relaxes, showing generosity.

Of the fish that concern the flats fisherman, bonefish are the smallest and probably the hardest to see. Water and light conditions dictate how they are to be sought with the eye, but again intuition eventually takes over. In the Florida Keys, where bonefish are characteristically seen swimming rather than tailing (and this is perhaps true everywhere), you must make a disciplined effort to look *through* the water surface. The water surface itself is something very inviting to look *at,* and the man who confuses angling with relaxation will let his eye rest here — and he will miss nine out of ten fish. In the beginning, especially, the task must be borne down upon, for it is hard work. Eventually you will learn to sweep, or scan back and forth, over the area of possible sighting. At the first sweep, your mind records the features of the bottom; on subsequent scans, if anything is out of place or if the small, unobtrusive, and utterly shadowy presence of a bonefish has interrupted those features in your memory, you will notice it.

Polaroid glasses are an absolute necessity. There is some disagreement about which color is best. Green lenses are commonest, but things show up a little better with amber. Many people find the amber lenses hard on their eyes on brilliant days and so confine their use to overcast skies. I have used the amber glasses on brilliant July days and been plagued by headaches and strobelike afterimages.

In very shallow water, bonefish manifest themselves in two other ways: by waking and by tailing. Fish making waves are often seen on the early incoming tide, and I think these are more important to the angler than the tailing fish. The singles make a narrow V wake, not always very distinct, and the pods of fish make a trembling, advancing surface almost like a cat's-paw of wind.

The most prized discovery, however, is the tailing fish. And wading for tailing fish is the absolute champagne of the sport. These fish can be harder to take than the swimmers — their heads are down and it is necessary to get the lure very near them so they may see it, yet this close presentation tends to frighten them — but the reward is commensurately greater and the fact that they are usually hooked in the shallowest kind of water makes their runs even more vivid. Since very often there is more than one fish tailing at the same time, the alarm of a hooked fish is communicated immediately and the companion fish will explode away from the site like pieces of a star shell.

The sound that a hooked bonefish makes running across a flat cannot be phonetically imitated. In fact, most of the delicate, shearing sound comes from the line or leader as it slices through the water. The fish will fight itself to death if not hurried a little and if great care is not taken in the release.

Anglers of experience speculate a good deal about the character of their quarry, doting on the baleful secrecy of brown trout, the countrified insouciance and general funkiness of largemouth bass, or the vaguely Ivy League patina of brook trout and Atlantic salmon. The hard-core smallmouth angler who accedes to a certain aristocratic construction to his sport is cheerful and would identify himself with, for instance, Thomas Jefferson, whose good house (Monticello) and reasonable political beliefs about mankind (Democracy) have been so attractive to the optimistic and self-made.

The dedicated trout fisherman is frequently an impossible human being capable of taking a priceless Payne dry-fly rod to an infant's fanny. One hardly need mention that more lynching has been done by largemouth bass anglers than by the fanciers of any other species, just as Atlantic salmon anglers are sure to go up against the wall way ahead of Indiana crappie wizards.

But the bonefisherman is as enigmatic as his quarry. The bonefish is as likely to scurry around a flat like a rat as he is to come sweeping in on the flood, tailing with noble deliberation. So, too, the bonefisherman is subject to great lapses of dignity. A bonefish flat is a complex field of signs, quite as difficult a subject for reading as an English chalk stream. The bonefisherman has a mildly scientific proclivity for natural phenomenology insofar as it applies to his quest, but unfortunately he is inclined to regard a flock of roseate spoonbills only in terms of flying objects liable to spook fish.

The bonefisherman is nearly as capable of getting lost between a Pink Shrimp and a Honey Blonde as the lone maniac waist-deep in the Letort reading his fly box from Jassid to Pale Evening Dun — though, because a boat is usually required, he may be slightly more oppressed by equipment.

As the bonefisherman is sternly sophisticated by his quarry, his reverence for the creature increases. Undeterred by toxic winds, block meetings, bulletproof taxicab partitions, or adventures with the Internal Revenue Service, he can perceive with his mind alone bonefish on remote ocean flats moving in the tongue of the flood.

A
WORLD-RECORD DINNER

I CONCEDE that "mutton snapper" is hardly a prepossessing title. The sheep, from which the name derives, is not much of an animal. No civilized person deals with him except in chops and stews. To bleat is not to sing out in a commanding baritone; to be sheepish is scarcely to possess a virtue for which civilization rolls out its more impressive carpets.

And it is true that the fish, as you may have suspected, is not at all handsome, with its large and vacant-looking head, crazy red eye, and haphazard black spot just shy of its tail. Yet it's brick-orange flanks and red tail are rather tropical and fine, and for a number of reasons it deserves consideration as major light-tackle game. When you have been incessantly outwitted by the mutton snapper, you cease to emphasize his vaguely doltish exterior.

To begin with, mutton snappers share with the most pursued shallow-water game fish a combination of hair-trigger perceptions. They are wild and spooky, difficult to deceive, and very powerful. Taken under optimum conditions, they are as enthralling as any species that haunts the flats.

Like most flats fish, the mutton snapper is primarily a creature of deep water, another individual thread in the ocean system that, following its own particular necessity, crisscrosses the lives and functions of the animals that share its habitat.

Which is to say that in looking for one fish you find another — and maybe in the end you find it all.

After a long winter's flats fishing, I had naturally acquired a ready facility for recognizing most anything that came along. A flat is a circumscribed habitat so far as larger fishes are concerned. The first mutton snappers I found were encountered while I was poling for permit on flood tides close to the keys. They were wild fish, hustling around in their curious way and pushing abrupt knuckles of wake in the thin water. Their red tails made them unmistakable.

They seemed so conscious of the skiff that it was hard to see how they might be taken on a fly rod. Besides, they were hard to find, somewhat harder, for example, than permit, and they were every bit as alert and quick to flush.

Last May, Guy de la Valdene and I began to fish for them in earnest, spurred on from time to time by the sight of brilliant red forks in the air. The fish often seemed hurried, and when we would pole to the place where we had seen a tail, there would be nothing. Most of the first fish we found were in a grassy basin south of Key West, a shallow place usually good for a few shots at permit. The basin was little more than a declivity in the long-running ocean bank that reaches from just below Key West to the Boca Grande Channel — and across which lie the Marquesas.

Early one hot day Guy and I began to fish this basin. A long convection build-up of clouds lay along the spine of the keys, like a mirror image of the islands themselves, all the way to Boca Grande, and then scattered in cottony streamers to the west. So we fished in a shadow most of the day, straining to find fish in the turtle grass.

With the leisurely wan hope that comes of being on a flat at no particular tide, I was poling the skiff. We passed a small depression on the flat and suddenly spotted two mutton snappers floating close to the bottom with the antsy, fidgeting look they so often have. Guy made an excellent cast and a fish responded immediately. My hopes sank as it overtook and began to follow the fly with the kind of examining pursuit we had come to associate with one of the permit's more refined refusals. But, with considerable élan, Guy stopped the fly and let it sink to the bottom. The snapper paused behind the fly at a slight forward tilt and then, in what is to the flats fisherman a thrilling gesture, he tilted over onto his head and tailed, the great, actually wondrous, fork in the air, precisely marking the position of Guy's fly.

I looked toward the stern. Guy was poised, line still slack, rod tip down. He gave the fish three full seconds, and I watched him lift the rod, feeling foredoomed that the line would glide back slack. but the rod bowed in a clean gesture toward the fly line, which was inscribed from rod tip to still tailing fish. Abruptly, the fish was level in the water again and surging away from us in a globe of wake that it pushed before itself; a thin sheet of water stood behind the leader as it sheared the surface.

The first long run ended with the fly pulling free. As Guy reeled in his line and backing, I let the boat drift in on the tide toward the little community of stilt houses standing mysteriously in spiderlike shadows off Boca Grande Key. Nearby, an old sail-powered commercial boat rusted on the bank that claimed it, a long row of black cormorants on its crumbling iron rail.

"Well," said Guy, "I guess they'll take the fly."

It was late in the afternoon and Guy was poling. I stood in the gun seat, as we had come to call the aft casting platform, trailing my loop of fly line. We were zigzagging around in our grassy basin, fishing out the last of the incoming tide and getting shots from time to time at permit. From directly out of the light, a large stingray was swimming toward us, and in front of it were two large fish, indistinguishably backlit. Because they were with the ray, these were necessarily feeding fish. I had time to roll my trailing loop into the air, make a quick false cast, then throw. The left-hand fish, facing me, veered off and struck. I had him briefly, but long enough to feel an almost implacable power, enough to burn a finger freeing loose fly line. Since mutton snappers frequently came into this basin from deep water with rays, we presumed that is what had taken my fly.

Whatever, it joined that throng of shades, touched and unseen, that haunt the angler — fish felt and lost, big ones that got away that are the subject of levity to nonanglers but of a deeper emotion to the angler himself.

Rays are a common sight on the flats. The game fish seldom follow the pretty spotted eagle rays, which have a perfection of shape and movement that is beyond quick description. They are dark and beautifully spotted like a fawn or leopard; as a wing is lifted to propel them the exquisite, creamy ventral surfaces are exposed. Spotted eagle rays mud less than stingrays; their oval mouths seem made for more exact procedures. When the boat is upon them they flush with long perfect sweeps of their wings, and when they are lost to the eye the swirls and turbulence of their deceptively powerful movements continue to disturb the surface.

The platitudinous stingray with his torpid, carpetlike movements, on the other hand, holds some special interest for game fish. Jacks, snappers, and permit will follow a feeding stingray throughout the tide, using the ray as a kind of stalking horse to scare up small fish and crabs. When a fish is found accompanying a ray, it may be assumed that he is feeding rather than traveling. A suitable presentation must be made.

We knew where we could find rays. We often saw them on the soft backsides of banks whose harder edges we fished for permit. We had a grandly complex set of banks that stretched from the Atlantic to the Gulf of Mexico; we had laboriously laid out its tortuous inner channels and developed some sense of the sequence in which permit used its individual flats and banks. But always we had fished the edges.

Today we wanted to go into the interior of the banks on incoming water and fish well up on the soft bottom. We made the long run from Key West in the early morning, the scattered keys looking deep, wet, and green on the slate sea. We passed Mule, Archer, Big and Little Mullet, Cottrell, Barracuda, Man, Woman, Ballast, and Boca Grande, on out past the iron marker, west into the first gut.

The flat was dotted with luminous slicks of mudding rays. Guy took the pole and we tracked down the rays one by one, finding them mainly alone, but here and there seeing the fleeting red forks or discovering the nervous snappers too late.

Eventually we found a single large snapper working a stingray. The ray was making such an extensive mud that it seemed unlikely the snapper could find a retrieved fly. In any case, the excitement of watching the tailing fish collaborate with the ray and the measuring in my mind's eye of the breadth of that fork went a long way toward totally eroding my composure.

The mutton snapper was tailing when I cast, and I threw well beyond the ray and retrieved the large fly through the edge of the slick. The tail dropped abruptly, and my first thought was that I had flushed the snapper. Then I saw the wake directly behind my fly and knew I was getting a follow. I hoped for a take straightaway but none came. I had to stop the fly and let it go to the bottom, an act that has always felt entirely unnatural to me. The fish tipped up instantly, tail entirely out of the water. I lifted the rod tentatively, then I came up tight and the fish was running.

Water streamed up the leader with a silky shearing noise, and the snapper peeled off in a bulge of water tinted by his own brick-red hue. The flat was a broad one and the snapper failed to clear it to deep water on his first run. At the end of that run he turned perpendicular to the line and held there for a while, implacable as a fire hydrant. Then, with an air of having made the decision himself, he allowed me to retrieve him at his own sullen rate. I began to look around for the net but found Guy one step ahead of me, the big net at parade rest.

My glances for the net were optimistic ones. There were a number of runs to be endured. With a fish badly wanted, it is always simple to imagine the hook pulling free, the leader breaking, the dead feeling in the slack rod. Five minutes later the fish was at the boat, succinctly netted by Guy.

It seemed quite big, bigger than I expected. A short time after landing the fish we ran into a local guide who weighed it: a little over fifteen pounds, the world record on a fly.

That night the world record was dispatched as follows: deprived of head and innards, he was stuffed with shrimp, shallots, buttered crumbs, parsley, tarragon, and mushrooms, then rinsed down the gullets of hungry anglers with gouts of cold domestic Chablis. I would wish a similar fate upon all world records that are not released at the boat.

The next day Guy took another big fish, this one thirteen pounds, and we began to feel we were getting the hang of it. This fish was given to a Cuban friend at the yard who remembered mutton snappers in the Havana markets. He carried Guy's fish around in a formal march, under the stored hulls, through the dry shed, and out to the carpenter's shop, before giving it the place of honor on the front seat of his pickup.

When we looked for the snappers in the next few days we could not find them. The rays came in on the same tides, but now they were alone. A week or so later the commercial fishermen found the snappers on the 120-foot contour offshore, 118 feet out of our depth. But we had had our glimpse and knew we would be waiting for them next spring on the flats.

TARPON HUNTING

IN THE KEYS by March you are thinking of tarpon. The fish have been around in small numbers all winter; not quite fishable numbers, somehow, when bonefish and permit have seemed the more logical subjects of attention. The night trollers and drifters have been taking tarpon in the channels and killing them for advertising purposes; they make the only sign a tourist will believe when hung up at the dock. The shrimp basin in Key West and the harbor always have quantities of fish; but these are domesticated brutes, feeding themselves on the culls of the commercial fishermen and rolling and burbling with the reptilian presence that half-tamed alligators used to have on Florida golf courses.

But usually, sometime in March, while we are permit fishing or bonefishing on an edge adjacent to deeper water, we spot the first string of migrating tarpon, often juvenile fish up to fifty and sixty pounds. Below Key West they inevitably appear to be travelers, pushing wakes and rolling with their eyes coming out of the water, so that you are absolutely sure they see you in the skiff, transfixed and watching them. The whole mystery of their cycle seems contained in the absolutely deliberate way they travel, deliberate as caribou or spring warblers.

Mystery is not an altogether misplaced word regarding tarpon. Much serious research on the fish was dropped when schemes for converting these unparalleled creatures to fertilizer and cat food were abandoned. There seem to be vertical migrations of fish from deep to shallow water, in addition to the fish that appear to be traveling from the south, very probably Central America. But facing a lack of hard information, the angler feels the invitation to elaborate his own sense of the fish's presence. An awareness arises of the distinction between a species like the tarpon and the offshore pelagic fishes with which, as a game fish, the tarpon is often favorably compared. But in the tarpon the aerodynamic profiles and chameleonic coloring of blue-water fish are replaced by something venerable; they are inshore fish, heavily scaled; they gulp air; and as if to seal their affinity for the land masses of the earth, they require fresh or brackish water to complete their reproductive cycle. They migrate, as many fishes do, and when we touch or intercept these migrations, we sense, subliminally, the dynamism of the biosphere: tarpon migrate by season, season is a function of planetary movement, and so on. Which is no more than to say you can face bravely those accusations of loafing when you have ruined a month chasing tarpon, racking your brain to understand their secret, sidling lives.

It is quite early in the morning. Not first light, because a higher angle of sun is required to see fish on the dark bottom that we are working today. But it is early enough that as we cross Key West the gas stations are being swept down by sleepy attendants with push brooms, and the Cuban men are over on their end of Duval Street drinking cups of their utterly black coffee and eating bollos. You can smell the smoke in the still air coming from City Electric on the other side of town. The ground swell of Latinate noise — that first of all things that make Key West another country — has not yet started, and as we go up Caroline Street all the side streets running down to the shrimp basin, marked for us because of the great trawling booms sticking up among the old wooden houses, are quiet.

The shrimpers always form first under the awning of the Fisherman's Café. There is no one there yet, though someone is arranging ship-to-shore radios and fathometers in the window of Key West Electronics across the street.

It feels like a tarpon day. Spring tides will give us a good push of water. The wind has swung almost into the full south and it is hot already. Up the keys the yellow mosquito plane will be skimming in over the mangroves, its cloud of spray hanging and settling in the still air.

There are sponges drying on the balconies of some of the old wooden houses, and as if you might forget that the town is at sea, gulls and frigate birds soar high over the streets. Next to Key West Oxygen Service, in an ugly asphalt parking lot that rivals the La Brea tar pits in midsummer, a bonefish skiff sits high on its trailer, bridging the imagination from the immediate downtown of Key West — which is both an outrageous honky-tonk and a memento of another century — to the gauzy, impossibly complex backcountry that surrounds. When you are at the drive-in movie in Key West, watching Adult Fare with all the other sweating neckers, the column of light from the projectionist's booth is feverish with tropical insects blurring the breasts and buttocks on their way to the screen. If it is low tide, you smell the mangroves and exposed tidal flats nearby and you are within a mile of sharks that could eat you like a jujube. When the movie is over and you have hung the speaker back on its post and are driving home, palmetto bugs and land crabs pop under the tires.

This morning, when we get to Garrison Bight, we turn off before the causeway and pull into the dry shed where my boat is stored. Across the bight at the ramp, we can see a skiff being launched behind a station wagon. I take out the binoculars and look. It's a Hewes guide boat. I see the chairs, the enormous engine, the push pole, the Teleflex steering up in the forward corner, and over me and my companion, Guy de la Valdene, comes that specific competitive tension you feel when another skiff is working the same country. If Saint Francis showed up with a guide boat behind his car, we would rather he stayed home. Every shallow-water fisherman down here is cordial on land, monstrous on the water.

It's not Stu Apte; his skiff has a center console. It's not Bill Curtis; his is yellow, and furthermore he fishes Key West mainly on permit charters. Woody Sexton is in Loggerhead today; so it's not him. Jim Brewer fishes out of a Fibercraft and this is a Hewes. Bob Montgomery has an offshore charter. Cal Cochran? He's supposed to have plenty of fish in his back yard at Marathon. Same with Steve Huff. Page Brown fishes out of a Mako and he would have told us if he was fishing Key West. It would be nice to know who it is so we could avoid running the same pattern. It might be one of the boobs from an angling club, chasing points, mounts, and records.

Richard, the manager of the boatyard, comes out and says, "Morning, Mister Tom," with that special look of philosophical resignation that is the hallmark of the Key Wester. He climbs up on the fork lift and heads into the shed for the skiff. I had it built right here at the yard only last winter, and the first rip of boat fever has not passed off. I love to watch the skiff come out on the fork so I can see the long, precise chine running from stem to bait wells. When the boat emerges, Guy says, "Yes, I know it's beautiful, but please don't say it again."

"I know, but —"

"Don't say it."

Richard rolls the fork lift forward onto the concrete dock and lowers the boat into the slick water. To the untutored eye, there is nothing to see that is exceptional about the skiff: bare nonfouling utility has been taken as far as the mind could create demands for the boat-builder.

The glass hull, brought down bare from the mainland, is white, low, and spare. From the side it looks like a simple linear gesture, the blade of a scimitar or an arrow. It is seventeen feet two inches long, not counting the integral bait wells.

The boat was built up from this bare hull with three-quarter-inch marine plywood, the arm-and-a-leg variety. From above, the skiff appears as a succession of bare surfaces, over which a fly line can blow without snagging; the forward casting deck is continuous with the broad, flat gunwales, The aft deck is set slightly below the gunwales and, like the casting deck, overhangs the bulkheads by half an inch. Set into the aft deck are the lids of two dry storage boxes, a battery box, and an insulated icebox. All topside surfaces are blue-gray.

The steering is forward and starboard, Teleflex with wheel set horizontal to the deck. Donald Duck's picture is in the hub; a pacifier hangs from the ignition. The throttle and gearshift controls are in a single lever, and there is a tachometer with which I pretend to monitor my engine's performance. I monitored my previous engine's performance, noticing not a thing right up until the idiot light turned on, a plug blew out of a cylinder, and the whole thing froze like a tractor in quicksand. There is a toggle on the dash for the power tilt, the 125 Evinrude on the transom being too heavy for hand-tilting as frequently as flats fishing requires.

Guy is at the gas dock, filling the stainless forty-gallon tank under the casting deck. I get a block of ice and put it in the cooler with our lunch and twelve soft drinks. The rods go under the port gunwale; rain gear is under the seat. The tackle box goes aboard with a couple of dozen of Guy's shock tippets rolled like surgeon's suturing materials. And now we're ready, feeling suddenly the anticipation that is the one return from the inputs of weather, readings from the Coast and Geodetic Survey tide book, and all the baloney and general hearsay from guides and other anglers about just where it is the tarpon might be.

Along the starboard gunwale, flexed tight against it, is the big kill gaff with its seven-foot hardwood handle, never to be used on a fish less than the world record, though Guy and I agree that the goal is to train oneself to release even that fish.

But at this early stage of development the gaff still goes along. Someday, when we have grown enough in the fishing, the gaff is to be nailed up over my desk, with the stainless-steel gaff head that I wrapped and epoxied myself, a rather handsome old souvenir of barbaric times. On top of the port gunwale, resting in two teak chocks and secured with aviation shock cord, is a seventeen-foot push pole.

Choked and started, the engine idles on the transom; the boat trembles and laps gently against the dock. Guy slips the lines and pushes us away from the dock and I put it in forward, easing us out past the crawfishing boats, two or three sponge boats with tongs laid across the seats; then out into the basin in the low angle of light. Idling along and sitting up forward, the boat rides low in the water with radically little freeboard; this is a skiff that will run forty miles an hour in less than a foot of water; offshore, it would be as reassuring as a waterlogged mahogany plank. Its design, derived from numerous other boats but primarily those built by Eddie Geddiman, is a pure indigenous product of the fishing conditions of the Florida Keys. It is a fast, shallow-water boat.

We pass under the Garrison Causeway as morning work traffic is beginning to rush overhead. We can smell its exhaust with the same emotions with which we perceive the hamburger stands over by the charter boat docks. Once on the other side, there is that damned guide boat we saw being launched, up on a plane now and way out at the front edge of a fan of wake. I hear the honking overhead and then a siren as a policeman runs down some sorry gob in a GTO. The brilliantly painted Cuban fishing boats are off to our left, gaudy as Arab smacks; behind them is the institutional slab of the navy BOQ, built with the military's usual flair for grace in design.

The guide boat by now has upped and gone. We don't know where he could be and are just hoping that our two skiffs don't go wandering over the ocean making the same

stops, tripping over each other as in some maltimed, synco-
pated dance step.

I run it up to 4500 rpm. The bow lifts; then the stern comes
up under the power and kicks the bow down. I slack off to
3600 and we bank and turn through the markers. Key West
drops quickly behind and finally clusters at the end of our
long arrow of wake. There is a sense of liberation as we run,
melting civilization away before us while another country, one
of mangrove keys, shallows, and open seas, forms around us.

When you pass them, the mangroves empty themselves of
cormorants; the birds drop down slapping the water with their
wing tips, then shudder after the first hundred feet or so, as
though it had been a close call. The backcountry is full of
pelicans, frigate birds, ospreys, bitterns, egrets, and herons;
not to speak of that mass of small shorebirds — plovers, avo-
cets, turnstones, surfbirds, phalaropes — and a number of
glamorous "occasionals," as the bird books call them: ibises,
eagles, and the utterly incredible roseate spoonbills that wheel
out behind a sandy little key, the color of a whore's lipstick.

We stake the skiff in a small basin near the Northwest Channel. The shrimpers are coming in sporadically from the Gulf
of Mexico, the trawling booms swaying and the diesel engines
sounding like farm tractors at this range. We are watching for
tarpon moving in the big channel to graze off or shortcut
toward the smaller channels shoreward of us. We are staked
— that is, tied to the push pole, which is shoved in the bottom
— along a sandbank that separates the channel from the
basin, knowing that it will deflect tarpon up into shallow water,
where it is hoped they will be moved to take the fly.

We are using the big rod; it carries a No. 12 saltwater taper
line and is a very effective rod for fighting a fish, if not exactly
a wand to handle. It is very powerful, double-wrapped, with a
second grip just short of the stripping guide. We have rigged
a grizzly-and-orange fly on a 3/0 hook, using an eighty-pound
shock tippet. Ten inches above that, the twelve-pound starts

and it is this breaking strength that brackets what pressure the angler can put on the fish.

We take turns with the rod, watching for incoming fish that can appear and blow by too quickly if one's alertness flags. Very early on, some tarpon roll in the big channel. They are clearly travelers though, and will keep right on going — to Mexico, for all we know.

After a bit, a good-size shark glides under the boat. Touched with the rod tip, he moves off in a surge. A little later a hawksbill turtle peers up at us from green water, then, frightened, races off at a speed one doesn't associate with turtles; his front flippers are a blur of effort, while the back flippers cross and trail.

Guy stands up on one bait well and looks intently through the binoculars. "The damned guide boat," he reports, "is sitting on our next stop." Sure enough, the skiff is at Mule Key, exactly the place where we would be getting the phase of tide we wanted in another half-hour. "And you know what else?" The answer was posed in the tone of his question.

"Yes," I said ruefully, "he's fighting a fish."

We start looking at our watches. We are not getting any shots on this spot and we are cut off on the next, but, we reason, when the men in the guide boat are done with their present fish, they very well might make a move to the place both boats would pick for the third stop. Guy looks through the glasses.

"What's he doing?"

"He broke the fish off," Guy said. "There are two of them. They're sitting in the boat to re-rig."

"I feel sort of frustrated here," I said.

"I do, too."

"If we don't crank up — I know this is irrational — if we don't crank up I'm afraid we're going to be watching that guy all day long."

"Let's slip the stake," said Guy, "and blow all the way to Big Mullet before he gets his nose out of that tackle box."

I slip the pole out of the bottom, coil the line on the bow, put the pole on its chocks, and secure it with the shock cord, then start the engine. I idle into Northwest Channel, then run it up to 5400 rpm, all the way to the stop, so that we are truly flying, running through the banks with a mean tide chop beating our back teeth loose.

We get two thirds of the way across Northwest Channel and the man running the guide boat can see the push pole on our gunwale and knows what is happening to him. He quick hands the rod he's rigging to his companion and starts the engine. Our problem is to hit the run-through channel in the Mule Key bank directly on the nose or we will be sawed off by the guide boat.

The guide boat wheels around and things are still at the educated-guess stage. From here the bank looks solid and we appear to be heading on a collision course — running aground. Now the guide boat is flying full tilt as well, on an interception course. It is sufficiently neck and neck that we will have to find another place to fish if I have to shut down the engine on the shallow bank and feel my way along for a place to run through.

But then a piece of the bank seems to peel away before our eyes and suddenly there is a little solid green creek running through the hard stuff. We cross the bank at 5000 rpm and shut off. In our new silence we hear the drone of the guide boat taper off to an idle a short distance behind us.

"You look back," says Guy with a smile. We are both of us pretending to survey the basin as though we hardly knew the other boat was in the country. I turn around and see the two men hunched in the idling boat, staring at us without love.

It is a far cry from the genial gatherings of anglers on the Test or the Itchen. When flats fishermen run into each other on the water, it is more like war, smiles and jolly waves notwithstanding. When information is asked for, a bum steer quite naturally springs to the lips. I rather suspect, though, that the true scoop on the Test and the Itchen would indicate that those anglers, tweeds and all, have the needle into each other as thoroughly as we do.

Soon we hear the guide boat running again, the big engine offering what we interpret as a mild trumpet of resignation. We've broken the maltimed syncopation, and now we can fish on our own. All is fair in this, and we fully expect to see them at another stop. Meanwhile, it is as quiet as can be, the water lapping gently on the sides of the skiff and pearly summer clouds along the horizon.

We tilt the engine and Guy begins to pole. He was a collegiate rower and poles better than I do, with a steady, persistent beat that is perfect for surveying an area when you are not absolutely sure of finding fish. Immediately we begin seeing life; clusters of spotted eagle rays bustle around like nuns, barracudas appear near the boat without ever having been seen in the act of swimming over, small sharks come, stingrays and houndfish. But not, for the moment, any tarpon. We're not talking very much. I feel the successive pushes of the pole and hear its steady rise and fall in the water. Occasionally we glide to a stop and I hear Guy lighting a cigarette behind me, and in a moment the boat surges forward again. The bottom is dark with turtle grass and we look hard to penetrate its surface. At the same time we try to survey a wide range for rollers and watch the surface for the faint wakes that look like a thumbnail pulled gently along under a sheet of silk. What you see more than anything is movement; the resting or sleeping fish are the toughest to spot.

There is a little breeze now and a few high horsetail clouds in the sky, brilliantly white and lacquered. A radiant drop curtain of fuchsia light stands on edge from the Gulf Stream south of us. East across the channels Key West can still be seen, like a white folding ruler, in sections on the blue expanse.

Guy says "tarpon" so quietly that I wonder if he means tarpon in general, but with a certain dread I realize he has spotted fish and a moment later I see a large single swimming with easy sweeps, quite black and bulky-looking, moving on a course that we will easily intercept. This means it will be entirely up to me. I am trailing enough line for my false cast and have already begun that rather tense process of trying to figure our range as it is modified by the progress of the skiff in one direction and that of the tarpon in another. That the fish itself looks about as manageable as a Cape buffalo is little help in the finer calculations of the mind. I know from experience that this peaceful meandering fish can offer a scarifying performance calling into question (if usually theoretically) whether or not the angler is actually safe.

Guy poles to an interception point and turns the skiff so that by the time the fish is in range we are at rest. The pole is down and away from where my backcast could foul it. I roll my trailing line into the air, false-cast, shoot, false-cast again, shoot, get my range, and cast. The fly falls acceptably and I strip sharply once to get the fish's attention, continuing with a quick, jerky retrieve. Then the tarpon turns almost imperceptibly. It is this point that enthralls and terrifies the tarpon angler — the moment when, unbelievably, the great fish alters its course, however slightly, to take the fly.

Now the fish is tight behind the fly, so close as to seem cross-eyed as he watches and follows it, a dense reptilian presence in pursuit of the streamer. Then comes his slight elevation and gain of speed, the mouth opening, and one last forward surge as the fly vanishes.

I strike him too quickly and feel little more than a bump as the fly comes free. The tarpon muscles about in confusion, making a depth charge of disturbance when he sees the boat, and turns over on himself clearing out. We should be fighting that fish now, one reflects gloomily. Yes, one is inclined to admit, one has blown off a good fish.

It would be Guy's every right to seize the rod with a pontifical sigh and hand me the push pole, but he remains in the bow, camera around his neck, ready to record each faux pas.

I return to my post in the stern with that special determination that surely prepares the angler for more garish errors than those which produced the determination. This is the vicious circle of angling, the iron maiden of a supposedly reflective pursuit.

We pole for a good long time without sighting another fish. We are beginning to lose our tide here, and it is time to think of another move. We sit down in the skiff, drifting under the dome of unsoiled marine sky. Guy hands me a sandwich and we have our lunch, chewing and ruminating like cattle. We are comfortable enough together that we can fall silent for long periods of time. A flats skiff is a confined place and one in which potentials for irritation are brought to bear as surely as in an arctic cabin, but this comfort of solitude enhanced by companionship is the rarest commodity of angling. Pure solitude, nearly its equal, is rather more available.

Lunchtime, between tides, with the boat drifting before the wind, our piddling inclinations toward philosophy begin to emerge. My recent failure with the fly rod exaggerates my proclivity for higher things. We talk about "the meat bucket." Originally, the term indicated a particular place in the water that held fish in quantity. Then, gradually, it came to mean whole rivers or bays or banks that were good and, finally, states and regions where someone could live who could not live where the country was all shot to hell. In the end, the meat bucket was a situation of mind where everything was going to be okay. When you had gone and messed up your intelligence with whiskey or worse, jacked yourself all out of shape, the meat bucket was the final pie in the sky, the universal trout or steelhead or permit or what-all run, the place where you always threw the perfect loop and never had to live with right-hand winds, cold rain, broken homes, and failed religion.

The meat bucket was Bill Schaadt pantomiming coming up tight on a fifty-pound chinook on the Smith River, saying, "I'm *into* one!" loud and reverent; the meat bucket was Russ Chatham making a precise delivery at a hundred feet with a hangover; the meat bucket was Jim Harrison screaming that his knees were buckling and *"He's got all my line!"* on his first hundred-pound tarpon; the meat bucket was Bob Weddell laying his ear to your Hardy reel that a twelve-pound steelhead was making scream, and saying with rapture, "They're playing our song!" The meat bucket was Bob Tusken's weighted Bitch Creek nymphs hitting you in the head when you tried to cast them, Guy de la Valdene skinny-dipping between two guide boats full of glowering anglers at Cutoe Key, Chico Horvath miming a gangbang in his waders on the banks of the Firehole, Rudi Ferris sleeping on the garage floor waiting for "the bite," Woody Sexton looking with horror at the bad housekeeping in my skiff, seawater and Lucky Strike wrappers in the dunnage box. In the end it was all the unreckonable fragments of the sport that became the reference points of an obsession that you called the meat bucket; or, among the archdiocese of angling maniacs you had come to know, more simply, the M.B.

The push pole is secured once more in its chocks; the engine is down and again we are running. This time we head southwest toward Boca Grande Key. The light is so good we can see the stilt houses from here. The spongers browse around in their little boats, standing in the bow and steering the outboard motors with clothesline tied to their waists. They rake up sponges like oceanic gardeners.

We are heading for Ballast Key, where we expect to find tarpon and where I have every hope that I will not fall apart and bungle either the cast or the hookup, or the sometimes appalling fight that ensues.

The keys down here have a considerably less swampy character than those above us along the Gulf of Mexico. They are higher, with, in some cases, headlands, beaches, and woods. In the spring they are great meeting places for migrant warblers headed for cool northern forests.

We shut off next to an empty beach of wild palms amid

clouds of wheeling white seabirds, and Guy begins poling down the face of Ballast. There is a wash here that raises and drops the skiff. The bottom is rock and packed sand, dotted with sea fans, a desperately difficult place to pole without falling out of the boat. When fish are spotted the poling is so noisy that tarpon are often spooked, and the boat cannot be easily or quickly positioned for incoming fish. So you abandon yourself to the combinations and hope they come up in your favor.

We find tarpon at Ballast at the far end, almost to Woman Key: a string of fish, they are traveling on a bright sandy bottom, as distinct as fractured sections of pencil lead.

We are in good position and it is now only a question of waiting for them to come within range. At first we see them from afar, splashing and marking their progress purely in surface movement. They are no more scary this way than a school of feeding jacks.

Then, as they approach, their above-the-surface presence of wakes and splashes is replaced perceptually by the actual sight of fish as specific marine entities, individual torpedos coming at you. It is hideously unnerving, if you care about fishing.

I like my cast and on the first strip two fish turn out of the string to follow. Then one of them quite aggressively takes the fly and turns off to the side. I continue the strip I started with my left hand until I come up tight. Then, with the butt of the rod in my hip and the rod tip low and to the side, I hit two or three times hard.

The fish is in the air, upside down, making a noise that reminds you of horses, thunderous and final; your eye remembers the long white rip in the ocean. Then a short accelerated run is followed by an end-swapping jump by a game animal that has pulled all the stops. At the third jump the run begins. The fourth jump would be better observed through binoculars; the line no longer even points at the fish.

The tarpon has burned off 150 yards in such a way that the centrifugal surge is felt in the reel, shuddering the arm. Now he must be followed in the boat. The backing goes onto the reel at the expense of a painful swelling of the forearm and the shirt clinging wetly. After some time the fish is within 60 feet of us, where we can reasonably exert some pressure. Guy keeps the boat parallel to him, silver and brilliant in the deep green water, and the fight goes on, interrupted by inexorable 50- and 60-yard runs from which we patiently recover. Now the fish makes a number of sloshing, head-rattling jumps, after which, in his new weakness, I can turn him slightly on his side.

In a moment he is beside the boat, bright and powerful-looking. I take the pliers and seize the shank of the hook, and with a twist the tarpon is free, though he is slow to realize it. I reach down and hold him for a moment, and I sense in this touch his ocean-traveling power. An instant later he has vanished.

Guy tells me it's my turn to pole.

MOLLY

I HAVE A seven-year-old pointer. When she was a puppy she was wild, flushing birds far from the gun. She ran deer and often didn't come home at night at all. My dog has six hunting seasons under her belt now and, if anything, she is worse than ever. Her remote barking in the deep forest is the sound of bird hunting to me.

But this was to be the year when my dog Molly and I would get it all together. We were starting out clean. She doesn't blame me, knowing I have worries. And I, who despise negative reinforcement and the electrical collar, have come to see my dog as a person as rich in neurosis as Oblomov. Like me, though, she aims to please.

I always have a kind of private opening day, simply because my vague orientation as a hunter keeps me from getting the news. My opening day is liable to be weeks into the season. This year was no exception. The first hard frost wiped out what was left of our garden. Last year the horses beat the frost by three weeks, moving brutally among the tomato vines and oak-leaf lettuce plants with their pie-plate-size hoofs and yellow piano-key teeth. Anyway, the garden was shot. Jack Frost was in the air, and the departure of a long list of summer houseguests and a long line of sour-mash dead soldiers was enough to send this sojourner into the field.

There is an unsuccessful motif that has long threatened to eclipse my hunting life. I feel it began one late fall day long ago in a duck blind with my father at the mouth of a Michigan river. We'd had a good morning's pass shooting. (Those were the days when blacks, redheads, and canvasbacks were not the sort of thing one was inclined to send to the taxidermist.) It was very cold, and my father kindly offered to pick up the decoys, with their icy lines, if I would clean up the blind.

While he rowed around in the blowing sleet, I tidied up. We had a Zenith radio to listen to the Lions game and a chaste little briquette fire upon which to smokelessly prepare various snacks between flights. I put the empty tins and papers in a neat pile next to the radio to take home. I leaned my 20-gauge in the homeward corner of the blind next to our limit of ducks. And, just how I shall never know, I set my father's 12-gauge butt-first in the fire.

Then I went outside and dawdled. Our blind was on a long, old dike of dredging from the construction of the Livingstone Channel. It spanned the U.S.–Canadian border. The inner-sanctum duck gunners in my hometown took licenses in both countries, owned a hundred cedar decoys, a sneak boat, and usually a layout boat. The prestige gun was a Winchester Model 12 with a thirty-inch full-choke barrel that was as close to riflery as shotgunners ever get. There was a mild kind of disparaging rivalry between Canadian and American hunters, and not much more fraternization between the lines than there was in the First World War between the Hun and the doughboy. We knew in our hearts that Canadians slaughtered ducks on the water, shot gulls, and guzzled weird diuretic ales in their Ontario public houses.

When my father brought the boat ashore and tilted the Evinrude down against the transom, I helped him pull the bow up against the granite dredging. He climbed out on the rocks and went into the blind. Then he came from the blind and asked me why I had done it. In his hands was his Winchester. Much smoke poured from the wrong end. The butt-stock extended about 2½ inches behind the trigger guard.

"I would have thought," said my father without rancor, "that you could have smelled the recoil pad burning. It's rubber."

I don't suppose either of us knew on that day, there in the driving sleet on the American frontier, that in some way the most resonant chord of my life as a hunter had been struck.

But, frankly, the hell with that. Out here in the northern Rockies the sky is big. Cowboys still gaze coolly upon the dudes from inside their air-conditioned Wagoneers. Out behind the old prefab the sage still turns blue in the spring. Here and there tranquilizer-junkie grizzly bears slump in the junipers with hypodermic projectiles buried in their fundaments. And I felt it was not unreasonable to think of a fresh start in hunting.

As I say, I had the dog. Molly. Born in Michigan of an old line of Arkansas hunting machines, the kind that roar in your ears and run up and down that kennel wire like orangutans.

The breeder had brought out two armloads of seven-week-old pointers, wrinkling their eyes in the sunshine and groaning. He put them all in the grass, where they began to wander around and pounce on each other. I had done my homework in gun-dog books, and had any number of Nash Buckingham—level prejudices of classical fanaticism. My opinions were emphatically not based upon the actual slumberous yard dogs of my own life and experience.

I knew how to spot a bold, promising pup and how not to take guff from wily dog handlers. But as I surveyed the tumbling fat puppies on the lawn, I began to notice an isolated case: a pup who didn't want to play, who was afraid, and who sat by herself blinking slowly — a dog with absolutely no future on the concrete runs of a serious kennel.

The wily dog handler could not believe his luck when I forked over hard cash for that one. My brother was with me, and my action inspired him to cough up for a pup himself.

We headed home with the speckled babies in the front of the car, crawling around the gearshift and crying for their mother. We were moved.

In no time flat I had my dog dancing to a bird's wing on a fishing rod. I also had a piece of clothesline, an Acme Thunderer dog whistle, and a blank pistol, props for an outlandish charade that was to last many many years.

In the meantime, another friend, Jim Harrison, had also acquired a pointer, a crazed muscle-bound hyena who once swam over the horizon in Lake Michigan while our wives wept on the beach. We would hunt our dogs in tandem that first fall on Mister Partridge, the Einstein of the northern forest.

I drove up to Jim's and brought Molly into the house. Molly and Jim's dog Missy did their best to recapture the magic of the tiger scene in *Little Black Sambo* where everything turns to butter. They did leg springs off the backs of chairs so that the chairs would still be doing figure eights in midair long after the dogs had left the room. They would lie side by side on their backs under the sofa and pull out all the stuffing. They would try to shatter glass with their voices when a car pulled into the driveway, micturating all the while on a couch, a pillow, a doily, or anything precious that they could evaluate. Jim explained that this was how it was with hunting dogs. Jim's wife had a reply that I sincerely believe it will someday be possible to print.

Zero hour. We roll through the cedar gloom of the northern fastness. The two dogs are looking out of the window. I have come to think of them as existentialists. Jim and I feel instinctively that the forest is stiff with birds of the grouse persuasion. We're bucking along in my Land Rover, whose odometer is giving 100,000 miles a long hard look.

We pull off the road into a grove of trees and get out of the Rover. Then we run all those numbers around the car that hunters like to get into: racking open the guns, donning ammo belts and canvas coats, last hits on the coffee thermos, and light war-zone chatter that is pointedly not about hunting.

The dogs are still inside the car, pouring around behind the glass, jumping from front to back, back to front, scrambling for traction on the upholstery.

A moment of silence, and Jim says, "Uh, shall we let the dogs out?"

"Sure," I say, almost gaily. I open the front door a little and am rudely slammed back as the two evil hounds vault for the forest like voltage jumping a gap.

Of all instruments, the Acme Thunderer seems the least appropriate for playing dirges, but over and again Jim tried, I tried. A bluish pallor fell across our faces. From the distance the yapping of the fun couple rang in the swamps.

Later Jim and I decided to go hunting. We walked miles in a forest less than entirely stiff with game birds. Ultimately, a partridge sprang into the air. Jim and I fired simultaneously; The bird fell. We ran from converging courses to the bird and came darkly close to having words. An autopsy with an examination of shot was considered. We would carefully shred the corpse with a carrot grater, placing each bit of shot on a sheet of white paper to be measured in the micrometer. But this was ruled out because we were both shooting 7½s.

The pitch of the dogs' barking suddenly changed. They apparently had treed a coon.

Later in the day our dogs came back to relax and warm up in the car. We sealed them inside the Land Rover, then wedged our way through the doors to be sure neither of them tried anything cheap like another forty-mile-per-hour swamp crossing. But the dogs were content to save themselves in the back, studying migrating songbirds high in the sky through the window and listening to the radio.

We crossed the country. A grouse had been seen in a cherry orchard that week, and we were headed for that cherry orchard. A short time later we were slithering up a wet clay road that ended in an open field. Jim instructed me to head across, toward the woods and orchard at the other side.

I shifted the Land Rover into low and started out onto the

level field. A minute later this machine, which had proven itself all over the world — in desert and in swamp — lurched to a stop within whimpering distance of a thousand white cottages. We got out and rather formally looked under the car. The differential was resting neatly in the crotch of a cherry-tree stump. I got back in and put it in four-wheel drive, compound low, and goosed hell out of it. Nothing. This went on for about an hour. Finally I got out of the car and the dogs shot between my legs and went shrieking into the sunset. We saw a grouse depart the orchard as they barreled through.

Sometime later we called a wrecker. How strange it all seems now, the big white wrecker in a level open field, hauling that safari vehicle off a cherry stump while the dogs prospected for county lines at incalculable land speeds. And how strange, finally, to be standing out there in the absolute middle of nowhere, presenting one's AAA card to a service-station attendant.

But why go over that? It's morbid to think that the past lays its dead hand on all our days. It's been twenty years since I burned my father's shotgun and more than five since the wrecker came. I've been in Montana for some seasons now. It's a different time, a different place. I have a private opening day to look forward to.

Molly is ready, too. She comes into my room and stares at my hunting boots for long periods of time. She howls when my son mistakenly shuts her in the bathroom. But, except that it is bird season, what was she doing in the bathroom anyway? And she does irresponsible things that indicate that her mind is not on the routine domesticities of out-of-season dog life. For example, yesterday she ate a two-volume edition of *Anna Karenina*.

This will be our day together.

My son's playmates are here, and as I have trained them, they are throwing things for the dog to make her run around so that on hunting days like this one she will be tired before we ever start and not so inclined to clear out on a strafing mission.

I put dog and gear into the same old Land Rover, now as thoroughly packed as a Spalding Dot, and head north of our ranch to an area of fertile, dry-land farming I know to be full of fat grain-fed pheasants.

The drive takes nearly an hour, and from time to time I study my dog's eyes for indications of lunacy and the grossly unpredictable. She looks as sound as a silver dollar. Even *I* feel a trifle seasoned. I wonder if she has noticed that, or if, in fact, she's found any little reason for admiring me.

I leave the Rover by a grove of thornbushes. The open country lies in fast-intersecting declinations that fall from the foothills of the Crazy Mountains. I am on a plateau and can see the Absaroka Range to the south, already snowy. It's slightly stormy, and plumes of snow are whirling out of the higher passes. But down here the sun plays all around us.

As I get ready Molly stays close to me, prancing like a cheerleader. A small cloud of butterflies dances across the tractor ruts and Molly makes after them like a rocking horse but returns to my side when I whistle.

All right, ready to go. "Find some birds," I tell her. She gives me one last look, as though from the cockpit of a fighter plane, and pours it on. I don't believe this. My heart begins to sink as she ticks off the first 880 and I realize nothing has changed.

I walk gloomily along a shelterbelt of Lombardy poplars with only the vaguest reference to the shrinking liver-and-white form in the distance. At the far edge of the field I see her stop, lock up on point, then selfishly pounce into the middle of the birds. Gloom. Gloom. Pheasants scatter. But wait — *my God!* They're flying this way.

Like the lowest kind of dry-gulch artist, I crouch in the hedgerow. The pheasants keep coming, Molly yelping along behind. At fifty yards I rise to the balls of my feet. At twenty I stand up out of the brambles and . . . *shoot a double!* Two cock pheasants tumble. I scramble around to gather them up before my dog can rend and eat them.

I hang the handsome birds from my belt. Their rich, satisfying odor keeps man's best friend trotting along at my side. Now and again I hear her teeth click lightly. There is a spring I know near the thorn grove where I gather some wild, peppery watercress for our game dinner.

At last that perfect symbiosis between a man and his dog! I finally feel that Molly is as good a hunter as I am.

We approach the Land Rover. The cloud of butterflies blows across the tractor ruts again, and I check myself from pursuit.

A
VISIT TO
RODERICK
HAIG-BROWN

For many who have seen angling as the symptom of a way of living, rather than a series of mechanical procedures, the writing of Roderick Haig-Brown has served as scripture. And in a sport with an ample but often abysmal literature of easy heroism and quasi-technical advice, the reader turns to Haig-Brown with the same general sensation he would have when the oxygen mask drops into his lap upon what is referred to on commercial aircraft as "a sudden loss of cabin pressure."

For one thing, at the center of each of his works is the conviction that the world will not cease its circumnavigation of the sun if no one goes fishing again. Fishing for Haig-Brown is sublimely without function and therefore, in its explication, without the perpetually wearying assumption that the angler is really hot stuff.

Haig-Brown is a famous fisherman in an era when famous fishermen scramble to name flies and knots after themselves with a self-aggrandizing ardor unknown since the Borgia popes. Anyone who has sat in on the bad-mouth sessions at fly shops and guides' docks will welcome the serene observations of a man more interested in fish than fishing, and more interested in the whole kingdom of nature than holding water and hot spots.

There is scarcely an angler so avid that he doesn't spend most of his time not angling; much of the time, because of the inclemency of the weather or the demands of work or the inferiority of actuality to fantasy, he pursues his sport in what is called "the armchair." There are any number of armchair anglers who do not own armchairs. These are harmless creatures whose minds have beaten out everything else for the control of things; and for them the theory of the sport lies heavily upon the sport itself.

Others use the armchair, sometimes an actual armchair, selectively to read and to think; and at such times, if they are anglers, they are susceptible to the guidance of men who have written about this peerless sport which affects the world's fortunes not at all. For them there is no better place to turn than to the writing of Roderick Haig-Brown.

That much has been clear for some time: Haig-Brown's prominence in this fugitive literature is seldom doubted. His great series *Fisherman's Spring, Summer, Fall,* and *Winter* is an integral part of the shelf of every angler who thinks about what he is doing. *Measure of the Year, Return to the River,* and *The Western Angler* amplify that great series and lead the angler to increasingly broad preoccupations within his sport, until he shares with Haig-Brown a continuity of perceptions, from the tying of small brilliant flies to the immeasurable and celestial movements of fish in migration. Finally, he treats the way the angler holds his fishing grounds in trust; because I suppose before anything else Haig-Brown is a conservationist — and not, I was to learn, one of the walking wounded of the ecology movement.

He lives in Campbell River, British Columbia; and one summer I decided to pay him a visit, not, I hasten to admit, without some trepidation. Sportsman, magistrate, English prose stylist of weight, Haig-Brown seems artfully contrived to make me feel in need of a haircut and refurbished credentials. I wanted to withdraw my novels from publication and extirpate the bad words, reduce the number of compliant ladies by as much as 96 percent.

As I winged my way north, the Rockies, in my present mood, unrolled themselves beneath me like skin trouble. A drunk boarded the plane in Spokane and chose the seat next to me. He wore a shiny FBI drip-dry DeLuxo summer suit and a pair of armadillo cowboy boots. He told me he couldn't fly sober and that since he was doing emergency heart surgery in Seattle that afternoon, he didn't have time to drive.

"At three o'clock," he explained, "I'm going to thwack open a guy's heart and I'm already half in the bag. I may have to farm this mother out. I'm totaled." He leaned over to look out the window. "Aw, hell," he said, "I'll end up doing it. It's my dedication. Think about this: when the hero of Kafka's *Meta-morphosis* wakes up and discovers that he has been transformed into a giant beetle, the first thing he does is call the office and tell his boss he's going to be delayed. Where are you headed?"

I explained about my trip. As a reply, I suppose, my seat-mate told me he had seen matadors in the Mexico City Plaza de Toros fighting a giant Coca-Cola bottle as it blew around the arena in the wind; ultimately it was drawn from the ring behind two horses and to resonant *olés*, just like a recently dispatched bull. "Tell that to your buddy Haig-Brown. He's a writer. He'll like that story."

My schizophrenia, my need of a haircut, the patch on my pants, my chipped tooth — all formerly coiled like a well-fed cobra — now began to move restlessly about far from the snake charmer of self-confidence. Haig-Brown seemed to loom in the northern fastness while I was being coached to tell him a story about a Coke bottle in a Mexican bullring. I felt entirely off on the wrong foot.

At this point, my companion confessed that he was not a doctor. He was an inventor. He had invented an aluminum ring that you put over the exhaust pipe of your automobile; stretched across the aluminum ring was a piece of cheesecloth.

It was an antipollution device. It had been patented in twelve states. "If you can come in with twenty thousand dollars," he said, "I can let you have half the action when we go public."

"Well, I don't know . . ."

"I've got a friend who sold ten million smackers' worth of phony stock and got a slap on the wrist from the Securities Commission. This is free enterprise, pal. Get in or get out."

"I just don't see how I . . ."

"How about your friend Haig-Brown? Maybe he can buy in. Maybe he can stake you and the two of you can split the action. What say?"

In Vancouver, I spent a long layover waiting for the small plane to take us to Campbell River. There were a number of people whose small luggage suggested a weekend trip to Vancouver, an enormously muscular girl in hot pants, and a number of loggers. At one point, I looked up from the book I was reading to see a familiar face. It was Roderick Haig-Brown, lost in conversation with the ordinary people around me, many of whom seemed to know him.

I introduced myself, and we flew north together, Haig-Brown describing the country of mountain ranges and fjord-like inlets beneath us with great specificity. Everything we saw reminded him of something he knew, and despite his modesty as a storyteller (and he is a meticulous listener), I was reminded of his two great strengths as a writer: his command of anecdote and his ability to reason.

I told him about the surgeon-inventor with whom I'd flown to Seattle. His chin dropped to his chest and he laughed convulsively. I began to be able to see him.

Haig-Brown is British-born and somehow looks it. Though the great share of his life has been spent as a Canadian, you are reminded of the "county" English for whom culture and sport are not mutually exclusive. To say that he is a youthful sixty-three suggests nothing to those who know him; he is neither sixty-three nor, it would seem, any other age. He is rather tall, strong, and thin. He is bald on the top of his head, and the prelate's band of hair that he retains sticks out behind like a merganser in profile. His eyes are intent and clear and so suggest seriousness that it is perpetually surprising how quickly he laughs. He has a keen appreciation of genuine wit; but he will accept whatever is going. He relished *Mister Hulot's Holiday.*

By the time we approached Campbell River, Haig-Brown was at my urging describing his origin as a lay magistrate in the British Columbia courts. "Well, my predecessor as magistrate was a teetotaler and didn't drive an automobile; and he was hard on the loggers and fishermen who were my friends."

We landed on the edge of the forest. Haig-Brown's wife, Ann, met us in a car that said on its bumper: LET'S BLOW UP THE WORLD. WE'LL START WITH AMCHITKA. Both Haig-Browns, I was to see, had a firm sense of Canadian nationalism, a sense of belonging to a distinct political and cultural entity, that seems so fresh among Canadians today as to be something of a discovery both for them and for Americans who see it. The inherent optimism is in some ways painful for an American in the 1970s. But to a man like Haig-Brown, whose formal judicial district is some ten thousand square miles, mostly wilderness, it would be difficult not to be touched by the optimism of a frontier.

The Haig-Browns headed home, caught up in their own talk, while I waited for my rented car. Later Ann Haig-Brown would ask me quite ingenuously, "Isn't Roddy wonderful?"

I was raised two miles from Canada; but this seemed to be the interior. Most of my trip from Vancouver to Campbell River had been over grizzly country; yet I had seen some of the ugliest clear-cut logging in those noble ranges. The woman who brought me my car had moved to Campbell River from the Yukon. My spirits rose. How did she like Campbell River? Very well, she replied, but the shopping plaza in the Yukon was better. I wondered if she would have the same chance to marvel at decimation's speed as we'd had at home.

From the largest seaplane base in North America, poised to

survey the roadless country around us, to the hockey hints in the newspaper and the handsome moored salmon boats with names like *Skeena Cloud* and *Departure Bay* (despite the odd pleasure boat with *Costa Lotsa* on its transom), I felt I was in another country.

During my week of visiting Roderick Haig-Brown, at some inconvenience to his intensely filled schedule, I began to see that I had little chance of discovering that precise suppurating angst, that dismal or craven psychosis that is so indispensable to the author of short biographies.

I had fantasized a good deal about Haig-Brown's life; angler, frontiersman, and man of letters, he seemed to have wrested a utopian situation for himself. It was with some shock that I perceived his immersion in the core problems of our difficult portion of the twentieth century.

I knew that his work with the Pacific Salmon Commission represented an almost symbolically tortuous struggle for balanced use of a powerful resource among explosive political forces. But the hours I spent in his court did as much as anything to disabuse me of any cheerful notions that Haig-Brown's clarity as a writer was the product of a well-larded sinecure.

A man was brought before him for reckless and drunken driving. The man allowed that he did not feel he was "speeding too awful much." His speed was established by the arresting officer as something like 300 percent of the limit. The officer mentioned that the man had been impaired by drink; he described the man's spectacular condition. "I wasn't all that impaired." A numerical figure from the Breathalyzer test was quoted, one that suggested saturation. The accused had heard these numbers against himself before. He reiterated doggedly that he hadn't been "impaired that awful much," and gave up.

A young logger and his girlfriend who had run out on a hotel bill appeared before Haig-Brown. What did he do, Haig-Brown inquired, referring to the specifics of the young man's profession. Boomed and set chokers. Haig-Brown nodded; he had been a logger too, one who had blown up his inherited Jeffries shotgun trying to make fireworks in camp on New Year's Eve.

"You are addicted to heroin, aren't you?" Haig-Brown asked the sturdy young man. The logger replied that he was; so was his girlfriend. He had always lived between here and Powell River, had only had eight dollars the last time he got out of jail, and so on. He and his girlfriend wanted to help each other get on the methadone program. He thought their chances of doing so were reduced if he went to jail.

The prosecutor wanted a jail sentence. Haig-Brown released the young man on promise of restitution to the hotel-keeper and adjourned to his chambers, where his mongrel dog slept in front of the desk. I noted that the prosecutor was anxious for something stiffer; and Haig-Brown remarked that the prosecutor thought the logger was not being sincere with the court. I asked him what he thought about the young logger. "He's probably conning me," Haig-Brown said, then added with admiration, "but he's a marvelous talker, isn't he?" We talked on until I discovered what is an essential axiom to Haig-Brown in his practice (he is frequently accused of leniency): a magistrate who risks an accused man's liberty risks his own honor.

Haig-Brown feels himself in the presence of the potentially ridiculous at all times. He does not seem to feel that his position as magistrate or as chancellor of the University of Victoria separates him by nature from the people who come before his court. And when he talks about the scheme to dam the Fraser River and wipe our the major run of Pacific salmon, a toothy smile forms around the stem of his pipe and he says, "Bastards!" as though to discover that his opponents cannot resist the temptation to be ridiculous.

After court one day, Haig-Brown and I stopped to buy some wine. While he shopped, I wandered through the store and discovered some curious booze called (I think) Wood-pecker Juice. I brought it up to the cash register to show Haig-Brown. "Bring it." He grinned. "We'll take it home and try it."

We spent a number of evenings in his study and library, where I prodded him to talk about himself. He would stand with one foot tipped forward like a cavalier in an English painting, knocking his pipe on his heel from time, trying to talk about other than himself: his children, Thomas Hardy, whom he knew as a child, his literary heroes like Richard Jeffries and Henry Fielding, the great Indians of the Pacific Northwest.

Eventually my persistence led him to sketch things in: his schooling at Charterhouse, his attempts to get into the then shrinking colonial service, his emigrating to Canada, his experience during the Second World War as a major in the Canadian Army on loan to the Mounted Police, a post that took him over the entire country — "The making of a Canadian," said his wife — his life as a logger, angler, conservationist, university administrator, and writer. As I saw him, standing amid an Edwardian expanse of well-bound books, sipping brandy and wearing a cowboy belt buckle with a bighorn ram on it, the gift of the Alberta Fish and Game Department, I began to be able to visualize that powerful amalgamation and coherence it takes to make a successful frontiersman. In Haig-Brown, a Western Canadian with roots in Thomas Hardy's England, I imagined I saw an exemplary instance of the genre.

He had just made his first trip back to his place of origin in England, wandering around the streams he had fished and the places of his childhood unseen in forty years. I wondered how it had been.

"It was like being psychoanalyzed," he said.

Such a life does not make sentimentalists.

SEASONS
THROUGH
THE NET

THE PUMP in the well kept shutting off. I messed around with the pressure switch to no avail. And when I restarted the pump by hitting the breakers, it belched rusty water into the sink and the pressure wasn't strong enough to sprinkle the garden. The pump is 180 feet down there with its own dark and secret life. I call the plumber.

An hour later the plumber is in the well pit. I look at him in that gloomy hole with his rusty wrench, the water up around his ankles, the pale tuberous roots of vegetation sticking out of the cold earthen sides of the well. He asks me how I've been doing; he means with fish.

I go out to the mailbox and run into a man taking in the sights with his wife. He wants to talk. They live in a trailer near Red Lodge, and he sells concrete animals for yards. He keeps a good quarter horse and is a weekend jackpot roper. He's looking to catch him a large trout, he says. It must be in the air.

I stood with fly rod in hand on my first day of trout fishing for the year. We were a mile above the bridge that leads to White Sulphur Springs. They were retrieving a strange souvenir of winter. A Texaco wrecker was backed to the bank, hauling a dead horse out of the river, hauling him up by his hind legs, swinging him out through the willows on the end of the boom in black, wet-meat totality. A sandbank had gone out from under him, and he was lost to the river as surely as today's water and streamside pasture.

When the ice broke up, the flooded river had returned to its banks and the broad, dull floodlands reshaped along the road in their loops and meandering symmetry. By June the spring storms were light-shot and prominent, quite unlike the homogeneous gloom of April: the first summer storms, perhaps. In the evening the Absaroka and Gallatin ranges overlapped like jagged sheets of palest slate under the pearly turbulence, and the river dropped from flood to a full canal gloss. Then, at last, the spangled river came out from under, braided in places like a glacial river, or lying along sandy bars in a green, bending slot of oxygen and trout.

Sunup got earlier and earlier, until you woke under blue windows full of blowing cottonwood seeds, always with the feeling you had overslept. The pass above the ranch was already dropping its long lever of candied light into day. You could hear the creek from the bedroom window, racing down stony terraces among dry junipers.

It was clear that if you weren't careful, another summer would slip through the net, trailing wasted time, mortgage payments, and a number of things you could have saved.

The river stayed out of color well past the Fourth of July on our stretch. We hiked into the canyon of the Yellowstone to catch the last days of the salmonfly hatch, carrying rods and packs around geysers and poison springs with deer skeletons on their bottoms, and into pine copses through which sulfurous steam blew, and down long switchbacks of scree and crumbly rhyolite. The far side of the canyon rose trail-less miles away with our slow descent. It seemed another world from us: absolute, remote, and changing color with every hour's shift of light.

We were a true phalanx of trout bums, since dispersed as

far away as New Zealand and as near as wives and families, that quicksand into which a troll's share is taken, generation after generation, spitting bamboo fragments and blue dun hackle, to join — with some decency — another of sport's secret mothball fleets.

Finally, at the bottom of this hot canyon, there is the river, a terrific surprise. And the switchbacks jut in to trail along its sides. The river seems quite literally a crack in the earth, here so exposed as to be principally rock. So while our home stretch of the same river is still brown with spring runoff and irrigation, slough-connected and meandering among old ranches, here it is a lightning fissure in rock, empyrean blue and slightly unearthly.

In the canyon the trout's range of travel is bounded by falls, sudden declivities, or change of altitude in the slab rock: the blue river turns green-white in a right-angle downward turn, a long ribbon of falling water, roaring and blowing away. The trout live above or below such a place; these are separate civilizations.

We cast our big, visible dries on the glossy rush, and quickly trout soar into focus and vanish with our flies. Rods bow and lines shear through the water. Handsome cutthroat trout are beached and released in the gravel, wriggling back into deep water and flickering invisibly into the pale water curtain.

A mile below the trail's end, we found a feeder creek that dropped almost vertically from pool to minute pool. And each pool held handsome cutthroats that took flies readily and leaped, dropping down the plateaus, until they were in the river itself. It seemed unfathomable to hook fish at eye level, watch their descent, then finish the fight under your feet. Many of these fish were in their spawning colors and shimmered in the current as brilliant as macaws.

We ended the afternoon's fishing in time to save an increment of energy for the climb out. A great blue lid of shadow had started down one wall, and the boulders and escarpments bore eccentrically long panels of shade. Above us, a few impressive birds of prey sorted the last thermals. In two hours they were below us, turning grave circles in polite single file.

At Tower Falls we stumbled out of the woods. It was getting dark and someone fumbled for the car keys.

Mirage on the road crowns as I spring along under sage-covered ledges; pools of water on macadam hills. Blackbirds scatter before my truck.

All the grass that seemed to indicate something about possibility, that turned up in mountain edges full of yellow-blossomed clover, was sun-dried like hard wire, annealed and napped in one direction or in whorls like cowlicks but distinctly dun-colored on the hard hills.

Now when the sheep yarded up in the orchard, their fetor hung slowly downwind with an edge that was less organic than chemical. In the heat of broad day I saw a coyote on a yellow grassy bench digging along the length of a pocket gopher's workings, throwing up an industrious stream of dirt behind himself like a beagle.

In midsummer big streams like the Missouri headwaters can come to seem slumberous and unproductive. The great sweeps of river are warm and exposed; and the fishing can be perfectly lousy.

Then, evening fishing on the spring creeks — streams that jump full-grown, quite mythically, from under ledges or out of swamp ground, and flow for miles before joining a river, often at some secretive or wooded confluence. The stub ends of such streams are seen by passing fishermen, who seldom suspect the trout network lying beyond.

The angler parcels out the midsummer months with pocket situations, good for a few amusing visits. I always make two or three trips to my nearby beaver ponds, wallowing through swamp and chest-high grass to the beaver houses, beyond which stands water full of small brook trout. In the still ponds are the gnawed stumps of trees, big enough in diameter to suggest the recently solid ground these advanced rodents have conquered.

If we fish here in the fall, we bring back wild crab apples for baking with the easily gathered creel of brook trout. The fish in these ponds live on freshwater shrimp and their flesh is salmon pink on either side of their pearly backbones. The trout themselves are as surpassingly vivid as fine enamels, and the few meals a year we make of them are sacraments.

The stream that flows through our place, Deep Creek, is lost in irrigation head gates by August, so it has no trout. Obviously, my son fishes the pretty pool next to our cattle guard, year after year increasing his conviction that trout are a difficult fish. Morbid friends say he is a sportsman of the future. I will explain to him as an acceptable realpolitik: if the trout are lost, smash the state. More than any other fish, trout are dependent upon the ambience in which they are caught. It would be hard to say whether or not it is the trout or the angler who is more sensitized to the degeneration of habitat, but probably it is the trout. At the first signs of deterioration, the otherwise vigorous trout just politely quits, as though to say, "If that's how you want it . . ." Meanwhile, the angler qualitatively lapses in citizenship. Other kinds of fishermen may toss their baits into the factory shadows. The trout fisherman who doesn't turn dangerously unpatriotic just politely quits, like the trout.

It's October, a bluebird Indian-summer day. Opening day for ducks, and you're going to need your Coppertone. It will be over eighty degrees.

Standing on the iron bridge at Pine Creek, I look upstream. I suppose it is a classic autumn day in the Rockies; by some standards, it is outrageous. The China-blue river breaks up into channels that jet back together from chutes and gravel tongues to form a deep emerald pool that flows toward me on the bridge with a hidden turbulence like a concealed shock wave. Where the river lifts upstream on its gravel runs, it glitters.

The division of the river makes a multiplicity of banks, but the main ones are shrouded with the great, almost heartbreaking cottonwoods that are now all gone to a tremulous, sun-shot gold, reaching over the river's blue rush. Where the pools level out, the bizarre free-traveling clouds with their futuristic shapes are reflected.

I can see my friend and neighbor, a painter, walking along the high cutbank above the river. This would be a man who has ruined his life with sport. He skulks from his home at all hours with gun or rod. Today he has both.

"What are you doing?"

"Trout fishing and duck hunting."

I feel like a man who has been laid off to be only trout fishing.

"As you see," says the painter, gesticulating strangely, "I'm ready for anything. I spoiled half the day with work and errands. I have to pull things out of the fire before they go from bad to worse." Across the river, the Absaroka Range towers up out of the warm valley with snowcapped peaks and gold stripes of aspen intermittently dividing the high pasture and the evergreen forest. My friend heads off, promising a report later on.

The last chance you get at overall strategy in trout fishing, before you lose yourself in the game itself, is during the period called "rigging up." I stand next to my truck, looking upstream and down, and remove the knurled brass cap from the aluminum tube. I am deep into the voodoo of rigging up. I draw the smoky-colored bamboo shafts from their poplin sack and join the rod. I fasten the old pewtery Hardy St. George reel my father gave me to the cork seat and knot the monofilament leader in place. Then I irritate myself over the matter of which fly to use, finally darting my hand into the fly box blindly. I come up with one I tied myself that imitates the effect of a riot gun on a love seat. I swiftly return it and take out a professionally tied spruce fly and attach it to my leader. I get into my waders, slipping the blue police suspenders onto my shoulders. Rigging up is over and there is fishing, or angling, to be done.

By the time my friend is out of sight, I am scrambling down the bank to the river, which here is in three channels around long willow-covered islands. By cautiously wading the heads of pools in these channels, one can cross the mighty river on foot, a cheap thrill I do not deprive myself of. Regardless of such illusions, I am an ordinary wader and pick my way over the slippery rocks, experiencing the various nuances of having my heart in my mouth. I have friends who are superior waders. One of them, significantly a former paratrooper, glides downstream whenever he loses his footing, until he touches down again, erect as a penguin all the while. At any and all mishaps when wading big rivers I tend to feel that I am too young to die, then fob off this cowardice as "reverence for nature."

This late in the year, the first channel crossing is child's play. I wade over to the long willow island that is decorated on this shore by a vintage automobile, a breakaway bit of Montana riprap, high and dry, with river sand up to the steering wheel.

The brush willows form an interior jungle, all the details of which contrive to slap you in the face over and over again as you bushwhack through. I come to a small clearing where a shallow sandy-bottomed slough has penetrated. A school of fry, a couple of feet wide and maybe ten feet long, dominates the end of the slough. With my approach these thousands of fish scatter toward the river; this is as fertile a nursery area as it is possible to imagine, dense and dark with infant fish.

I continue across the island, sweating in my waders, and

end up at a broad, bright channel. The tenderloin of the spot is a 150-foot bevel of current, along the edge of which trout persistently hang. I wade into position, false-casting the necessary amount of line to get under way. Then I make my first cast, up sun, and coronas of mist hang around the traveling direction of the line. I mend the line, throwing a belly into it to make the streamer continually present itself broadside to trout holding upstream in the current. I have a short strike early on, but I miss it.

Then nothing except the steady surge of the river against my legs until I can feel it bending with enormous purpose toward North Dakota and its meeting with the Missouri. In the green of the river, the ghostly orbs of white boulders are buried in running channels. The river is a fluid envelope for trout, occasionally marred by the fish themselves rising to take an insect and punctuating the glassy run with a whorl that opens and spirals downstream like a smoke ring. The boulders are constant, but the river soars away to the east.

After a period of methodical fishing, I finally come up tight on a trout. He holds throbbing for a long moment, then without any run at all is suddenly aerial. Four crisp dashes later and the trout is vividly alive and cold in my hand. As I return him to the river, I bend over and watch him hold briefly in the graveled current between my feet; then quick as light he's gone.

I stand up and I feel that mild, aching joy of the first fish and I look to the long river moss in the crystal gravel channels, streaming and wavering like radio signals.

I return to the bridge and court my soul, gazing into the rapids. The painter appears within the hour, empty-handed. Today he is both a duck hunter and a trout fisherman, so that when he says "I want a drink," he does so with such simplicity it is like a dog's bark, "IWANTADRINK!" When we have had some drinks, we begin to talk faster and faster, with less and less simplicity, frequently interrupting each other.

The painter pours out his origins as an angler on the California streams, fishing the Truckee with revered uncles and cousins. The palmier days in the Golden State were good to anglers who wandered the great drainages from Sierra to Pacific. Now California has gone on to bigger stuff, helping our republic to really pour on the coals. Some of the trout the painter caught were heading for the sea. As a midwestern angler, I feel the pinch conversationally, and so lay great emphasis on the native brook trout we tracked down in the swampy headwaters of our own cedary and painfully recalled streams.

The thing is this: my trout memories precede my actual sighting of a trout. They go way back to a time when, inflamed to angling by rock bass and perch, I read hunting and fishing magazines and settled upon the trout as the only fish worthy of my ability. Also the broadbill swordfish. I had examined the Rockwell Kent illustrations in my father's copy of *Moby Dick*. I didn't for the moment see what I could do about the white whale. Among my friends a rumor persisted of giant squid in the Humboldt Current that assaulted cabin cruisers and doused anglers with black ink before sinking a parrotlike beak into their brain pans. Not even this enormity could compete with the trout for my attention, though putting the gaff to a wilderness of tentacles had its appeal for a bloodthirsty child. Finally, I fished for trout in ways other than my fantasy and for many ruinous years haunted Michigan's cheerful trout rivers. Now, here, the painter and I were loath to confess we'd moved family, bag, and baggage, to Montana for the sake of, well, *not even a mammal.*

We walk back, one trying to outremember the other. I can see the sun roosting deep in the aspens and spruce. Chickweed and wild roses flow down out of the forest carpet around the garden and up the sides of the compost heap. A sleeping bag floats on a clump of laurel, sunning out. You can walk in any direction of the compass from here and sooner or later you will run into a trout. And you see, at some point, that you will keep making that walk.

The Indian-summer day ends with an edge; and during that night the temperature falls forty degrees. In the morning you squint out the kitchen door into a snowfield. The orchard looks like a corsage, and the poles in the corral are snow-capped in stillness. Trout season is over.

ANGLING
VERSUS
ACTS OF GOD

THIS WAS ONE of the ways a fishing trip could begin. The airline smashed my tackle, and in less than twenty-four hours after starting I lay in bed at our hotel in Victoria, food-poisoned.

Frank, my companion, was speaking to the house physician. "It came on him very suddenly," he said. *"He didn't even finish his drink."*

I lay there, the poisoned pup of American angling, and wondered about the long flight north the next day. At that moment our itinerary seemed to lie heavy upon the land. We were going up into the Skeena drainage, and I realized that if I could stop vomiting (and rueing the prawn dinner that had precipitated this eventuality) I would see matchless country and have angling to justify all the trouble. It would be the perfect antidote to food poisoning and all the other dark things.

As it was, the trip seemed a trifle askew. Coming in from Seattle, I had inadvertently been thrust among the members of an Ohio travel group; a mixed bag, coming from all parts of the country. "We're with Hiram Tours," one man said to our stewardess as we flew north from Seattle. "Is that Alaska down there? Or Oregon?"

The stewardess began a quick and voluntary rundown of the glories of Our Neighbor to the North. "There is a mountain in Banff," she explained momentously, "that they've named Mount Eisenhower." She paused to look first at the blank uncomprehending faces, then at the sullen Pacific beneath us. She exhaled audibly. "After your former president, that would be."

We flew on for some time in silence.

One of the tour group looked up beaming from the map on his lap. "Strait of Juan de Fuca!" he cried.

I could take it. I was ready for this kind of thing. I was going to virgin country and I still hadn't got food poisoning and my companion hadn't yet had to call the house physician to say, *"He didn't even finish his drink."*

They had been to San Francisco and were doing the résumé now: "Filthah hippahs!" said a lady from Little Rock. Then a young man bound for Vietnam announced, "Well, I'm off to defend my country!" in tones that seemed less than totally sincere. So the tour group, for this and other reasons, grew restive and was ready to pile off the plane by the time we arrived at Victoria.

I registered at the Empress Hotel, a stupendous Victorian edifice where the bellhops scurry and the waiters in the dining room murmur any number of hopes about your meal; exactly the place to have an RAF mustache. Frank, my fishing companion, arrived and we talked about our trip north. Then early to bed, with glimpses of the curious Victoria skyline, a pastiche of the high-rise and the venerable.

Every traveler here soon discovers the considerable piety about the British connection. If the queen ever gets run out of England, this is where you're going to find her holed up; the Victoria Chamber of Commerce will have drawn its wagons in a circle around her.

In addition to the good transpositions like the unmatched gardens of the city or the numerous bookstores, you get double-decker buses imported from London, a lot of stuff about coats of arms in woolen-store windows, and tea and crumpets bombarding the eye everywhere from the Empress itself to the Rexall drugstore.

But to emphasize the town's studied dowdiness is unfair. It is a tourist trick. It is obvious that Victoria is a town of what used to be called graciousness, and any ride around its perimeter will put the traveler's back to the unparalleled gardens and, in contrast to such cultivation, his face to the headlands of the San Juan Islands.

There had been heavy weather immediately prior to our arrival, and long golden log booms, the shape and color of egg yolks, had been towed inside the bays for protection. Beyond, handsome trawlers were moored under clouds of gulls. If you squinted, it looked like Anchorage or Seattle or San Francisco or Monterey or — squinting tighter — Mazatlán: the Pacific community seemed continuous.

That first morning I picked up the menu downstairs in the hotel. A number of breakfasts were described: "The Charlotte," "The Windsor," "The Albert," "The Edward," "The Victoria," and "The Mountbatten."

"I'll have The Mountbatten," I said, "over lightly."

Frank made a number of order changes in his Edward.

"If you're going to substitute oatmeal and an extra egg on your Edward," said the waitress, "you might just as well order à la carte."

I was hungry and ate The Mountbatten abruptly.

We spent the day driving around as far up the coast as Saltspring Island. At one of the ferry crossings, watching the wind-striped water and high, beautiful fjords, I innocently poisoned myself with a prawn.

A local prawn? I don't know.

Within hours I had failed to finish my drink. My companion was on the phone to the house doctor. My vision was contracting. My gorge was rising for the tenth time. I felt the Canadian Pacific was not what it was cracked up to be.

*

We were going north to Smithers by way of Williams Lake. The fellow passengers were more promising than the tour group — a few sports like ourselves, some surveyors, timber cruisers, a geologist. The minute the aircraft had elevation, a country revealed itself that was so tortuous, folded, and empty that some trick of time seemed to have been done.

The sky came down to a jagged horizon of snow, and for 360 degrees a coastal forest, baleful and empty, rose to the mountains. Past the bright riveted wing, the ranges succeeded each other to the north in a blue eternity.

We landed at Williams Lake on the Fraser River, dropped off passengers, taxied, flew a few yards, landed again, taxied again, took off again, and landed. The pilot came out of the cockpit with his shirt unbuttoned and remarked with appalling candor that the plane felt like a Model A.

They sent us into Williams Lake to eat while they fixed the plane. In the cab we learned the airline we were using was bankrupt. It had come to seem so. But at the restaurant they told us to return to the plane immediately.

When we boarded, the pilot said, "I hope it goes this time. Occasionally you're not lucky."

So we flew over the increasingly remote wilderness, hoping that we would be lucky and that the plane would work and be better in all ways than a Model A.

At Smithers, the seaplanes rested very high on their pontoons beside floating docks. A mechanic tapped away at a workbench nearby as we boarded a De Havilland Beaver.

Within a short time, we hung, it seemed precariously, over a long, gravelly mountain ridge. The pilot craned around looking for mountain goats, while Frank and I exchanged nervous glances and judged the drop.

On either side of us, implacable-looking peaks and ridges stood, while, underneath, blue and green lakes hung in saddles and rock-walled cirques. Occasionally the entire groundscape shone amid delicate water meadows, and in a short time we had landed and were taxiing toward our fishing camp. I thought of the trout under our gliding pontoons.

We met Ejnar Madsen, the camp's co-owner.

"How is the fishing?" Frank inquired routinely.

"Extremely poor," said Ejnar.

"Really?"

We put our luggage down on the dock. It began to rain. There had been an Act of God and we could not be philosophical about it. I asked what had happened. The biggest summer rain in many years had raised the lake and turned the river almost black with runoff.

Next day we floated disconsolately down the slow, ineffably northern river in a twenty-five-foot, Indian-built spruce riverboat. The rain poured off our foul-weather gear and made puddles in our laps.

Between long spells of silence we burst into absurd conversations:

"Neighbor's cat crawls under the hood of the car. Next morning the neighbor starts the car. The fan does a job on the cat."

"Apropos of what?"

"Wait a minute. They take the cat to the vet. He shaves the cat's whole tail except for the end. The cat looks like a lion. Pretty soon the cat thinks he's a lion."

"In what way?"

"Forget it."

Now the rain was going sideways. You'd cast a fly and it would vanish long before it got to the water. We knew gloom.

Some very small, very stupid trout came upon our flies and ate them. We caught those trout. Of the large smart trout known to live in the lake, we took none. Some hours later we sat around the Air-Tight heater, for all purposes blanked.

We were fishing for rainbows in their original watershed. In such a situation they can be expected to be magnificent fish, quite unlike the hatchery imitations, which have, in effect, besmirched the species. They are strong, fast, and rise freely to a dry fly. We were, moreover, in an area that produces fish of a rather large average size.

In the spring and early summer the fish here herd and pursue salmon fry, including the sluggish little alevins, which are the very young fry, tadpole-shaped, with their still-unconsumed egg sacs. Ideally, the big rainbows are to be found chasing the bait on top, where they can be cast to, rather like pelagic fish. We liked this image. We would cast, fight, land, and release until our arms were tired. The rainbows could also be taken on dry flies; there were mayflies and grasshoppers to imitate and there were stoneflies in the lower stretch.

We had not made much of a beginning, but our hopes were still running high. The next morning we were fishing by six, hunting feeding rainbows. It is "hunting" if you are finding something. If you are not, it is driving around the lake in an outboard.

"We should have brought the water skis."

"Oh, come on."

We continued hunting, as it were. And we didn't find anything; not one thing. When more of the unseasonable rain blew in from the exaggerated sky, we sat, fly rods in hand, like drowned rats. I began to take an interest in the details of the bilge.

Sometime later, when it had cleared a little, we headed down the lake to an Indian village that is inhabited by a branch of the Carrier tribe — so named because the widows of the tribe once carried the charred bones of their husbands around on their backs. The village is prettily sited on a high series of hills and looks out on the lake and river where the two are joined. There are a couple of dozen buildings along a wooden walk and a small Hudson's Bay store.

When we passed the upper part of the town, an Indian girl in an aniline-blue miniskirt was pulling sockeye salmon from a net. Nearby, a man worked on his outboard; ravens and gulls screamed and circled overhead, waiting for a chance at the offal from the gutted salmon. There were a hundred thousand or more sockeyes in the river now. Many of them came up out of the wilderness with bearclaw marks on them.

We docked at the lower end of the village, hurried up the hill, and got under the eaves of the wooden schoolhouse as the rain started in hard. There was a notice in the school window.

To Whom It May Concern:
During the absence of the schoolteacher, this school building must be closed. It therefore cannot be used for dances, bingo games, or any other social gatherings. Anyone asking permission to use the school will be refused.

> R. M. McIntyre
> Superintendent
> Burns Lake Indian Agency

In two or three places on the walls of this wilderness school were dabbed the letters LSD, which did not stand for League of Spiritual Discovery. The letters were doubtlessly put there by someone who spoke English as a second language.

When the weather relented a little, we hiked up the hill to the old cemetery, mostly overgrown. The epitaphs intrigued us: "To the sacred memory of our brother killed by a gunshot wound." I found two old headmen's graves. "Chief William" and "Chief Agusa." The titles were purely titular; the Carriers gave their chiefs little power. The cultural overlay seemed rather bald on the last stone I looked at. Beneath a conventional crucifix it read, "In memory of Ah Whagus. Died 1906. Age 86."

We walked around the village. The shy people smiled at the ground or stayed inside when we passed. On the boardwalk someone had written "Big Fat Sally Do Your Stuff." Beyond the LSD graffiti and the noise of a transistor radio playing Dolly Parton as she sang "I'm a lady mule skinner from down ol' Tennessee way," black-shawled Indian women were taking the salmon down the river to a lower island and smoking them against a winter that was probably more imminent to them than to us. The older people were locked in some intense dejection, but the children played with familiar, maniacal energy in the deep wet grass with their salmon-fattened dogs.

It had rained enough that our simple cabin with its Air-Tight heater acquired a special and luxurious glamour. When we got good and cold, usually the result of running the boat in one direction while the wind took the rain in another, we would head for the cabin, put some wood in the heater, douse it with coal oil, and throw in the magic match that made everything all better. This was the romance of the heater. We played with the flue, adjusted the draft, and while the logs rumbled and roared inside we tuned the thing like a violin. One afternoon, when a view through any of the windows would have suggested that the cabin was Captain Nemo's vessel and that we were at the bottom of the sea, Frank leapt to his feet with an expensive Japanese camera in his hands and began to take picture after picture of the tin heater rumbling peacefully with our wet laundry hanging around it in homage.

One of the exhilarations of fishing new places lies in rendering advice into some kind of obtained reality. Cast the fly, you are told, right along the bank and the trout will rise to it. So you cast and you cast until presently you are blue in the face and the appealing syllogism you started with is not always finished. When it does not work, you bring your vanquished person back to the dock, where there is no way to weigh or measure the long face you have brought instead of fish. At the first whiskey, you announce that it has been a trying day. Then someone elsc says that it is nice just to get out. Irrationally, you wonder how you can get even for the remark.

But once, when the British Columbia sky made one of those spectacular partings we associate with the paintings of Turner or the handing down of stone tablets, we saw what had been described to us in the beginning.

Large fish, their fins showing above the water, were working schools of salmon fry: a setup. We started the engine and ran upwind of them, cut the engine, and started to drift down. We had the goods on them. When in range I false-cast a few times, made a long cast beyond them, and gently retrieved into their midst.

I hooked a fish instantly. It made a strong first run, then mysteriously flagged. I reeled. It came obediently to the boat, where Frank netted it.

"What is that?" he asked. In the net was some kind of giant minnow.

"It looks like Martha Raye," I said bitterly. Later we learned that it was a squawfish. No one ever caught one on purpose.

It was not until almost our last day that the river began to disclose itself. We made a drift past the Indian village, where we were seeing occasional rises. The problem was that the river was so clouded that the fish were unable to see a fly. The condition was blamed on a stump desert left by nearby logging.

We began to drift, blind-casting large Wulff flies ahead of us, mending the line to keep the river from bellying it and dragging the fly. In very short order, a bright band appeared beneath my fly, moved downstream with it, and inhaled. I lifted and was solid to a very good fish, which was netted some minutes later. It bumped heavily in the bottom of the boat until I could get the fly out and release it.

We were startled. A short time later another came, boiling the fly under with a very positive, deep take — and was released. There were no rises to be seen any longer, though fish rose fairly well to our own flies, until we had six. Then the whole factory shut down, and nothing would persuade a trout to rise again. While it had lasted, all of British Columbia that existed had been the few square inches around my dry fly. With the rise over, the world began to reappear: trees, lake, river, village, wet clothes.

I remembered how when I watched movies as a child the theater seat — everything — would vanish, leaving me floating disembodied before the images on the screen. And it was this sort of possession you looked for when angling: to watch the river flowing, the insects landing and hatching, the places where trout hold; and to insinuate the supple, binding movement of tapered line until, when the combination is right, the line becomes quite rigid and many of its motions are conceived at the other end. That stage continues for a time that is dependent on the size of the trout and the skill of the angler. When the initiative changes hands, the trout is soon in the net, without an idea in his head until you release him. Then you see him going off, looking for a spot, and thinking. We had this only briefly: our trip was over.

On the way out we got a Cessna instead of a De Havilland and the airline didn't lose my luggage until Seattle, where it vanished through the looking glass of computerized bungling. A week later it surfaced in Bozeman, Montana, and we were reunited. I took a good look at the suitcases. Someone unable to stand the pressure had enjoyed himself with a ball-peen hammer.

I opened my luggage on a hot Montana day and all the woolens began to steam. I was home again.

ANOTHER
HORSE

G ENE WAS SURE there were enough horses. When I called him I said my friend Scott wanted to come and we would need another horse. I told him I had the saddles: a Mexican roping saddle and an A-type, marked *Montana Territory*, in case we met any antiquarians in the mountains.

I drove south in the Yellowstone Valley the next morning; Scott got the gate and we headed up the road to the ranch that Gene stays on. It was a cold late November day; Gene and Keith were putting the horses in the stock truck to take them up to the trailhead in Tom Miner Basin. Gene had a bandanna tied around the crown of his hat to ward off nimrods and was wearing green chaps he won bullriding in Williston, North Dakota, in 1965 (it said so on the chaps). He was wearing a gun.

Keith was dressed in his National Park Service coveralls and it was he who discovered we were shy a horse. Scott and I were hikers, though not so committed that we'd forgo the one horse. So I said we'd take that and they could pack our gear in the panniers and we'd meet them in camp.

Keith had secreted his little camp up some six-inch creek in the Gallatin Range; so we all hunkered around a clean piece of bare mud and scratched out directions. I made sure Scott and I had matches. We were going through an area of some grizzly concentration. I don't know what you bring for that, unless it is Librium and a glass of water.

We put the territorial saddle on a bunchy short mare that jumped every time you took off your coat, though Gene said she was "a good little bitch"; and I noticed she tipped up her left hind hoof when you walked around her. She pulled back all the time when you used her in the pack string; and when Gene had tried to cure her by securing her to his pickup truck with a logging chain instead of a rope, she rared until she broke the logging chain. Then didn't go anywhere.

"What kind of logging chain, Gene?"

"Just a damn logging chain."

I wanted to wear my John B. Stetson hat with the big feather in it; but my ears hurt already; so I put the hat away and with it a certain portion of my self-esteem and pulled on a woolen hat instead.

Keith and Jim (another fellow from Bozeman) headed off in the pickup carrying the pack saddles, panniers, and all the gear. Scott and I went with Gene in the stock truck. When we got halfway down the ranch road, Gene spotted his dogs following us in the rearview mirror. He hit the brakes, jumped out of the truck, drew his gun, and fired. The dogs hightailed it for the house. I looked at Scott.

We crossed the Yellowstone and headed up Tom Miner Basin, struggling for traction on the long, snowy canyon road. We parked the trucks at the top. Somebody had a tent there; and there was a small corral with four bales of hay in the snow.

Jim said, "Can you throw a diamond hitch?"

I said I could.

Scott and I led the four saddle horses and the two pack-horses up to the corral and tied them. There was a lot of snow and we were going up another three or four thousand feet, Scott and I trading off on the antiquarian saddle, being too big to double-team the twitchy mare.

Some hunters came up to the head of the road in a little Jeep, packed inside, all guns and hot orange hats.

"I don't see nothin' hangin'," said the driver.

"We're only starting out," one of us said; though the truth was, Scott and I were just going to make a bloodless round trip to see the Gallatins under snow.

Gene knew where Keith's camp was for sure. Scott and I knew where it was on the mud map back at Gene's place; but there was more snow than we thought there would be and trails would be obscured. So Gene went ahead to cut a trail. Jim and Keith agreed to pack up and follow when they were done; and meanwhile Scott and I would start, trading off on the mare.

We started up the easy grade along Tom Miner Creek, Scott getting the first ride, up through the bare aspens and gradual snow-covered slopes dotted by dark knots of sage. We could see the snowy Absaroka Range across the Yellowstone.

Then the canyon steepened during my turn on the horse, as I saw Scott fade, trudging behind in six inches of snow. The trail contoured around high on the north side, really quite steep; and I remembered two years before in the summertime with Keith, taking two riding horses and a three-year-old that had never been packed between us, me in front. The young horse banged the plywood panniers on a tree and panicked, chasing my horse headling down the skinny trail, the creek sonorous in the deep canyon below me. Finally, my horse swerved up on a short leveling of the slope and stood crooked and not half so unnerved as me. The young packhorse shot on through, bucking and emptying the panniers of everything from sleeping bags to Pepsodent and a German chocolate cake.

Today it was relaxed, with the snow muffling the horse's hoofs and the altitude beginning in the cold air to produce the radiant and astringent combination of air and light that is year after year fecklessly pursued by the manufacturers of beer calendars. I noticed that riding was colder than walking; my toes were a little numb, as were my nose and cheek points; my ears, thankfully, were warm, due entirely to the abandoning of my High Lonesome hat down there at Headquarters. I stopped and waited for Scott.

When Scott caught up, he confessed to thinking about grizzlies. "If one came after me," he said, "I would dodge around in those aspens, in and out, in and out, until somebody came and rescued me."

I trudged along behind as he gradually disappeared ahead. I noticed the snow getting heavy; and now the sky was deeply overcast and snow was beginning to pour down the canyon in a long sweep. After a while, I could see it streaming into the horse tracks, obscuring them. I transferred the matches to an inside pocket and mentally reviewed Jack London. I thought, When I get back, I'm going to buy a whole mess of horses so we never run out.

My eyes flicked to the brushy creek bottom for grizzly sign; just like one of those fang mongers to come on a man having a hard enough time as it was. I had the strange thought that nothing could happen to a person by way of grizzer charge or vanishment beneath snowbank who had as many magazine subscriptions as I do. But it was getting to be grim out here. I could see about fifteen inches ahead of me.

The snow was deep enough that it was a struggle to walk, and my boots were full. If I had stayed home, I could have watched the Colts and Dolphins play, up in my room with snacks and the Sunday Livingston *Enterprise* and cozy telephone calls to my friend the writer down the road as to the relative greatnesses of Tolstoy and Dostoevsky. Or I could read an off-color comic from San Francisco.

I caught up with Scott in about half an hour. I climbed on the horse, not describing to him what he was in for as to wallowing. I noticed, though, that my boots disappeared into the snow, stirrups and all, making wakes. Scott remarked the horse looked like a cocktail waitress. So it was beginning to get to him, too.

In two tradeoffs, we made it to the top. We looked back into the immense valley of the Yellowstone and rode (or walked) through the trees on a kind of plateau, Buffalo Horn Pass, where the Indian hunting parties crossed; and then to the western slope and a tremendous view of the Gallatin drainage with white, jagged ranges angling in from the north.

The snow let up and we were in deep powder. When it was my turn to ride, I started down a long switchback that ended in the trees. Scott, on foot, decided to run straight down. At about the point I reached the trees, Scott was pinwheeling in a cloud of snow. Then the horse fell; though fearing getting hung up in the stirrups, I ejected before she hit the ground. The snow was so deep and soft that Scott and I and the horse wallowed around and made no very great attempt to get to our feet again.

The sun came out and the raucous birds of the high mountains started in with some brazen appreciation of the general impovement.

The horse was getting silly. When one of us rode ahead and the other reappeared, she jumped back in horror as though from a representative of a dog-food concern. And on the steep switchbacks, she slid down the snow on her haunches. I felt she was stunting and might pull anything next, an Immelmann turn, for example.

Then Scott galloped off through the trees, the trail making a soft white corridor and the speed of his departure producing a sun-shot curtain of snow. The laden boughs poured white powder in the sunshine; whole sections of snow dropped from the treetops onto the trail with a soft concussion. Suddenly we were in camp: a wall tent half buried in powder and a pole corral.

Gene was cutting "standing dead" for the sheepherder stove in the tent and we took turns splitting it. (You had to have all your terms straight if male self-respect was to survive in a hostile world. When you went fishing, you went "out"; when you went to the mountains, you went "in.")

Keith and Jim arrived almost immediately with the pack

stock. Keith complained that Gene had cut the trail too close to the trees, so that the pack animals banged the panniers all the way up; then, to Scott and me, he allowed as how the snow had been unexpectedly deep.

"Did the horse fall?"

"Yes."

"I saw the place. See any game?"

"Gene saw two moose."

Jim said, "The sorrel packhorse fell and slid forty feet on its stomach and got up straight without spilling anything."

We all admired that.

"How many of these horses you want to picket?" Gene asked Keith. Keith looked around and shared with us the idea of losing horses in all this snow.

"All of them," Keith said. "Then let's butcher up a good mess of wood. It's going to get cold."

The sun was starting to go down at that. We had one more tent to put up. It took an hour to shovel the snow out of the site and get the ridgepole in place. The pile of split wood, fresh and lemony-smelling, was building in front of the first tent. And by about sundown the second tent was up, the heater in place. We threw in two shovelfuls of dirt so the bottom wouldn't burn out; put the sheet-metal tubes together to form the chimney and ran it up through the asbestos hole in the roof. We built a fire in it; and the snow inside started to melt in the warmth and form the mud hell that was necessary until the tent had aged a few days.

We went to the other tent about sundown. It was very cold; and we started to work on making dinner, spacing the job out with bourbon and one of those ersatz wines that is advertised right in there at half time with Gillette razors and the Dodge Rebellion. Some of us were swaggering around with cigars.

Scott and I peeled potatoes and onions. Keith and Gene cooked some elk, sliced up a head of lettuce with a hunting knife. Jim explained how he had expelled Allen Ginsberg from a coffeehouse for running down America.

We ate, greedily, for the first time that day. The mud was starting to deepen in the tent.

Somebody hauled some feed to the horses; I looked out the tent flaps and saw them picking precisely through the snow with their front hoofs for the pellets.

I was pouring bourbon into cups full of powder snow; Keith would drink half a can of Seven-Up and pour whiskey down through the triangular hole into the can and say, "Right on!" to no one in particular.

Gene rose imperfectly to his feet and began doing six-gun tricks, whirls, drops, spin-and-draws, fanning back the hammer.

"Is that loaded?" I peeped.

"Yes."

We all backed away into the corners, fearing a general O.K. Corral. Finally, Gene, winded, put the gun back in its holster.

Jim dropped his elk steak on the floor. When he picked it up, it was covered with mud and had a few mothballs stuck to it. "Go ahead and eat it," everyone encouraged him. He said he wasn't hungry.

Jim took the bucket of heated water off the sheepherder stove and started washing the dishes. In passing, he explained that Dave Brubeck liked to pinch girls' bottoms.

"Where's Keith?" I asked.

No one knew. After a while, I went to look for him. He was asleep in the other tent, laid out in the mud in his sleeping bag next to a pile of saddles. I put a couple of pieces of wood into the heater and the base of the chimney glowed cherry. When I walked back to the other tent, I stopped in the cold, still air and looked up at the stars. They seemed to swarm a matter of inches over my head.

Scott came out. "That's Orion," he said. "See the belt and the sword there?"

I said I did; but the truth is, I never could make those things out much, beyond the Big and Little Dippers and the North Star if I didn't take my eyes off of it. I heard a coyote. I thought, I am on top of the earth and I don't work for the government.

Jim, Gene, and Keith all slept in the same tent because they were going to get up before dawn to look for elk. Scott and I rolled out our bags on the floor and turned off the Coleman lantern. For about half an hour, we could hear the banked-down stove crackle and see the rectangle of bright light around its door.

When the stove went out, the mud froze. I wished I had flattened out some of the mud under my bag because it froze in shapes not reciprocal to my body. I pulled the drawstring up tight around my face. I was warm in the good Ibex bag; but my head felt as if it was in a refrigerator. I put on my wool cap, feeling for it among my frozen, board-stiff socks and the hiking boots that were as rigid as building blocks.

I could hear when I woke up the next morning the other three crunching around outside, wrangling the horses and falling silent as they drank coffee in the tent. It was insultingly cold.

Scott said, "Oh, no!" from the interior of his sleeping bag.

"What?"

"I have to go to the bathroom."

We got up shortly and had a crackling fire going in the sheepherder stove. We made a pot of coffee and lazily divided a vast sheet of Missus So-and-So's breakfast rolls. I thawed my socks and boots in front of the stove; rivers of steam poured from them into the stove's open door.

When I stepped outside, I could see where the snow was trampled from the morning's wrangling. Their trail led across the small open meadow and over the rim, a soft trough in the perfect basin of snow. The light was tremendous, and the sky formed an impressive light-shot blue dome, defined on the side of our camp by a row of snow-laden pines, and opposite us by the glittering range of the Gallatins. A big lone spruce stood between us and the newly risen sun; full of snow and ice crystals, it exploded with the improbable brilliance of an Annunciation. There weren't words for it.

We put the bags in stuff sacks, straightened out the tent, and let the fire die. I printed a note and left it on a pannier, weighted with a jackknife.

Boys,
We're going to work our way back. We'll leave the horse in the corral at Tom Miner Basin.

Tom and Scott

We got the bridle and saddle and headed out for the mare. A pine bough had shed its load of snow and her back was white and powdered with it as she stood in the glittering mountain light. I swept her dry while Scott warmed the bit in his hands.

We saddled the mare and took the long way home.

MY
MEADOW
LARK

DO YOU KNOW what it is to be boat sick? To hang upside down through a hatchway to see how they put that shapely cedar planking through the turn at the bilges? To watch someone take hot white-oak frames out of the steam box and bend them down against the form so that when they've cooled they bear the transept of the hull's flowing sheer, yet hold the shaped planking against green, wind-driven seawater, against careenings, groundings, and the attritional violence of years' usage? Have you ever walked on a laid teak deck, sprung to the sheer, then fitted to a king plank at the center as though all the planking had grown that way, gathering in sweeps around the catwalks, up the foredeck, and around the samson post with passionate simplicity? Now, once you have seen that, do you know how to keep from offering the traditional arm and a leg for some authentic artifact of a very old allegiance between wood and water?

In 1948, L. Francis Herreshoff, the mandarin genius of American yacht design, issued from his literal castle at Marblehead a set of plans for what he called a poor man's yacht, designed for those "who can visualize a different type of yachting than ocean racing." Today, when a great number of the stock sailboats available are compromised for the cruising sailor by designs that aim to capitalize on gaps in racing regulations and rating systems, Herreshoff's dictum has a certain pungency, and the sailor with even the vaguest aesthetics turns with refreshment from the emetic details of the swollen, winch-encrusted racers to the wholesome lines of this poor man's yacht.

Herreshoff called his creation the Meadow Lark, a shoal-draft boat that could, he said, "skim over the marshes and meadows as the joyful bird of that name does over many of our fields which border the Atlantic." The boat derived in main from the old New Haven sharpies, fast, capable, hard-chine oyster boats that were popular in the nineteenth century. And it quite possibly derived from the experiments of Commodore Ralph Munroe, a south Florida pioneer who in the late nineteenth century built the legendary Presto boats.

The Meadow Lark was ketch-rigged, thirty-three feet long, and, instead of a keel or centerboard, had leeboards like the Dutch Boier yachts, winglike things that are alternately dropped and lifted when tacking. The draft of the boat was fifteen inches, a wondrous fact in a thirty-three-foot sailboat and a statistic which opened a world of cruising grounds that seldom see a sailboat.

The Meadow Lark, said Herreshoff, was for those who would like to spend their vacations "in pleasure." It is amusing to speculate upon those who like to spend their vacations otherwise. One suspects that here Herreshoff again meant the racing sailors, surfing the big screamers with their sail bins, tower-of-power spinnakers, and wilderness of madhouse equipage with names like "reaching struts," "shroud releases," "spider blocks," and "boom vang tangs." It is reasonable to wonder if someone wailing away on a two-speed Barient pedestal winch is spending his vacation in pleasure or (you see the old man in his Marblehead stone tower, grinning) *in pain.*

One thing Americans have done surpassingly well is design boats, and the apotheosis of this national trait is in larger-than-life figures like the Herreshoffs (Captain Nat and L. Francis),

S. S. Crocker, William Atkin, and John Alden, to name a few peaks. The moment you examine an activity like sailing and sense the variability of aesthetics and performance and finally the long, noble tradition of preoccupation in its unbroken stream, you begin to sense there is something beyond sport and pleasurable vacations.

The Meadow Lark is almost an aside in Herreshoff's career, though the old man, with his penchant for variety (from sail skis to serene canoe yawls to world sojourners like the Marco Polo), is a little hard to pin down. Where today's highly trained naval architect will describe some negative trait in a boat's performance in terms of, say, section and flow, Herreshoff will simply note that it is "annoying" and tell you how it is avoided. The annoying is to be avoided just as the vacation is to be spent in pleasure. The best thing when you are out at night in a strange anchorage is "not to be worried." That sounds simple enough, but the sailor who has watched the compass shift slightly with a dragging anchor in the darkness and the ocean rumbling spookily on a lee shore knows that to sleep without worry is a concept clogged with meaning.

Key West is a noisy town. A realtor once told me not to worry about the fantastic racket in the drumlike nineteenth-century house she was showing me; the exhaust pipe of every car that passed in the street outside seemed to be routed via some stereophonic magic into each room. "You use the air conditioners to drown out the noise," she explained. And since Key West is surrounded by water, I found myself concentrating upon the theme of silence as the principal verity of the eternal sea. The eternal sea has other verities, but in a bustling, Latinate town like Key West, silence is the big one.

For me this was the fissure through which boat lust entered. Marine reading increased to the point that my bedside looked like headquarters for the junior-high paper drive. I would have many vessels, if I could, and in my spare time I would build a lissome traditional schooner, thousands of feet of deck and planking pouring from my back-yard miter box.

Instead, I built a dinghy which the designer called "the acme of simplicity." I fitted secondhand fire hose from the Key West Fire Department to its gunwales so my son could ram things, as is his wont. The boat worked fine. Then he wanted a window in its bottom, so I installed one. At the relaunching the dinghy headed for the bottom, so I slobbered aquarium sealer all over it and it floated, the sea's verities passing the plate-glass window.

But while I ripsawed through the three sheets of exterior-grade plywood that comprised, finally, the dinghy proper, I was seeing ketches, schooners, and yawls slipping down the ways into green seas whose silence was not a byproduct of air conditioning. I knew in my heart that at the very moment my wife was asking me not to get glue on the furniture, some cheerful circumnavigator was busting a magnum of Mumm's on the oaken stem of an oceangoing brute.

My fantasy had finally focused itself. It took little originality for me to worship Herreshoff's sense of line. And living in an island city surrounded by so much thin water — the city's earliest economy was based on salvage — called out for a shoal-draft boat in a voice reminiscent of the noise of oak against coral, a gargling squeal not even approached by the late Janis Joplin. Everything pointed to a Meadow Lark. I instinctively trusted Herreshoff's desire that its owner spend his time aboard "in pleasure" and not be "annoyed."

But what was the use? I didn't see how I could afford to have one built, though a handsome glass model was being turned out on Buzzards Bay in Massachusetts. The state of Florida doesn't have a great nose for traditional boat building, so unless I could convert to a taste for pop-top cabins and LSD color schemes, I would just have to keep a lonesome eye on used-boat columns.

I did so for a long time and once in a while a Crocker or an

Alden or another Herreshoff would surface among the two-seater runabouts, the metalflake zombiecraft guaranteed to blow every rich hedonist off the lake or your money back.

Sometimes I would see pictures of Meadow Larks in remote places. I was a sick acquisitor in a capitalist madhouse. I'd pick up a boat magazine looking for a Meadow Lark at rest in a summery Nova Scotian cove, its owner visibly spending his vacation in pleasure. Instead, I'd find a fold-out advertisement for a pea-green multihull powerboat tail-walking across the wakes of other pea-green multihulls, the drivers all looking strangely annoyed. In another, a boatman rose from what looked like either a half-swamped torpedo or a scale model of the *Merrimack,* and aimed a fiberglass crossbow at a sleeping carp. These boats weren't called Meadow Lark or Friendship or Bluenose or Sharpie or Skipjack, in the old manner. They were called things like Avanti, Sport Fury, Cobalt, Marauder, Luger, and Mark IV. In their ads, sweet little things surrounded the control panels with their piquant breasts. They are removed from the boat after the sale or I wouldn't be talking this way.

I did know that when I bought a boat I didn't want to discuss the "standard accessory grouping" and I didn't want a day in it to be a sort of space probe. I didn't want a floating vinyl madhouse backed up by fifty-six distributor centers where I could stand in line with my dissatisfaction printed out in twenty-five words or less. Reading Joshua Slocum caused me to undervalue boats that were presented as, for example, fully carpeted. One boat company claimed its product as a modern classic because its interior was color coded. Another company said its product was the only choice for "blowing the others out of the water." Its performance was described, with simple American eloquence, as "hellacious." I couldn't quite appreciate boats whose various enigmatic details were "foamed in place." I didn't want to be "the superstar of revolutionary performance features." It had long since occurred to me that none of Herreshoff's boats was equipped with Flo-Torq. And the discovery that the builder of your boat was a division of a company like General Foods was, I thought, potentially disconcerting. Who do you call if she goes to the bottom? Betty Crocker? Aunt Jemima?

My voice, crying out "You won't believe this!" still seemed to hang in the air. My wife's eyes grazed off among the familiar appliances of an American breakfast. Her lips parted for a moment before she spoke:

"There is a used Meadow Lark in the paper."

"How could you have known that!"

You wonder about the money and where it is going to come from. You look at your child and suddenly he seems to be eating too much.

But you catch yourself at these thoughts. You nurse a certain unspeakable dread behind baleful eyes which you arrange like forlorn olives in the Peter Lorre manner. Similar eyes — expressing withdrawn hope interchangeably with shattered dreams — have been used to great effect beneath elms, in simple rock gardens, and in old, rather ornate elevators of a kind once found in New York hotels. Somehow — and let me be the first to confess this — they just didn't come off among the English muffins and Smucker's marmalade jars.

My wife said, "Why don't you give him a call?"

I remarked that a telephone chat never hurt anybody, then whirled the dial with my forefinger.

The owner of the boat possessed a certain gift for meticulous description. He started with the hull, rigging, and general equipage, then went on to lay out the cabin from companionway to forepeak. It had been built with meticulous attention to Hereshoff's plans: white-oak frames, double-planked long-leaf-yellow-pine bottom, white-cedar sides, and mahogany joinery. The mast trucks and leeboard fittings had been made by L. Francis himself in his Marblehead workshop.

I wondered if I would be able to bear to go up to see it, what with the child and the pets eating like there was no tomorrow, not to mention my wife's sibylline remarks flung at me over the marmalade. I decided to have a look.

I met the owner at Matheson Hammock, where his boat, still bearing its Marblehead trailboards, stood out among the sailing Clorox bottles like a sore thumb. The sails were neatly hidden in covers and the halyards tapped lightly on the two raked white masts. In a way quite different from my three-sheets-of-plywood dinghy, the Meadow Lark was the acme of simplicity. Save the ignition system of the auxiliary engine, the boat was devoid of electrical wiring. The cabin lights were oil; so were the running and riding lights. I agonized over that cabin with its bowed, coach roof and chaste white paint. And under the cockpit sole and the floorboards of the cabin the bilge was sweet and dry, bearing that final distinction of a well-planked hull: cobwebs.

Calvinist reserve and a near-perfect capability for imagining disaster kept me from a prompt decision. The boat owner quite understood and lent me Herreshoff's plans for perusal.

I went back to Key West to make up my mind. My home had achieved the atmosphere of an isolation booth on a quiz show. I spoke to my family as though from behind a thick plate of glass.

I bought the boat. All I had to do was bring it 150 miles from his house to my house and that would be that. But I hadn't sailed in fifteen years and in nothing larger than boats half the size of the Meadow Lark. Two friends agreed to go up with me, and the owner would give us a brief shakedown on handling the boat. But when we got there, the owner, unfortunately, had broken his foot; all he could do was hand over the documents, the key to the auxiliary, and a map of the utterly Byzantine contours of Biscayne Bay. We took three days coming down to Key West. We were becalmed, spent hours under small-craft warnings with the lee rail pouring foam, were becalmed again, and finally, rarity of rarities in the keys, we were caught in a fog. We listened to the big diesels of shrimp boats moving about us and knew we could be run over before we saw a boat coming. We were nearly home but took a straight inshore tack to see if we could tell where we were by fetching up on the beach at some point we'd recognize.

We headed through the cotton, under power, totally disoriented. Suddenly the mangroves were in front of us and we were in two feet of water: Saddlebunch Key. We knew where we were, but night was falling and we had some distance to go. We headed out of the shallows, where but for the extraordinary shoal capabilities of the Meadow Lark we'd have gone aground, and darkness fell in fog around us.

Finally the lights of the desalinization plant appeared like a switchboard in the sky and we turned in to Stock Island and a safe mooring. Toward the end the wind had blown weirdly through the fog and we sailed blind at a pace that was unnerving. Then we were in and secured. We fussed over the springlines, gave the Meadow Lark one last look, and headed home.

The last thing to be done before attempting to fit the big sharpie into our routine was to make an extensive shakedown cruise; not me and my competent companions, but me and my family, including my hysterical if glamorous bird dog, Molly.

We began to get things ready: fresh water, groceries, charts, books and blankets, a collecting net for our son, dog food, and a first-aid kit. As we prepared, the weather got steadily worse. It rose to Condition Two and stayed there. We kept eating the perishables among our trip groceries and replacing them and waiting and eating the perishables again. Every morning we got up, one ear on the wind, and sure enough it would continue to howl and the dry palm leaves rattled against the house and the same iron sky poured at us from the northwest at forty miles an hour.

We decided to go anyway. Our plan was to sail west to Boca

Grande and look for a protected anchorage there. We loaded the latest groceries into the car and deliberately took the shore road to Stock Island, where the boat was docked. Breakers were rolling toward Key West from the horizon, and the only craft we saw, commercial fishing boats, appeared and disappeared in explosions of white water.

The groceries went into the Meadow Lark, and I started the auxiliary, noticing the clatter of shrouds and rigging overhead. We freed the lines, reversed into the basin, and picked our way out through the commercial fishing boats crowded in because of the weather. At the end of the long channel by the desalinization plant, I could see the weather and white water, but we'd been waiting a week or more and we were just going to go.

The last protected water swept by us. We were still under power when we hit the first big waves. The boat began lifting and plunging down through it. A couple of times green water broke over the deck and poured down and out the scuppers in an organized way; most of the heavy spray that we knocked into the air blew across the deck ahead of the house. We stayed fairly dry.

I wanted to get out of the commercial channel before attempting to get the sails up, but by chance I glanced at the engine temperature gauge. Perhaps I had smelled something first. The water pump had failed and the engine was dangerously overheating.

I shut it off and we lay in the seaway, heaving with the rollers that passed under us as they raced for the Key West shore. I rigged our heaviest anchor on the foredeck in case the worst happened and we got blown toward the beach. The beach itself was making a low rumble to our right, and we could see the green water race, elevate, whiten, and break on the shore.

I put a reef in the mizzen and raised it. The main and mizzen on the Meadow Lark are rigged with small gaffs, so I felt like a one-armed paperhanger keeping the two halyards in order while the wind tried to wrap them around the masts. Once the mizzen was up and trimmed, the boat turned like a weather vane into the wind and hove to. I began to feel in control. I put up the working jib and immediately the boat swung out of the eye of the wind and began to sail, always a magical moment. A part of you still asks, Why are we moving upwind?

At this point my dog Molly, who had long stared at me in complete distrust and antipathy, began to howl. But I sat down at the tiller and purposefully headed us for Boca Grande. Eventually, my helmsmanship brought her howling to a stop and she went back to bed. And my own thoughts of baiting crawfish traps with her carcass passed, too.

Even under jib and jigger, the Meadow Lark made good speed, and we sailed along the Key West shore a mile or so out. In the green breaking troughs, amid screaming sea gulls, the wind singing in the shrouds, I kept looking shoreward and feeling the inordinate contrast of traffic, passing buses, and well-rooted trees.

My next zone of fear was Northwest Channel, the main ship channel. We had to cross it to get to the area of uninhabited islands, at the end of which lay the long, verdant island of Boca Grande, with its beach and shelter. I knew a spring tide would be falling toward the Atlantic and that seas would be especially heavy there.

Right at the corner where the island meets the channel and where a point of shoal ground has built up from tidal action, a New York fireboat at least a hundred feet long had gone aground. The fireboat was headed south to be converted into a yacht and had landed on the spoil bank. Seaward of the fireboat, about a quarter of a mile behind, an oceangoing tug was maneuvering. I decided to tack between the stern of the fireboat and the tug.

We started our tack, sailing toward the bleak-looking ship

as the seas beat into its side. We were about two hundred yards from the fireboat when a lifeboat suddenly appeared from around its stern and two men waved us frantically back. And at that point a surge drew the cable taut that connected the tug and the fireboat.

We had gone too far to tack to seaward of the tug as well as the fireboat; the angle was wrong, we couldn't make it. We were blowing down steadily and losing time. Molly reappeared in the companionway, driving up the tension.

I started the auxiliary and it immediately overheated. That was out. The lifeboat stopped and rolled in the sea a hundred yards away and watched us bear down helplessly on the ship.

The bottom here was hard sand and if I anchored, it would be a long drag before we grabbed, if we did at all. It was then I remembered Herreshoff and Commodore Munroe and the gospel of shoal-draft boats, of sharpie mail boats that skimmed the inlets at West Palm in the 1890s in impossible conditions.

I changed direction and headed around the bow of the boat. As we closed the distance, I could see a line of breaking water between the bow of the fireboat and Key West. There was rock close in. I asked my wife to shut the cabin so that I wouldn't have to see my dog watching me, and I picked the tightest line to the fireboat I dared and sailed on.

Before we ever got to the boat we could see bottom. Rocks and sponges raced under us and once or twice the leeboard tapped and lifted. A good way to sound your way through thin water, Herreshoff had said. The men in the lifeboat stood and stared whenever their boat lifted high enough for them to see us.

We tacked right in under the bow, hearing the sea roar and break around us, and out to deep water again. We let the dog out of the cabin and then sized up the huge rollers coming into the main ship channel. A minute later we were in the first ones and the boat began to lift and work and pick its way through the big green haystacks as they raced at us. The boat made such a premier performance in these conditions that we were suddenly able to let down and enjoy it. The waves coming from seaward were so big we were afraid to look at them. Instead, we waited to feel them lift the boat, then watched their backs as they raced, roaring, away from us toward Key West.

Then the main ship channel was behind us, too, and we were sailing the blue-green waters inside the reef toward Boca Grande. We were actually having fun. We had sandwiches. Our son fell asleep, and the verities of the eternal sea did not seem to be the same verities that have brought us salami or penicillin.

We rounded Boca Grande in early evening and anchored in a little channel that offered us a bit of lee. I laid two anchors on a good scope of line. The Meadow Lark pitched and hunted about, but, in all, we were comfortable. We went below and ate sumptuously. Just at dark, two young Cubans who had a crawfish camp on the island rowed out to us with great effort and asked if there was anything we needed. We said that there was not and thanked them, rather moved by this kind of frontier courtesy.

We lit the oil lamps in the cabin at dark and talked till late about our personal greatness as adventurers. I read a few chapters of Herreshoff's *The Common Sense of Yacht Design* and we all fell asleep in the howling wind.

SMALL
STREAMS IN
MICHIGAN

THE FIRST FLY ROD I ever owned was eight feet of carpet beater made by a company whose cork grips were supplied by my father. My father worked for a Portuguese cork company whose owners swam at Estoril and supplied our family with innumerable objects of cork, including cork shoes, cork boxes, cork purses, and unidentified flying cork objects that my brother and I threw at each other. In our living room we had large cut-glass decanters of Burgundy, long soured; and my brother and I would have a couple of hits of that vinegar and head for the cellar to throw cork.

Everyone in our family had a huge brown fly rod with a Portuguese cork handle and identical Pflueger Medalist reels of the size used for Atlantic salmon. As I look back, I am touched by my father's attempts to bring us to sport, *en famille*.

I remember when he and my mother canoed the Pere Marquette in that early phase. Passing underneath the branches of streamside trees, my mother seized one of them in terror. The branch flexed, the canoe turned sideways in the current and began to go under. My father bellowed to let go of the branch; my mother did. The branch shot across the canoe like a longbow, taking my father across the chest and knocking him overboard.

With his weight gone, one end of the canoe rose four feet

out of the water and my mother twirled downstream until my father contrived to race along a footpath and make the rescue.

When it was done, two rods with Portuguese cork grips were gone. The canoe was saved until the time my brother and I could use it for a toboggan in snow-filled streambeds and beat the bottom out of it.

At that time, we lived down on Lake Erie, where I conducted a mixed-bag sporting life, catching perch and rock bass on worms, some pike on daredevils, some bass on a silver spoon. In the winter, I wandered around the lake on the ice and shot crows.

But when we went up north with our Portuguese cork handle fly rods, I knew the trout were there. And so I spurned worms, had a fly box, and espoused purist attitudes, which, in their more mature form, nauseate folks all over.

There was a lake near the cabin, and I would paddle out upon it trailing all my fly line and a Mickey Finn streamer. Then I would paddle around the lake, trolling that fly until I caught a trout. This is about the minimum, fly-wise. But I do remember, with a certain finality, what those trout looked like lying between the canoe's varnished ribs; and how in the evening it felt to put the trout and jackknife on the dock, pull the canoe up on the beach, and clean my catch.

I don't doubt that for many fine anglers the picture of what could be, in fishing, begins with a vision of worm gobs lying in dark underwater holes, the perfect booby trap. The casters I used to see, throwing surface plugs in flat arcs up under the brushy banks, made that kind of fishing seem a myth. And I even once could see the point of fishing with outriggers. But now trout seem to be everything that is smart and perfect in fish, and their taking of a floating fly or free-drifting nymph is a culmination in sport to be compared to anything. But what interests me is how I came to believe that.

I recall grouse hunting near the Pere Marquette when I was very young. It had just snowed, and I had killed one bird, which bulged warm in the back of my coat. I kicked out a few more birds in a forgotten orchard and couldn't get a shot; then walked down a wooded hill that ended in a very small stream, perhaps two feet wide, but cut rather deeply in mossy ground. A short distance above where I stood, the stream made a pool, clear and round as a lens. In the middle of that pool, a nice brook trout held in the cold current. With a precision that still impresses me, it moved from one side to the other to intercept nymphs, always perfectly returning to its holding position in the little pool.

Not long after that, during trout season, I waded the Pere Marquette one hot day on which not a single rising fish was to be found. I plodded along, flicking wan, pointless casts along the bank.

The river at one point broke into channels, and one channel bulged up against a logjam, producing a kind of pool. I had always approached this place with care because trout often soared around its upper parts and if a cast could be placed very quietly on the slick bulge of water, a take often was the result. I crept up, but no trout grazed under its surface waiting for my Lady Beaverkill to parachute in.

But salvation was around the corner. The deep shadowy color of the pool seemed to hold a new glint. I stood erect. There was nothing near the top of the pool for me to spook, but clearly trout were deep in the pool, moving about enough to send their glints up.

I remembered the brooky in the minute fissure of stream when I had been grouse shooting, and I recalled how steadily he had held except to intercept a free-swimming nymph in the icy water. It occurred to me that something like that sudden lateral movement and return must be what was sending these messages to me from this large pool in the Pere Marquette.

I tied on an indeterminately colored nymph and shot a cast up to the head of the pool. The nymph dropped and sank, and the point of my floating line began its retreat back toward me at current speed. About a third of the way back, the line point stopped. I lifted and felt the weight. A couple of minutes later, I trapped a nice brown trout against the gravel at the foot of the pool with my trembling hands.

This was before I had learned the thrill of the release, of a trout darting from your opening hands, or resting its weight very slightly in your palms underwater, then easing off. So three nice trout went from the pool into my creel and then, after a decent interval, into my mouth.

Anyway, the connection was complete. And even if I couldn't always put it together, I saw how it was with nymphs. Years of casting and retrieving made it difficult to slackline a tumbling nymph — the forms of manipulation in trout fishing are always so remote — but I realized that fishing a nymph invisible under the pools and runs on a tensionless line was not inferior in magic to the dry fly.

It was after that we found a long beaver pond covering many acres of ground in a dense mixed forest of pine and conifer. There were, I had heard, good-size brook trout in the pond which had migrated down from the stream itself.

Beaver ponds are a mixed blessing, having only a few years of good fishing. Then the standing water turns sour and the size of the average fish gets smaller as his head grows proportionately larger. But this pond was only a couple of years old, with a soft bottom covered with drowned leaves.

I had some trouble locating the pond but ended up tracking its source through the cedars. It was almost evening when I got there, and huge columns of light came down through the forest. There was a good hatch of mayflies in progress along the stream, with small trout rising to them and cedar waxwings overhead hovering in the swarm.

The pond was perfect. Some dead trees stood ghostly in its middle, and the pond itself inundated small bays around the water-tolerant cedars. Best of all, big easy rises were in numerous places, slow takes that produced an actual sucking noise.

I cautiously waded for position. The pond was so smooth that I anxiously anticipated the fall of line on its surface. I had a piece of inner tube in my shirt and I used it to thoroughly straighten my leader.

Every time I moved on the soft bottom, a huge cloud of mud arose, carried behind me, and then filtered down through the beaver dam. It was a cool summer evening and I wore a flannel shirt; I shivered a little and tried to keep from looking up when one of the big rises opened on the pond.

I tied on my favorite fly, the Adams, a pattern that exemplifies my indecisive nature. The Adams looks a little like all bugs. It's gray and funky and a great salesman. My fly box is mainly Adamses in about eight different sizes. In the future, I mean to be a fine streamside entomologist. I'm going to start on that when I am much too old to do any of the two thousand things I can think of that are more fun than screening insects in cold running water.

You have a problem making a first cast on delicate water. You haven't warmed up and it may be your most important cast. I had the advantage on this glassy pond of being able to see a number of widely separated rises, and I felt that, at worst, I could blow off one fish and still keep my act alive for one or two more.

I looked around, trying to find a place for my backcast, stripped some line, and false-cast carefully until the instant a rise began to open on the surface. I threw and dropped the fly very much closer than I deserved. I poised myself not to break the light tippet on the strike, held that attitude up to the descending moment I realized the fish wasn't going to take. Another fish rose and I covered him, waited, and got no take.

I let the line lie on the water and tried to calm down. My loop was turning over clean and quiet; the leader was popping out straight. And the Adams sat cheerily on its good hackle points. I refused to believe the fish were that selective. Then I hung up a cast behind me, trying to cover a fish at too new an angle, and a lull set in.

You never know about lulls. You ask, Is it my fault? Do the trout know I'm here? Have they heard or felt my size-twelve tread on this boggy ground? Is my casting coarse and inaccurate? Where can I buy a drink at this hour?

It was getting dark. I didn't have a fish. The rises kept appearing. I kept casting, and I never got a take. There is a metallic loss of light one feels when it is all over. You press to the end but it's kaput. I left in blackness. A warm wind came up and gave the mosquitoes new hope. I lit a cigar to keep them out of my face and trudged through the forms of the big cedars along the stream, trying not to fall. I snagged my suspenders on a bramble and snapped myself. The moon was full and I was thinking about the TV.

The next evening I was back earlier. This time I crawled to the edge of the pond with the light at my back and had a good look. The first thing I saw was the rises, as many as the night before. I remembered how they had failed to materialize and checked my excitement. As I watched, I caught a rise at the moment it opened; and saw the fish drop beneath the ring and continue cruising until it was beyond my view. The next rise I caught, I saw another cruiser, moving immediately away from the place of the rise and looking for another insect. I began to realize my error of the night before. These were cruising fish, waiting for something to pass through their observation lane. There were a good number of them traveling about the pond, hunting for food.

I retreated from my place beside the pond, circled around below the dam, and waded into my position of the night before. I tried on another Adams, but this time a rather large one. I cast it straight out into the middle of the pond and let it lie.

Rises continued to happen, picking up a little as evening advanced and as the cedar waxwings returned to wait, like me, for the hatch. My Adams floated in its same place, clearly visible to me. I could see the curves of my leader in the surface skin of the water and I waited for a trying length of time. I had to see my theory through because, like many a simple-minded sportsman, I see myself as a problem solver.

The fly dropped out of sight. I didn't respond until the ring had already started to spread, and I lifted the rod and felt the fish. The trout darted off in a half-dozen chugging didos in the dark water over drowned leaves. I landed him a moment later, a brook trout of a solid pound. I studied him a moment and thought what a bright, lissome, perfect fish this little American char is.

Brook trout are cheerfully colored in deep reds, grays, and blues, with ivory leading edges and deep moony spots on their fins. They are called squaretails elsewhere, after the clear graphics of the profile. I reached in for my Adams and felt the small teeth roughen the first knuckles of my thumb and forefinger. Then I let him go. He sank to the leaves at my feet, thought for a minute, and made off.

I rinsed the fly carefully. That long float required a well-dried fly. Then I false-cast the fly a moment to dry it, applied some Mucilin dressing, which I kept smeared on the back of my left hand, and cast again. This time I stared at the fly for ten or fifteen minutes, long enough to notice the Adams changing its waterline. But then it sank suddenly and I had another fish.

Since casting was nearly eliminated from this episode, the fishing did not seem fast. But at the end of a couple of hours, I had taken seven fish. The takers were all solid, confident, and deep. I released all the fish, and by the time I had hiked out of the boggy forest that night, I could feel glory all around me.

It would be one thing to say, pragmatically, that in still or nearly still waters, feeding trout cruise; and that in streams and rivers they tend to take a feeding lane and watch a panel of moving water overhead, elevating to eat when something passes; and that the repeated rises of a holding trout in a stream are as unlike the disparate rises of my beaver pond as they are unlike the deep glintings of nymphing trout. But the fact is, these episodes are remembered as complete dramatic entities, whose real function, finally, is to be savored. It is fine, of course, to escalate them toward further successes; but in the end, angling has nothing whatsoever to do with success.

Nevertheless, by the time the aforementioned had been met and dealt with, I had come to think of myself as a pretty smart fisherman. I had a six-cylinder black Ford, a mahogany tackle box, two split-cane rods, and Adamses in eight sizes. I had cheap, clean lodgings within quick reach of the Pigeon, Black, and Sturgeon rivers, where you ate decently prepared food with the owner, one or two other fishermen, and perhaps a young salesman with a line of practical shoes and a Ford like mine.

From here, I'd pick a stretch of the Pigeon or the Black for the early fishing, wade the oxbow between the railroad bridges on the Sturgeon in the afternoon. Then in the evening I'd head for a wooden bridge over the Sturgeon near Wolverine.

Below the bridge was a large pool deeply surrounded by brush and inhabited by nearly nocturnal brown trout. A sandy bottom shelved off into the undercut banks and it was a rarity to find a feeding fish here in the daytime. But shortly after dinnertime in the summer, when the hatches seemed to come, the trout would venture out into the open pool and feed with greater boldness.

I stood on the bridge itself and rigged my rod with a relatively short, heavy leader; the fish were not leader-shy this late. And I tied on a fly known locally as a "caddis," though it was anything but an actual caddis. This was a huge, four-winged fly with a crosshatched deer-hair body. Lying in your open hand, it covered the palm, and when you cast it, the wings made a turbulent noise like a bat passing your ear.

The trout liked it real well.

What I appreciated was that I could fish from this wooden

bridge in the black of night without fear of falling in a hole, filling my waders, and passing on. I'd cast that big baby until two or three in the morning, guessing at the rate at which I should retrieve to keep up with the fly backing down on the current toward me. I had to strike by sound every rise I heard. Five out of six rises I struck would just snatch the fly and line into a heap at my feet. But that one out of six would be solid to a trout, and some of those trout were big by my small-stream standards.

Finally, something would end the fishing, an especially baleful frog in the swamp, a screech owl, or a train a couple of miles away, and I'd reel up for the evening. I'd take my trout and lay them out in the headlights of the Ford and think how sweet it was. Then I'd clean them with my pocketknife, slitting them to the vent, separating the gills at the point of jaw, and shucking those fastidious entrails; I'd run out the black blood along the spine with my thumbnail so it wouldn't change their flavor, restack them in the creel, and head back to my lodgings.

The first time I met my wife's grandfather I was twenty and a full-blown trout snob. Pomp, as he was called, was a gifted bait fisherman, and he took the position that I fly-fished because I didn't want to get worms on my hands.

Pomp and his wife live near Kaleva, Michigan, which is one of the numerous Finnish communities in the state. They had a cabin overlooking Bear Creek on a small piece of ground next to a gradually approaching gravel pit. And they lived a through-the-looking-glass life, to which we all tried to annex ourselves.

My wife had a better line on the situation than I. She had summered in a jungle hammock with her grandparents, helped bake pies for the raccoons, been accidentally locked in the sauna of the neighbor's farm, now abandoned, with nothing inside but a moth-eaten Korean War infantry uniform.

Moreover, she could report to me the kind of trout fishing Pomp was capable of — upstream bait-fishing, the deadliest in the right hands. He had great hands. Secondly, he belonged to that category of sportsmen who will stop at nothing.

Bear Creek ran through a large corrugated culvert under a country road. Pomp had located a very large trout living there, a spotted brute that finned forward in the evening to feed in the pool at the upstream end of the culvert. How he knew about that trout, I can't say; but for sure he knew it by indirection. He had great instincts about trout, much envied by the locals. Pomp was from farther south in Michigan; and even among the old-timers, there was a competition over who was from farther north than who. Now it has become a perfect frenzy as the footloose Michigander wages the war of roots with fellow cottage builders.

Anyway, he crept up and hooked the thing and quickly discovered it was bigger than he suspected. The trout fought its way down the culvert. At the far end, it would be a lost cause; the line would be cut through by the culvert itself. I was a fly-fisherman, new to Pomp's world, when I first heard this story; and I confess that I reached this point in the narrative without beginning to see how I would have landed the fish. But Pomp had a solution.

He had his wife lie across the far end of the culvert. He fought the fish to a standstill inside the pipe and landed it. As I say, this was early in our experience together; and the reader will remember that it was his opinion that I fished with flies in order to keep from touching worms.

Heretofore, I had hoped to outfish him in our already burgeoning, if covert, competition. But his emplacement of his wife at the far end of the culvert in order to beat that trout — well, it showed me what I was up against.

And, in fact, as a bit of pleasant foreshortening, I ought to say that he consistently outfished me, all along, right through the year of his death, the news of which came as usual in some pointless city, by telephone.

I had accumulated some ways of taking trout, above and below the surface. We would start at dawn with shots of bourbon from the refrigerator, cold to take away its edge in the morning. Then trout, potatoes, and eggs for breakfast, during which Pomp would describe to me and to my fly-fishing brother-in-law the hopelessness of our plight and the cleanliness of worms.

Then on into the day, fishing, principally, the Betsey, the Bear, and the Little Manistee rivers. Usually, we ended on the Bear, below the cabin, and it was then, during the evening hatch, that I hoped to even my morbidly reduced score.

The day I'm thinking of was in August, when the trout were down deep where only Pomp could reason with them. I dutifully cast my flies up into the brilliant light hour after hour and had, for my pains, a few small fish. Pomp had a lot more. And his were bigger, having sent their smaller, more gullible friends to the surface for my flies.

But, by late afternoon, summer rainclouds had begun to build, higher and blacker, and finally startling cracks of thunder commenced. We were scattered along the banks of the Bear, and as the storm built, I knew Pomp would head for the cabin. I started that way, too, but as I passed the lower bridge pool, I saw trout rising everywhere. I stopped to make a cast and promptly caught a trout. By the time I'd landed it, the trees were bowing and surging, and casting was simply a question of rolling the line downwind onto the pool. The lightning was literally blasting into the forest, and I was suddenly cold from the wind-driven rain. But the trout were rising with still more intensity.

When I was a child, I heard that a man was killed by lightning that ran down the drainspout of a bus station. And ever since then, lightning has had a primordial power to scare me. I kept casting, struck, misstruck, and landed trout, while the electric demon raced around those Michigan woods.

I knew Pomp was up in the cabin. Probably had a cigar and was watching the water stream from the corner of the roof.

Something would be baking. But I meant to hang in there until I limited out. Well, I didn't. The storm stopped abruptly and the universe was full of ozone and new light and I was ready for the cabin.

Outside the cabin, there was a wooden table next to a continuously flowing well, where we cleaned our trout. The overflow of the well ran down the hill to the Bear, and when we cleaned the trout, we chucked the insides down the hill for the raccoons. I laid my trout out on the table and went in to get Pomp.

Pomp came out and said: "What do you know about that!"

SAKONNET

BECAUSE THIS WAS a visit and a return, I might have had the nerve, right at the beginning, to call it "Sakonnet Point Revisited" and take my lumps on the Victorianism and sentimentality counts, though half a page of murder and sex at the end would bail that out. But if you are to cultivate a universal irony, a Edmund Wilson told Scott Fitzgerald to do, you must never visit anything in your works, much less revisit — ever.

But when you go back to a place where you spent many hours of childhood, you find that some of it has become important, if not actually numinous, and that universal irony might just have to eat hot lead for the moment, because there is no way of suppressing that importance. Also, there is the fact of its being no secret anyway. A Midwestern childhood is going to show, for instance, even after you have retired from the ad agency and are a simple crab fisherman by the sea, grave with Winslow Homer marineland wisdom. Sooner or later someone looks into your eyes and sees a flash of corn and automobiles, possibly even the chemical plant at Wyandotte, Michigan. You can't hide it.

Still, there was one thing certainly to be avoided: to wit, when you go back to the summer place everything seems so small.

You protest: "But when I got there, everything *did* seem small . . ."

Don't say it! The smallness of that which is revisited is one of the touchstones of an egregious underground literature in which the heart is constantly wrung by the artifacts of child-hood.

Concentrate on all that dreck on the beach that didn't used to be there, won't you? Get the usual garbage, but lay in there for the real nonbiodegradables, too. Be sure the aluminum cans and the polystyrene crud show up on the page. The great thing, ironists, is the stuff is really there! So questions of falsi-fication and literary decorum are both answered satisfactorily.

I had neared Sakonnet Point thinking, This place is loaded with pitfalls, and I had visualized a perfect beach of distant memory now glittering with mercury, oiled ducks, aluminum, and maybe one defunct but glowing nuclear submarine. And I met my expectations at my first meal in the area: The Down East Clam Special. The cook's budget had evidently been di-verted into the tourist effluvium inspired by the American Revolution that I saw in the lobby. The clams that were in my chowder and fritters and fried clams were mere shadows of their former selves, in some instances calling into question whether they had ever been clams at all.

On my plate was universal irony in parable form, come to haunt me. I knew at that moment that I had my imaginative rights. As a result, I actually returned to Sakonnet Point half thinking to see the whalers of the *Pequod* striding up from their dories to welcome me. And, truly, when I saw the old houses on the rocky peninsula, they fitted the spangled Atlan-tic around them at exactly the equipoise that seems one of the harmonics of childhood.

I had my bass rod in the car and drove straight to Warren's Point. There was a nice shore-break surf and plenty of boiling whitewater that I could reach with a plug. Nevertheless, I didn't rush it. I needed a little breakthrough to make the pursuit plausible. When you are fishing on foot, you have none of the reassurances that the big accouterments of the sport offer. No one riding a fighting chair on a John Rybovich sportfisherman thinks about *not getting one* in quite the same terms as the man on foot.

Before I began, I could see on the horizon the spectator boats from the last day of the America's Cup heading home. The Goodyear blimp seemed as stately in the pale sky as the striped bass I had visualized as my evening's reward.

I began to cast, dropping the big surface plug, an Atom Popper, into the white water around boulders and into the tumbling backwash of waves. I watched the boats heading home and wondered if *Gretel* had managed a comeback. During the day I had learned that an old friend of the family was in Fall River recovering from a heart attack and that his lobster pots still lay inside the course of the cup race. I wondered about that and cast until I began to have those first insidious notions that I had miscalculated the situation.

But suddenly, right in front of me, bait was in the air and the striped green-and-black backs of bass coursed through it. It is hard to convey this surprise: bait breaking like a small rainstorm and, bolting through the frantic minnows, perhaps a dozen striped bass. They went down at the moment I made my cast and reappeared thirty feet away. I picked up and cast again, and the same thing happened. Then the fish vanished.

I had blown the chance by not calculating an interception. I stood on my rock and rather forlornly hoped it would happen again. To my immediate right, baitfish were splashing out of the water, throwing themselves up against the side of a sea-washed boulder. It occurred to me, slowly, that they were not doing this out of their own personal sense of sport. So I lobbed my plug over, made one turn on the handle, hooked a striper, and was tight to the fish in a magical burst of spray. The bass raced around among the rocks and seaweed, made one dogged run toward open water, then came my way. When he was twenty feet from me, I let him hang in the trough until another wave formed. I glided the fish in on it and beached him.

The ocean swells and flattens, stripes itself abstractly with foam, and changes color under the clouds. Sometimes a dense flock of gulls hangs overhead and their snowy shadows sink into the green, translucent sea.

Standing on a boulder amid breaking surf that is forming offshore, accelerating, and rolling toward you is, after a while, like looking into a fire. It is mesmeric.

All the time I was here I thought of my uncle Bill, who had died the previous year and in whose Sakonnet house I was staying, as I had in the past. He was a man of some considerable local fame as a gentleman and a wit. And he had a confidence and a sense of moral precision that amounted for some people to a mild form of tyranny. But, for me, his probity was based almost more on his comic sense than on his morality — though the latter was considerable.

He was a judge in Massachusetts. I have heard that in his court one day two college students were convicted of having performed a panty raid on a girls' dormitory. My uncle sentenced them to take his charge card to Filene's department store in Boston and there "to exhaust their interest in ladies' underwear."

He exacted terrific cautions of my cousin Fred, my brother John, and me, and would never, when I fished here as a boy, have allowed me to get out on the exposed rocks I fished from now. His son Fred and I were not allowed to swim unguarded, carry pocketknives, or go to any potentially dangerous promontory to fish, which restriction eliminated all the good places.

And he had small blindnesses that may have been infuriating to his family, for all I know. To me, they simply made him more singular. By today's or even the standards of that day, he was rather unreconstructed, but this makes of him an infinitely more palpable individual in my memory than the adaptable nullities who have replaced men like him.

His discomfiture will be perceived in the following: He invited Fred and me to his court in Fall River. To his horrified surprise, the first case before him was that of a three-hundred-pound lady, the star of an all-night episode of *le sexe multiple*, and included a parade of abashed sailors, who passed before Fred's and my astounded eyes at the behest of the prosecution. Unreconstructed in her own way, the lady greeted the sailors with a heartiness they could not return.

After the session for the day, my uncle spirited us to Sakonnet to think upon the verities of nature. For us, at the time, nature was largely striped bass and how to get them. But the verity of a fat lady and eleven sailors trapped in the bell jar of my uncle Bill's court fought for our attention on equal footing.

I hooked another bass at the end of a long cast. Handsome: you see them blast a plug out at the end of your best throw. I landed the fish as the sun fell.

I was here during the hurricane that made the surf break in the horse pasture across the road from the house. Shingles lifted slowly from the garage roof and exploded into the sky. The house became an airplane; unimaginable plants and objects shot past its windows. The surf took out farm fences and drove pirouettes of foam into the sky. My cousins and I treated it as an adventure. Uncle Bill was our guarantee against the utter feasibility of the house going underwater. And if it flooded, we knew he would bring a suitable boat to an upstairs window.

Late that day the hurricane was over, having produced delirium and chaos: lobster pots in the streets, commercial fishing boats splintered all over the rocks, yards denuded of trees and bushes, vegetation burned and killed by wind-driven salt water.

My cousin Fred and I stole out and headed for the shore, titillated by looting stories. The rocky beach was better than we dreamed; burst tackle chests with more bass plugs than we could use, swordfish harpoons, ship-to-shore radios, marine engines, the works.

Picking through this lovely rubble like a pair of crows, we were approached by the special kind of histrionic New England lady (not Irish Catholic like us, we knew) who has got a lot of change tied up in antiques and family *objets* that point to her great familial depth in this part of the world. She took one look at us and called us "vile little ghouls," which rather queered it for us, neither of us knowing what ghouls were.

I kept fishing after dark, standing on a single rock and feeling disoriented by the foam swirling around me. I was getting sore from casting and jigging the plug. Moreover, casting in the dark is like smoking in the dark; something is missing. You don't see the trajectory or the splash. You don't see the surface plug spouting and spoiling for trouble. But shortly I hooked a fish. It moved very little. I began to think it was possibly a deadhead rolling in the wash. I waited, just trying to keep everything together. The steady unexcited quality of its movement began to convince me that it was not a fish. I lifted the rod sharply to see if I could elicit some more characteristic movement. And I got it. The fish burned off fifty or sixty yards, sulked, let me get half of it back, and did the same again.

I began to compose the headline: LUNKER FALLS TO OUT-OF-STATE BASSMASTER. " 'I clobber them big with my top-secret technique,' claims angler-flâneur Tom McGuane of Livingston, Montana," etc., etc.

The bass began to run again, not fast or hysterical, but with the solid, irresistible motion of a Euclid bulldozer easing itself into a phosphate mine. It mixed up its plays, bulling, running, stopping, shaking. And then it was gone.

When I reeled up, I was surprised that I still had the plug, though its hooks were mangled beyond use. I had been cleaned out. Nevertheless, with two good bass for the night, I felt resigned to my loss. No I didn't.

I took two more bass the next day. There was a powerful sense of activity on the shore. Pollock were chasing minnows right up against the beach. And at one sublime moment at sundown, tuna were assailing the bait, dozens of the powerful fish in the air at once, trying to nail the smaller fish from above.

Then it was over and quiet. I looked out to sea in the last light, the white rollers coming in around me. The clearest item of civilization from my perspective was a small tanker heading north. Offshore, a few rocky shoals boiled whitely. The air was chilly. It looked lonely and cold.

But from behind me came intimate noises: the door of a house closing, voices, a lawn mower. And, to a great extent, this is the character of bass fishing from the beach. In very civilized times it is reassuring to know that wild fish will run so close that a man on foot and within earshot of lawn mowers can touch their wildness with a fishing rod.

I hooked a bass after dark, blind-casting in the surf, a good fish that presented some landing difficulties; there were numerous rocks in front of me, hard to see in the dark. I held the flashlight in my mouth, shining it first along the curve of rod out to the line and to the spot among the rocks where the line met the water, foaming very bright in the light. The surf was heavier now, booming into the boulders around me.

In a few moments I could see the thrashing bass, the plug in its mouth, a good fish. It looked radically striped and impressive in the backwash.

I guided the tired striper through the rocks, beached him, removed the plug, and put him gently into a protected pool. He righted himself and I watched him breathe and fin, more vivid in my light beam than in any aquarium. Then abruptly he shot back into the foam and out to sea. I walked into the surf again, looking for the position, the exact placement of feet and tension of rod while casting, that had produced the strike.

One of my earliest trips to Sakonnet included a tour of The Breakers, the Vanderbilt summer palazzo. My grandmother was with us. Before raising her large family she had been among the child labor force in the Fall River mills, the kind of person who had helped make really fun things like palazzos at Newport possible.

Safe on first by two generations, I darted around the lugubrious mound, determined to live like that one day. Over the fireplace was an agate only slightly smaller than a fire hydrant. It was here that I would evaluate the preparation of the bass I had taken under the cliffs by the severest methods: eleven-foot Calcutta casting rod and handmade block-tin squid. The bass was to be brought in by the fireplace, *garni*, don't you know; and there would be days when the noble fish was to be consumed in bed. Many, many comic books would be spread about on the counterpane.

We went on to Sakonnet. As we drove I viewed every empty corn or potato field as a possible site for the mansion. The Rolls Silver Cloud would be parked to one side, its leather backseat slimy from loading stripers.

The sun came up on a crystalline fall day; blue sky and delicate glaze. I hiked down the point beach, along the red ridge of rock, the dense beach scrub with its underledge of absolute shadow. As I walked I drove speeding clusters of sanderlings before me. If I did not watch myself, there would be the problem of sentiment.

When I got to the end and could see the islands with their ruins, I could observe the narrow, glittering tidal rip like an oceanic continuation of the rocky ridge of the point itself.

A few days before, the water had been cloudy and full of

kelp and weed, especially the puffs of iodine-colored stuff that clung tenaciously to my plug. Today, though, the water was clear and green, with waves rising translucent before whitening onto the hard beach. I stuck the butt of my rod into the sand and sat down. From here, beautiful houses could be seen along the headlands. A small farm ran down the knolls, with black-and-white cattle grazing along its tilts. An American spy was killed by the British in the farm's driveway.

My cousin Fred came that evening from Fall River and we fished. The surf was heavier and I hooked and lost a fish very early on. There were other bass fishermen out, bad ones mostly. They trudged up and down the shore with their new rods, not casting, but waiting for an irresistible sign to begin.

When it was dark, Fred, who had waded out to a far rock and who periodically vanished from my view in the spray, hooked a fine bass. After some time, he landed it and made his way through the breakers with the fish in one hand, the rod in the other.

At the end of a fishing trip you are inclined to summarize in your head. A tally is needed for the quick description you will be asked for: so many fish at such and such weights and the method employed. Inevitably, what actually happened is indescribable.

It is assumed that the salient events of childhood be inordinate. During one of my first trips to Sakonnet, a trap boat caught an enormous oceanic sunfish, many hundred pounds in weight. A waterfront entrepreneur who usually sold crabs and tarred handlines bought the sunfish and towed it to the beach in an enclosed wooden wagon, where he charged ten cents admission to see it. I was an early sucker — and a repeater. In some way the sight seems to have taken like a vaccination; I remember very clearly ascending the wooden steps into the wagon, whose windows let water-reflected light play over the ceiling.

One by one we children goggled past the enormous animal

laid out on a field of ice. The huge lolling discus of the temperate and tropical seas met our stares with a cold eye that was not less soulful for being the size of a hubcap.

Many years later I went back to Sakonnet on a December afternoon as a specific against the torpor of university. I was walking along the cove beach when I saw the wagon, not in significantly worse repair than when I had paid to get in it. And, to be honest, I never made the connection that it was the same wagon until I stepped inside.

There on a dry, iceless wooden table lay the skeleton of the ocean sunfish.

It seemed safe to conclude in the face of this utterly astounding occasion that I was to be haunted. Accommodating myself to the fish's reappearance, I adjusted to the unforeseeable in a final way. If I ever opened an elevator door and found that skeleton on its floor, I would step in without comment, finding room for my feet between its ribs, and press the button of my destination.

THE
LIFE AND
HARD TIMES
OF CHINK'S
BENJIBABY

THE MODERN cutting-horse contest, of which Chink's Ben-jibaby has been a star, requires some explanation. Since the days of the trail drives, a horse with the mind and physical ability to sort sick cattle and strays from large herds has had great practical value and is usually ridden by the most accomplished cowman in the outfit. Individual cattle don't want to leave the herd, however admirable the reasons, and they are quick and clever enough to test the horses trying to drive them out. As for the rider, there really isn't time to rein the horse from one spot to another, moving the cattle — once the cut has been made, it's up to the horse to make the reflexive decisions necessary to drive the cow into the open.

It has long been correct for even the most "horseback" rider to hold on to the horn; the stresses, G-forces, and lateral loads on the rider make it necessary. Gradually, under the pressure of wagering, a controlled contest evolved so that one cutting horse could be tested against another, one rider against another; and the unanswerable question arose as to who was to get the credit, horse or rider. It is said that a great cutting-horse rider can always trade horses with you and beat you. It is also assumed that the horse does it all. The truth is that the relationship between horse and rider is so intricate that one of the fundamental problems of a cutting-horse rider lies in controlling his own mood. Controlling your mood when a horse turns so sharply as to stick your spur in the ground is occasionally a matter of controlling fear.

Over the years, there have been legendary cutting horses: Jesse James, Poco Lena, Sugar Vaquero, Mister San Peppy, and Hollywood Gold, among the modern greats. And in my time, a mysterious black mare, reported to be crazy, Chink's Benjibaby, the product of rejection and indomitable greatness, a horse who has waged unremitting mind war against cutting-horse riders.

Why would anyone call a horse Chink's Benjibaby? Well, her mother's name was Chink and her father was an old cutting-horse stallion named King Benjiman. She was born in California in vaguely suburban circumstances of the densest kind of Texas blood, King and the legendary Old Sorrel. And her subsequent history would indicate that she was not born for life in the Golden West. Her original owners had her in a chain-link pen and threw her feed over the top. She was considered unpredictable even as a baby. But her refined face and slick-black form highlighted in chestnut maintained a tenuous line of credit for a horse destined to drive people crazy.

One early owner complained that she destroyed his box stall. So he had one built of cinder block by a contractor. She tore that down, and the contractor, who had guaranteed the stall would hold her, accused the new owner of being a psychopath who stole out at night with a pickax to tear down his work. When the new owner decided to haul her to a cutting, Chink's Benjibaby disliked his trailer and destroyed it. And yet, from the beginning, no one suspected her of meanness. It was agreed that she was a kind and capable horse who hated confinement, machinery, and the twentieth century.

Nevertheless, for the first time in her life, Chink's began to be rejected. Her conduct was sometimes amusing, as when she stood up on her hind legs like a kangaroo and watched the humans; or, when boredom overtook her in her box stall, she decided to leave hoofprints on the walls, twelve feet off the ground. But sometimes a darker mania overtook her, and she raised Cain until her eyeballs rolled and she fell soaked with sweat into a deep and troubled sleep. Some said that she wasn't meant for a life in stalls and pens, that she was a cowboy's horse.

Jerry Vawter is one of the premier stallion men on the West Coast, and his long string of great quarter-horse studs is the imprimatur of his authority. He first saw Chink's Benjibaby at Rancho California as a green cutting horse who had nothing to show for herself but her desire and chaotic genius. To a less practiced eye, she was probably ridiculous. Impatient with slow cattle, she reared, sank on her hocks, and vibrated in the hopes of getting something done for herself and for her rider, breaking all the rules, but revealing the intensity of "cow" — that quality of inclination to break down and work cattle — that Vawter remembered from her great sire, King Benjiman, when the part-Indian Ray Thomas rode him to glory on the West Coast. Vawter bought the horse immediately. Unfortunately, the mare came into Vawter's life at a time when his business was changing toward halter horses, and he sold her after six months.

Bill Baldwin, a cutting-horse photographer as well as a rider, took Chink's on trial. He concluded that she was great if you had time to ride her twenty miles to take the edge off before you went cutting. She walked the fence all night like a stallion and seemed to have some intense drive that no one could focus. "She was a cowboy's horse," said Bill, "and I didn't feel cowboy enough to keep her."

Chink's Benjibaby was shipped to two different cutting-horse trainers in the Southwest, top hands each, and was promptly rejected. Finally, a man in Kansas bought her and hauled her to Pat Jacobs of Gate, Oklahoma, for a last try; but the Kansas man went bankrupt and the most ignominious thing that can happen to a horse happened to this unlucky mare: She was repossessed by the bank.

What happened to Chink's Benjibaby after that is the subject of contradictory stories. I had been interested in the mare since acquiring her half sister, Benjistripe, another brilliant horse. Later we bought King Benjiman, her sire, and hauled him here to Montana, and thus became the recipients of Chink's Benjibaby lore. When Pat Jacobs invited us to Gate for Thanksgiving, my wife and I decided to go for a number of reasons: one of them was to find out what happened to Chink's after the bank got her. The other, as Pat promised, was to eat wild turkey and drink Wild Turkey.

Gate is in the Oklahoma panhandle. And the only way we could get there that weekend was by small plane. Things are a little slower in that part of the world. The front bedroom of Pat's last lease-ranch, for instance, was the former office of the Dodge City–to–Tascosa, Texas, stage line. When you come in from the west across the flat farmland of eastern Colorado and western Kansas, the monotony of rectangles and center-pivot sprinklers is hypnotically boring. Then it changes and the whorls of seasonal runoff in the empty sand hills, all russet against a pale fall horizon, have a beauty unmarred by the weathered homes and corrals of ranchers who are there to stay.

We dipped over Pat's ranch to let him know we'd be landing soon. I could see the rows of stalls and runways. Every runway had a cutting horse, and the sight seemed incredibly exotic: these ponies are as strange and special as falcons. In one pen, a curious black figure ran in circles at the sound of the airplane: Chink's Benjibaby.

The aerial view of the Oklahoma panhandle and the wonderful topography gave way as we made our approach, and soon the bare horizon was all that stood out around the little airfield. In a moment, Pat was there, muddy M. L. Leddy boots to his knees, spurs jingling like in the song.

A word about Pat: Pat is a cattle trader and cutting-horse trainer. Most trainers now are assembled around big population centers — Dallas–Fort Worth, Phoenix, Los Angeles — where displaced people spend money on cutting horses out of some kind of regional memory. Pat still lives out in the sticks, trading feeder cattle. He still believes that the King- and Leo-bred horses, who are the foundation of the sport, are better than the omnipresent Doc Bars, who represent the impact of California on the world of cutting. I see him leading a Doc Bar stud; the horses refuses to go into the arena: "This sumbuck's got so much cow he can't go in there and face it." Pat won't ride the fashionable Buster Welch saddles because of their flat seats, and rides instead a Price McLauchlin stock saddle with a built-up ground seat, claiming the Buster Welch model was designed to accommodate the inventor's hemorrhoids. And he likes to see a horse athlete enough, like the great Sugar Vaquero, to blow by a cow a little before cracking around, to master the cow even in the difficult corners; as opposed to trying to win in the middle, however elegantly, with what the old Spanish bullfighters referred to contemptuously as "dancing."

This is not the modern school, where the trainer meets you at the airport in a limousine. Pat's forte is open horses, the mature cutting horses who go down the road year after year, who stay tough until eighteen and older. Cutting today, it must be admitted, is focused on the futurities, where three-year-old horses are shown for the first and sometimes the last time. The most successful futurity horses often go quickly from brief stardom to breeding programs. At three years of age, Chink's Benjibaby was still walking on her back legs. She was destined to be an open horse or die in a can.

Pat lives with his wife, Nellie, his contraction of Ganell, her real name. When they were dating in the fifties, he was simultaneously seeing a girl named Raynell and he feared getting his sweet nothings crossed up. I never met Raynell, but I am sure Ganell was the right idea. She has been riding with him, turning back cattle, and helping with his colts for eighteen years.

The house is obviously the residence of cutting-horse mania. There is a big wall clock made out of trophy buckles, and trophy saddles are scattered around. The panhandle horizon is visible in any window. There is a desk set cornerwise, with a phone, note pads, and pocket calculator, everything a cattle trader needs: the rest is under his hat.

This is cattle country. The country seems shaped to that fact; that, and oil. The pragmatists learn the business by the seat of their pants, or at the hands of an older trader. That's what Pat did, swapping cattle out of an abandoned Champion gas station. The romantics head south to ride the rough string on ranches like the Four Sixes or Swenson's or the Matador. Everybody cries when they hear Bob Wills do "Faded Love." As to oil, here and there is some old kid living off a hundred thousand a month out of those iron jackrabbits pumping crude in the pastures his father and uncles pushed cattle all over, never suspecting. There are good old kids and bad old kids who fly stewardesses up from Oklahoma City three at a time and have rooms with purple walls, round sofas, and decorative planting to protect them from that empty panhandle horizon.

The subject of Bob Wills, the master of Texas swing, comes up as we are sitting in a little bottle club on the Texas–Oklahoma line. We are guests of Frankie McWhorter, who broke horses for the Four Sixes and who is an absolute master of Texas swing fiddle. On the way to the club, we dropped a horse with Frankie to "untrack" by riding her to cattle in the hills. A good young mare, she's been working in cattle pens so long she's forgotten how to lope. Pat used to travel with Lefty Frizell's band as a guitarist, and this was an opportunity for Pat to give us his good rendition of "Please Release Me." Then he sits down. "When I was rodeoing," he says, "that was the lowest scum on earth. So I went into music and the ranchers thought that was sissy. I had an inferiority complex most of my life." Nellie looks at the ceiling and laughs.

Pat bought Chink's Benjibaby back from the bank. I asked, "How did you train the mare?"

"I didn't," says Pat. "I never won a fight."

Pat talked all through that weekend about this strange horse, about getting under her skin to form enough of a team to get somewhere. Part of the excitement of riding cutting horses is this quality of collaboration. Human beings are species-lonely, relying on pushovers like dogs and cats to connect them to the earth's other inhabitants. But you learn something very different from horses, who, unlike dogs and cats, are born wild; and if they're any good, they keep that wildness throughout their lives to one degree or another. Chink's has, shall we say, a glint, a quality of that unlost wildness. One look at a tractor or an airplane too close and she throws a fit, suggesting she doesn't quite belong to this century.

She also had from the beginning a rather aristocratic self-esteem. Pat got his first look at this when he hired what he called "this little old hippie town kid" to feed for him. He cautioned the boy to feed Chink's first. The boy ignored the advice and was soon back in the house in panic to announce that Chink's was dying. Chink's was fine; she was simply so offended at not being fed first that she hurled herself on the ground and held her breath until she was given her grain.

In the beginning, Pat had a fine cowboy named Windy Spurgeon working for him; and between Pat and Windy there was a lot of plain ranch riding to be done. So instead of keeping Chink's in a pen and riding her in an arena, they rode her out hard, day after day, for six weeks. She accumulated wet saddle blankets and lived on ordinary rations. She was getting treated like a cow horse, working cattle under the cliffs of the Cimarron, down along the quicksand on the North Canadian, in the brush, in the heat, and by the lonely windmills that are the principal monuments of the panhandle. Chink's thrived on it and began to show a sense of purpose that rekindled Pat's hopes of her settling down as a cutting horse.

It was time to prove it; Pat set out for the El Paso Coliseum, home of a prestigious stock show cutting. It is necessary to understand the atmosphere at one of these important cuttings to understand what Chink's did. They have often been compared to funerals for their near silence; for unlucky riders, the muffled steps of their horses' feet on the coliseum floor sound like a cortege. But all is decorous, the judge in his place, pencil poised, ready to mark your horse down for losing a cow, leaking out from the herd too far, slinging his rear in his turns instead of cracking over his hocks, or just standing up too straight. The herd holders are in solemn attendance, the turnback men poised facing the herd.

At the El Paso show, Chink's was tied along the fence under saddle, a safe distance from the cutting. For some reason, she broke her reins and went on a high-speed tour of the coliseum. In the words of Jerry Mills, a tough nonpro rider, "A black beast was loose." She ran through the middle of the cutting and reduced it to chaos. Pat Jacobs watched this from the bleachers, eating a bag of popcorn. Finally, a large group of people circled the mare in the middle of the arena and contained her. Pat came down from the grandstand and pushed through the crowd, which was trying to identify the horse. "That's Jerry Mills's horse," said Pat.

When the cutting resumed, Pat barricaded Chink's in a roping box. She fixed him: *splinters*. Then she tried to leap out of the coliseum, high-centering on the sides; and finally she succeeded. The first description I ever had of Chink's Benjibaby was that she was the horse that jumped out of El Paso Coliseum.

I finally saw Chink's perform at Longmont, Colorado. Pat's stallion was getting a rest from the road. Rosie, Andy, and Wade, the Jacobses' three smart and unique children, were all showing cutting horses. So, of course, were Nellie and Pat. Pat knew of my fascination with Chink's and he led the mare up to me. It was inside a barn at night and the horse is gleaming black. She's not terribly big; but she has a narrow, beautiful head and a kind, if slightly possessed, look in her eyes. I was tired from traveling and I just stared at her. "Tom," said Pat, "here's Chink's Benjibaby."

When Pat showed her the next day, I knew what she could do. She turned around with cattle so quickly that it looked like an optical illusion. And the angle of her body to the ground was so drastic I couldn't see how she ever regained her balance. In fact, she never slipped a foot. I knew from Pat she thrived on impossible conditions like deep mud or slippery hardpan. And she hunted cattle like a cat, deliberately overshooting on her turns, stopping, and watching out of the corner of her eye for the last split second before running, sinking into her dying stop, and catching them up. When the cattle wouldn't try her, she sometimes jumped up and down in frustration.

Cutting is ruled by its judges; and its judges are ruled by the fashions of cutting or, shall we say, prevailing opinion. It's not like racing, where the first horse over the line wins. Human judgment as to what constitutes a great horse and a great ride will always spell the difference. But some judges are too sorry to assess the bravery of reckless horses like Chink's, and so they become all-or-nothing horses; because, with judges as with other men, there are none so blind as those who will not see. Nevertheless, as Pat began to go to cuttings, it soon became clear that Chink's Benjibaby could finish last at a cutting and be the only horse anyone remembered. Horses like that pit the fans against the judges; they change the history of cutting.

Trying to find out more about her in the atmosphere of the Jacobs household was not easy. Something was always going on. The youngest boy, Wade, sat around reading *The Art of*

Deer Hunting, then got up the next morning and bagged a record-class buck. Andy went to endless basketball practices, conferred with his coach, considered a college scholarship, and fed horses when Wade wasn't feeding horses. Rosie practiced barrel racing, needled me, helped her mother, and remarked there would be good cutting-horse judges when the judges quit reading cutting-horse magazines. Nellie's mother, Minnie, who'd had eleven children and who had more energy in her seventies than the rest of us have at thirteen, cheated at cards, hid beer, cracked jokes, baked desserts, and, when Rosie tipped over her glass, cheerfully admonished, "Now you'll never be a virgin!" They all eat or sleep when they're tired or hungry. There is no schedule, and I guess the connection is this: after being sold every six months of her life, Chink's Benjibaby landed on a ranch where a horse who didn't do things by the book could be understood by people who didn't care *who* rejected her.

Pat took me out and showed me some of the country Chink's ended up in: an old hangman's cottonwood, a place where a German sat all night long on a tractor seat affixed to a post, watching the stars rotate, acquiring enough information to paint the solar system all over the walls of his house. We visited Bill Spurgeon, Windy's brother, on his little ranch and talked about the great calf-roping horses he has trained. It seemed I kept meeting thoughtful, intelligent people with a lot of character in a part of the country widely considered Nowhere. "This is where the hoot owls make love to the chickens," says Pat.

I suppose that when Pat told me he never won a fight with Chink's, he meant in the parlance of that trade that he "got with" the horse as opposed to making a push-button horse, one you can control with your feet and hands at the expense of the horse's ability to think. He has a special opinion of King Benjiman's daughters as genius cow horses who will "fall off a cliff looking at a bird." But they have made-up minds in some ways, and you don't go rebuilding them. The reward is that about the time you figure them out, they figure you out. You have to get this close to cutting horses to do anything.

I think Pat has been sorely tested by Chink's. About the time he thought she was going to behave like other horses and join the twentieth century, Chink's stalked and attacked a derelict Model T Ford, striking it with her front feet and tearing out the upholstery with her teeth. Then she'd win a cutting going away. Pat still saw her greatness.

For a great part of the West, outside the Southwest and California, the most important exhibition for cutting horses is the Denver Stock Show. Pat decided to take Chink's Benjibaby, gambling that what he saw in her would come out.

In front of a coliseum filled with thousands of spectators, some sophisticated about cutting and others knowing no more than that it was a man horseback working cattle in the rites of an old collaboration, Chink's left the lesson beyond doubt with her optical-illusion turns and the sliding stops where her graceful body seemed to sink in front and behind all at once, drawing feints and moves out of cattle they might never have had on their own. A century ago in her present home on the panhandle, between the Cimarron and the North Canadian, Chink's and Pat might have helped one another sort cattle in the vast herds of that time. But today the roaring crowd, now standing on the bleachers and shouting, prevented Pat from even hearing the signal that his run was over. People walked toward them across the arena to tell him that the time was up. But Pat and the crazy mare were head to head with a single cow, absolutely alone in an old dance.

A cowboy's horse had come home.

WADING
THE
HAZARDS

LATELY I've been having trouble with golf. Which of us has not? Traced upon the minds of many of our countrymen are the perimeters of a golf course, a last frontier, a wonderful great lawn whose spacious nocturnal gloom always served the fantasies of young trespassers when nothing else in the republic did.

I'm thinking now of a middle of the night when Pete Waldeck, Mike Starling, and I were wading the water hazards; we were presumed asleep in our beds. Two of us hunted for golf balls in our bare feet, feeling in the muck and filling our pockets, while the third sat on the bank with the flashlight, pulling twenty or thirty humongous leeches off his legs. Only the previous week, Francis Kootsillas's neighbor had gotten a sixty-pound snapping turtle out of the same water hole. It had been living on water snakes and mallards and had the head of a malign regulation football and could hiss like a Belgian goose. The turtle remained unmentioned. The bloodsuckers, however, made your throat constrict and were said to have a ghastly ability to exchange their own blood with yours, sending weird spores and leech eggs coursing for your brain.

At that point in our still-simple lives, what kept us going were three brands: Spalding Dot, Titleist, and U.S. Royal. The latter ball was associated with the United States of America. It was the brand you would take aboard a fighter plane if you were going up against the Communists and felt, for some reason, you needed golf balls. The other two were fine brands but, we thought, basically belonged to a time when the Cold War was over and happy golf tournaments were the order of the day and none of us knew, but each of us really did, from which end of our bedrooms the flash from an atom bomb would come.

Our golf club was very important to us. In the wintertime we would break in the windows to steal cigars from the bar; then climb the tall elms around the frozen ponds, clear to·the top in the winter sky, to smoke and watch the freighters pushing pack ice on the river. In early spring the northern pike ran in the ditches and we speared them by lantern light and smoked the last of our stolen cigars while planning great lives in foreign lands.

We all had been caddies; but carrying double eighteen for doggedly cheap doctors who tipped you a Hershey had driven us to balls. Usually you hunted them in the rough, hoping for top brands without smiles. Bad smiles you slashed open with your jackknife to watch the rubber filaments crawl, then got the little ball in the center, which was sometimes liquid-filled and exciting. The good ones you took out at night — when Jack Orlick, the kid-hating greenskeeper, had gone home — and cleansed in the ball washes, drying them carefully on a towel. There were two types of ball wash: one a metal thing on a stand that you cranked, whirling the ball on a rubber wheel in sudsy water. Then there was a wooden job with a plunger, which we thought was old-fashioned and not as good.

We stalked the tees with pockets full of bargains, the best brand in the pocket of whichever hand you favored. Our friend Paul had deformed hands and carried them against his chest like a kangaroo. We got to know our customers and tried to avoid doctors; but all of the golfers beat us down on our prices. And if we stuck to our guns, they kicked us off for trespassing. When we got to a safe distance, we always yelled "Eat it!" to show our defiance and solidarity.

But that night, wading the hazards, we were having our first real fiscal breakthrough in the used-golf-ball business. Behind us, we felt, were the penny pinchers in loud plaids; behind us, the dour orthodontists, their forefingers stirring palmfuls of tiny change. We were wading the hazards and finding dozens of balls, most of them smile-free big names. We stayed half the night, and when the sky paled, we set out for home. In the morning we forgathered to examine our finds. We had nearly a hundred balls and, except for a very faint bluish pallor in strong light, they were as perfect as werewolf hair.

For selling our balls, the fairway on the fourth hole was the best spot. It was long and level with no changes of contour to hide a golfer from our view. Also, its tee had the best weekend pileup, producing milling, confused golfers for us to sell to. In some ways, the first tee was a better bet. But it was right in front of the clubhouse and middle management ran us off for creating a low-rent atmosphere.

By midmorning we fanned out to sell our golf balls. We had my dog Gret, and the beautiful golf balls were lying in the grass like birds' eggs, sorted as to brand and condition; each of us next to his own pile at the edge of the fairway, watching for golfers. By noon we had nearly sold out. And by afternoon I had gone to McComb Street and spent all my money on bass plugs. I had a few balls left, so I returned to the golf course to work the back nine. Whether or not the wind sang in the elms is something I cannot be expected to remember.

I guess I knew something was wrong when one of the first group of golfers called out, "There's one of those kids!" as I approached with our mechanical "Ya wanna buy a golf ball?" He came up to me with the kind of throbbing face we associate with the Yalta Conference and said, "I've got one of the longest drives in the club."

"Sir?"

"With these balls you sold me I'm goddamned lucky to get forty feet. They're *waterlogged.*" My dog Gret stared at the exchange. "Now give me my money back."

"I spent it, sir."

He held up two balls, one a brand-new fresh-out-of-the-cellophane U.S. Royal; and next to it, one of our finds. "I ought to shove this blue sonofabitch down your throat."

I crept off down the fairway, regretting my plug binge on McComb; and in a short time I heard the aggressive baying of the inconvenienced golfer: *"Fore!"* The clean buzz of a smile-free top brand burned the air over my head. I saw it carry and bound down the fairway; and I began to run, Gret racing out in front of me, running backward in dog glee, until there it was with the perfect, tiny, embossed "U.S. Royal" turned to a cloudless sky. I leaned over and picked it up.

In golf, one never touches the ball after one's tee shot: I could already hear the shouting. But by now I was sprinting for the woods, down through the skunk meadows and smoky snake hideouts, past the dead elm we blew up with stolen dynamite. There were hawk nests in the hardwood trees and Indian mounds that we climbed to shoot our .22s — woods through which the Underground Railroad had spirited slaves.

It was the perfect spot, but I knew from the beginning I would be found. Gradually the steps invaded my silence and the weaving progress of the unhappy customer, with his driver aloft, could be seen past the sumacs. I sat and stared at the space behind my hideout in which I knew he would appear, branding its soon-to-be-lost emptiness on my mind. For an unfathomable reason, Americans on the verge of cruelty like to say, "I'll teach you." And my golfer was no exception. Having said that, he began to swing his club at me; but just as he started his swing, Gret hit him in the chest. There is no finer memory of my childhood than of that golfer arcing backward with an oath more resonant than his grandest "Fore!" and the departing kiss of his cleats from the woodland floor.

We made our escape and I clutched my U.S. Royal till the end. A year later, a deer hunter shot Gret. So, like the man said, if the first one don't get you, the second one will.

ROPING, FROM A TO B

I GREW UP in the Midwest and despised horses. The ones I rode struck me as stupid and untrustworthy. I went to Wyoming when I was young, and the ones there were worse. On a cold morning, two out of three would buck you down. They were, I felt, an ugly necessity for where a truck wouldn't go.

I've been kicked, stepped on, and bitten. Bitten I liked least. My most trustworthy saddle horse leaned over once while I was cinching him up and clamped on my upper leg, turning the thigh into what looked like a Central American sunset. I threw him down on the ground, half-hitched his feet together, and put a tarp over him. I let him up two hours later; he thought I was the greatest man in the world, one he wouldn't think of biting. Horses only remember the end of the story.

Once I went with a girl who rode jumping horses. I sat in a box with her parents and, since I was a teenager, I was usually, secretly, drunk. I remember a little fellow in a homburg and red livery tooting a horn, horses hopping over poles, polite applause, and discussions of the Pan American Games. I wanted to head for the Sunday drags at Flat Rock in my 270 Chevy stick-shift and watch rail jobs, not horses.

But I was often slipping off to the Rockies, mostly Wyoming, but New Mexico, too, as well as Montana and a little Idaho. A lot of us read Jack Kerouac, and if you read Jack

Kerouac and were an American of a certain age, you felt you owned the whole place. There has been a great effort to discredit Kerouac, but I won't hear a word against him. He trained us in the epic idea that the region was America, and that you don't necessarily have to take it in Penciltucky forever just because you were there when your hour had come round at last. It was called *On the Road*.

Kerouac set me out there with my own key to the highway and I ended up in this same region, endlessly bumping into the despised nags, and there were times when there was work to be done and you had to get on one. I began to think in terms of making a deal.

I bought a saddle horse named Cayenne who is supposed to go back to Yellow Jacket; and for the first time I began to ride in the normal course of things — knocking around, going in the hills, checking ditches and head gates. I still have this horse. He's a big easy-keeping sorrel with a blaze on his face; above all, a sensible horse.

He really taught me the coming and going aspects of a using horse: how their feet move in the rocks, when they're winded, how much water they need when they're hot, how you shouldn't let them eat when you're gathering cattle or they learn to dive at a gallop because idle hunger has struck; why you should get down when your lariat is caught under your horse's tail, why nose flies make them throw their heads in your face, why geldings make that noise at a trot, why Old Paint will always walk off and leave you; how a horse will, finally, sell out for grain, how a horse can get you home from the mountains in the dark when a mule can't; and above all how, when you do such things long enough with one horse, you begin to see things in him, to look deep in his eyes and to make your deal, which is a kind of interchange of respect.

Once when I was trimming Cayenne's feet, I thought he was leaning his weight on me and I thumped him with the rasp. He wouldn't eat for the rest of the day. The rasp cer-

tainly didn't hurt him. Now that I think of it, I offered him
oats and he never sold out. There was a specific deal between
that horse and me; and I had violated it. I never did it again.
There was no question that I had hurt his feelings. At the
same time you should know that it was this horse, a few weeks
later, who made a cheap postcard of my thigh when I went to
cinch him up.

You could rope a little bit off this horse. He was better than
I was, anyway. He wouldn't jump out from under a rope and
you could heel calves off him. But you couldn't go to contests
on him. He didn't like blasting out of the box with his ears
pinned. He would jog up to a bunch of calves and let you
snake them to the ground crew. He was kind of a working-
man's horse. You could turn him out for the winter and wran-
gle him in the spring and he'd be solid. I haven't had a vet bill
on him yet. Last year I tied a huge red ribbon around him
and gave him to my son for Christmas. He looked at Cayenne
in the snow, stunned, and I tried not to let tears come. None
of this meant anything to Cayenne.

The very little roping I did when young was what they called
doctor roping and had to do with dabbing a loop on a cow's
head to immobilize her long enough to provide medical aid.
In addition to a rope, a lot of cowboys carry a plastic gun in
the saddle for sending pills down troubled gullets; no six-
shooter. Doctor roping is also done for calves with the scours,
and these little brutes are "heeled"; their back feet are roped
and they are skidded to the branding fire — in my experience,
a blowtorch. Dehorned, branded, castrated, vaccinated, they
are turned loose traumatized. Most people nowadays use a
chute and turn the calf on a table to do those things to him.
But a lot of ranches don't have a table and they need someone
so in love with roping he will heel calves all day long until
lather forms around the latigo and cinch dees and linear rope
burns form up and down the back of his hand from dallying.

"Dally" is a word that comes from the Mexican *dar la vuelta* — meaning to take a turn, a wrap around the saddle horn with the lariat to stop the creature in question, out there on the end, in the loop. The transposition of *dar la vuelta* into "dally" is in the great Western tradition of corrupting language into the grunting of the midland yokel who levels the same Mortimer Snerd suspicion upon all human products, but starts with language. Similarly, the rope which the Spanish hackamore horsemen wound and tied into reins and lead rope, the *mecate,* becomes, by the time it gets here to Montana, the "McCarthy."

When I first roped, I didn't know anything about dallying. It was hard and fast, the rope tied to the saddle horn. That's how contest calf ropers rope. They have to: they jump down and flank or leg the little cow and tie three legs with the pigging string, then throw their hands in the air. I don't like to get down and run all over the place like that. I'm getting too brittle. I like to stay mounted. Single steer trippers also rope hard and fast, but dally roping — *dar la vuelta* — is an ancient and beautiful craft still understood by a large number of people, handed down from the days of the old-time vaqueros, the Mexicans and Californios, who nobody much remembers but who, with their hair-trigger spade-bit horses and braided *riatas* were the absolute best hands in the long and crazy history of the American West. The horses and vaqueros are dead and gone; but something remains: hackamore reinsmen and dally ropers.

When I first started to rope that way, the lunacy of roping six-hundred-pound Corriente steers — Mexican horned cattle — without tying the end of the rope to the horn was obviated by the fact that I had misconducted my life to the point that it was, shall we say, in smithereens, and the prospect of losing a couple of fingers because I couldn't get my wraps didn't seem as catastrophic as it would have when I was happy and had my accustomed, highly excitable fear of pain. This is the background of stoicism everywhere.

Times got better, but as luck would have it, there came a day when I couldn't find the saddle horn and broke my thumb in a few places, tearing the end off it. When I went to the emergency room, the nurse said, "Miss your dally?" and I said, "Just tell the doctor I hate pain." Nevertheless, he pulled my thumbnail out with a pair of needle-nosed pliers and told me I was going to lose it anyway. But I had started to learn to dally, with that crazily loose-ended lariat, relying on wrapping the rope around the saddle horn to stop heavy running cattle.

Then, of course, there is the matter of your horse. If he's a good horse, he hits wide open on his second stride out of the box. Everything is moving; and staying loose and not tensing up is the roper's biggest obstacle. My own mental drill is based on an idea from a fine old roper: "Remember one thing when you back your horse into the box. There are nine hundred million Chinese who don't care whether you catch the steer or not." This helps; though, in the heat of a big roping, it's hard to picture those indifferent Chinese.

This same roper told me another wonderful thing, which is, really, about the mental atmosphere of dally roping as opposed to hard and fast: "Don't pitch your rope like you were through with it." When you first catch a steer you halfway wish you were through with it; the steer is hauling ass and that hard nylon rope heats to seeming incandescence when you run about eighteen inches of it through your hand. At the same time, you have to run it a little; the steer is moving away and you need to let it slip as you start down to dally. Fundamentally, you should know how to run the whole rope and let it go, if you have to, without getting a turn around your hand. It's easy to lose a finger roping and almost as easy to lose a hand as a finger.

Montana is a place with a sense of itself, and a very strong one. There is a vivid antipathy for Washington, D.C., "Californicators," "dudes," and "pilgrims." There is also a lot of dopey

complacency and Old West presumption that results in Californicators and their ilk cleaning up when they rodeo in Montana.

Nevertheless, Montana is my home, and anyone who has
moved here from somewhere else has had to endure a bit of
patronizing. Over the years, though, many local pontiffs have
turned in the old homestead for a snappy burger franchise
where seldom is heard a discouraging word. *Hold the mayo!*
Side of fries! and like that.

Montanans kicked their horses out into the hills in the
1920s, with the advent of the automobile. After the Second
World War, they went up and caught them again. These days,
Hondas and Ski-doos are pressing the stock horse once again.
You can get a bit of pressure now for having horses at all. But
a lot of the old boys are still around, hard-bitten romantics
with Red Man coming out of the corners of their mouths who
want to be "plumb mounted" on some shining pony that goes
back to studs like Old Sorrel or Oklahoma Star or Joe Han-
cock or My Texas Dandy or Midnight or Zantanon ("the Mexican Man o' War"). The thing is to be mounted and that is *not*
on a Honda or a Ski-doo.

These stragglers, hands, itinerants, despised old nighthawks
from big outfits, have nothing but their skills and prospects of
unemployment. They *always* do something for fun, unlike the
people on foot they call dirt savages. Among the things they
do for fun is jackpot roping in East Jesus arenas built off
somewhere out of plank and railroad ties. Some of these ropers are ranchers, some of them were born on ranches and are
now boilermakers on the Amtrak or surveyors on I-90, shooting in four-lanes. But between them and what ails them is that
good pony, maybe living on baled hay out behind the IGA
store, and that hard rope they're forever handling.

But out of — let's say — nowhere, but mostly California,
where dally roping is oldest, there come a lot of new ropers,
some of them hauling horses behind weird hot rigs; profes-

sionals, rope hustlers, cowboys in their twenties wearing King Rope hats from Sheridan, Wyoming, hats advertising Camarillo Ropers' Products, Powder River portable corrals, the LA Dodgers; and down in the pens beneath a streaky Western sky, a kid will be moving Corriente steers toward the chute in a T-shirt that says "Amazing Rhythm Aces." You can tell these new ropers by their aggressive style, too, standing straight up in the stirrups, holding their reins and coils down close to the horse's neck, sitting only when they dally. And they often run well-schooled horses that don't look abused, horses they have broken themselves.

When I turned to arena roping, I was exhilarated by these sourceless ropers. *I* felt sourceless for sure, born in the Midwest of New England Irish parents, my own son born on the West Coast. And when I saw some of these hot ropers, my ambitions, not just the ones fortified by alcohol, Charlie Russell, or *Western Horsemen* magazine, but the ones that started the first time I ever roped a calf, in the fifties, on a borrowed horse in Wyoming, my low rider parked in the draw, out-of-state plates, blue suede shoes, red nylon jacket, and flyer's glasses, my own ambitions returned as against the droning of the local-color types: *"Been here long?"*

Now, here's the way jackpot roping works: The steer chute is in the middle. Facing the chute to the right is the header's box and to the left is the heeler's box. I'm making a long story short. The header nods for the steer. The gate opens and the steer burns down the arena. The header ropes him and ducks off after dallying; he should "bump" the steer, that is, skid a foot or so of his rope on the horn so that the steer isn't jerked into bucking and becoming a more difficult target for the heeler. The heeler ducks in with the steer just behind him, throws his trap, ropes the back feet, dallies, and stops the horse. The header turns to face and the team is flagged for time, the steer stretched out.

It's hard for the header because everything is moving so fast. It's hard for the heading horse because he has to duck off with the steer, leaning into five hundred or six hundred hurtling pounds. It's hard for the heeler because those flying feet are hard to catch. It's hard for a heeling horse because he has to do that free-form crack-the-whip with the steer when the header sets him, then stop the steer and the head horse after the heeler has thrown his trick. That can be close to a ton hitting the end of thirty-five feet of seven-sixteenths-inch nylon.

Is roping the proper concern of mankind? Let's dust this one off. Roping teaches us about horses, cattle, and eternity. Sherwood Anderson wrote about horses. Not airplane saboteurs, serial orgasm, or "LA space." One atavism in rural roping, and maybe it's everywhere, is the business of hexing other ropers, making signs against the competition in the dirt, writing the name of the enemy on ceremonial mounds, and the general directing of black-magic signs and semaphores as well as jinxing, spitting, upside-down crosses, and the evil eye aimed at horse, rider, or the saddle horn. One arena owner said, "I don't believe none of that stuff. I *do* throw fellows out for hexing other ropers because it seems to upset folks."

When I'm at a roping, everybody looks so normal — ropers, trailers, horses, families, six-packs of Great Falls in the cooler. It's always a shock to find Dad behind the pens with his partner, drawing hexes in the dust.

Anyway, my boy now owned Cayenne and I was looking for a heel horse. I finally found one, named Dan, and I bought him: sixteen hands, buckskin gelding, 1,220 pounds; by a quarter-horse stud out of a thoroughbred mare. I liked him because he was big and still catty. He reined well, got into the ground on his stops with everything he had when you asked him, and was, in general, a horse who liked to hunt cattle. Also, he didn't pack his head so high I couldn't see where I was roping. He was a hard-knocking horse in every respect and his eight years had given him a lot of contusions: splints on his front legs, bursitis, and a navicular fracture. He had to be specially shod in front, bars across the bases to control heel expansion, rolled toes, and set at exactly fifty-four degrees. He had spent years gathering bucking horses in the hills, and though it showed, he was a horse who never ever blew his cool, even to standing like a rock when he got gored in the shoulder or when a wild steer wrapped his legs with hard nylon. Once when a steer flipped in front of him, he vaulted the steer and in three circling jumps had me back in position to rope.

A dog went by, a sore leg carried in the air. A roper walked along behind, doing little reverse whirls and tricks with his lariat; looked at the dog, then me.

"I call that dog Arithmetic."

"?"

"Because he puts down three and carries one."

Over at the stock scale, I had just lost a dollar betting on the weight of my own horse. "I don't seem to have a gift for this," I said, walking off.

"Same dog bit me," said the roper. Dogs in the air. One was in the heading box on the fourth go-round and had to be carried out like a baby, four feet in the air, looking sheepishly into the stands.

It was an eight-steer roping. We had a steer kick out on the seventh; then my header broke the barrier and we lost sixty bucks.

He said, "That was quick."

We'd been roping all day and the horses were steaming. There was no change at the concession stand and the coffee was gone. It was dark and the general call for a grudge match, "One steer for a fast go," was ignored. The dog guy walked past and said, "I could use some goddamned day-money. I live clear to Miles City."

I had a nice rope burn from where my horn wrap had

slipped. I loaded my horse and went to the Emigrant Saloon. I drank three "depth charges" with a bunch of ropers at the bar and played all the Jimmy Buffett as well as a couple of songs a couple of girls said had been written for them. After depth charge number three, I had a wave of affection for my horse. I went out to the trailer and opened the little door and looked into one of his great eyes.

"Hello," I said and went home happy.

Last June, I bought ten Corriente steers. They had wintered in Mexico and were gaunt and wild, leggy high-speed desert cattle with horns carried high on their heads like antlers. I turned them out in a small pasture across from the house, maybe twenty acres, to put on some weight; and they vanished. I thought they had jumped the cattle guard. But when I rode across, I began to spot them, every once in a while, popping up out of brush that couldn't hide a dog. They were completely wild cattle, could live on anything, thrifty.

They were also what is called breachy; a fence meant almost nothing to them. And so I was always driving one down from a neighboring ranch. They were the UFOs of my area, with those antlers, fabulous speed, and an uncanny ability to disappear.

As time went by, we named many of them: Old Blue for his color, Crazy because he gored the horse first time he was roped, Al Capone for his rugged Americanism, and A-2-Gas for his blaze of early speed.

Al Capone earned his stripes the day he took a hard right through the plank sides of the arena. Then he went through some fences and moved into the deep grass of a nearby ranch. When we went to get him, we planned an attack very carefully because there was no telling where he'd stop if we got him running again.

We approached in deep grass that swept our stirrups. It was evening and the individual peaks of the Gallatins were propped against their shadows. Somewhere ahead of us, we knew, Al Capone listened for our minatory footfalls, ready and willing to fool with our expectations. Steadily, we advanced: me; Allen Ray Carter, my roping partner; his brother, Little C.; and Paul Lyman, who used to ride broncs on the West Coast.

The wind swept the grass down. We saw the black tips of Al Capone's horns moving in precise abrupt arcs. Our plan was to move in with steady and unexcited progress; at the last minute, Little C. would race in and fire a head loop, one of us would back him up, and Al Capone would go home in a trailer.

As we moved in, the rotary movements of Capone's horns grew more intent. We got incredibly close. It was time. Little C. spurred his horse forward and Capone vaulted from the grass. Little C.'s loop snaked out and caught the horns.

But Little C. missed his dally and Al Capone was burning to the east, trailing a twenty-dollar heading rope. Allen Ray overtook him once on his big buckskin, roped him, and missed his dally, too. Capone was eating into our outfit.

When he reached Route 89, he broke the fences on both sides of the highway, trailing wire and sixty feet of three-eighths-inch nylon, not to mention lathered horses, and riders whose irrational babbling increased with every rod of gopher-riddled ground.

Capone hit the upper Yellowstone River and turned right. Things were beginning to tell. He merely dogtrotted past the dining room window of the last ranch we passed. And no one seemed to be sure whether or not he had his heart in it when he dove into the fish pond. In any case, he made an easy target for ropers, with nothing but horns and nostrils above the surface as he dog-paddled through the aquatic weeds. We took him home and named him. The horses were spent; and we've all been a little proud of that steer ever since. He's now in a big band of roping cattle; and when, at a jackpot, we see him in the chute, banging his horns against the steel just to be mean, we glance at each other and one of us says that revered name: *Al Capone.*

When I was studying literature under professors who told us about everything but the happy quackery of art, we were always talking of "rites of passage," which we said in French, *rites de passage* — which is French like the French in an Updike novel, where the eternal flame on Kennedy's grave becomes the *flamme éternelle.*

But roping has been a little of that, for me, after all these years in Montana. I don't know why. My favorite concept is that the proof is in the pudding: what you do. The vulgarity we call the "sense of place" is a fairly nelly sub-instance of schizophrenia, saving up facts, preferably inherited, about locale. It's like when Southerners talk about losing the war. It always made me very suspicious that *no one* from Yoknapatawpha ever went to Miami. Faulkner certainly left no stone unturned for himself; but the denizens of his books he locks up in this morbid Cloud-Cuckoo-Land where everybody has mule trouble while the author rides up and down Sunset Strip in a convertible.

I like to gesture at the cloverleaf ramps and exclaim, "The earth is good, Pablo." And like a lot of other ropers, I like to get a leetle loaded and rope horned cattle.

It is definitely not a case of wanting to be the Marlboro Man. The West is getting to be a number of other things. When I complained about the double-wides dotting the hillsides, my son reminded me that a lot of nice people live inside them, and what was the difference if they were painted flamingo or aqua? I've been to the aluminum door of many a double-wide to pick up ropers and, in years past, social diseases.

My boy thinks the West is a collection of wonderful places to pop wheelies. Horses are unreliable, and as to roping: "I like my fingers, Dad. Look at your hand."

I looked at my hand, crooked thumb, rope burns, enlarged knuckles, and I felt good because I was afraid, as a writer, I would always have these Ivory Snow hands; and, in fact, some cur said I had *writer's hands,* which really got to me, as I am someone who wants to be a rugged guy in the West and not some horrid nancy with pink palms. At the same time, you don't want to be the one roper they call Flipper. This is just a message to other arty types out there in the Rocky Mountains: roping is a good fast way to acquire local-color hands. A header up north felt that way; but he overran a steer, threw his horse, burst his spleen, and died, turning colors as he staggered after his steer dragging a lariat. There's no need of going that far. He'd just sold the ranch to have more time to rope; then bought the farm.

This is me at the Gardiner, Montana, rodeo. I had a number of reasons to be nervous. It was a one-steer roping, no average. We were roping Sunday after all of Saturday's ropers and the entry fee was high. My partner, Allen Ray Carter, was thinking about that entry fee. His wife was about to have a baby, and there was some feeling that paying out sixty bucks was a real instance of pounding sand down a rat hole.

Then, when we were unloading our horses, two of the state's best ropers came by and the heeler said, "We're going to *take your money."*

My girl was up from Alabama and she always covers her face when I go into the box with those nine hundred million Chinese.

My son sat on the rail and took a perspective of clarity only a ten-year-old has for his father. "You can beat those assholes, Dad."

"Don't say assholes, Tom."

"Ropers."

In effect, nobody wanted me to come out of the box and just be a writer about it. Nor did I, if I could help it. I wanted

Allen Ray to turn that steer like lightning so I could double-hock him and stop the clock.

I went down where the doggers started to go, to check out the cattle. It was the end of the summer and the steers were big and sour. They were setting up and the doggers were having to just kind of get down and shock them before the steers could set back and knock out their teeth. I noticed the hazers seemed to be trying to squeeze the cattle right up against the dogging horses. And, in general, there were numerous signs that these were indeed sour cattle.

When we entered, they told us we had to wear long-sleeved shirts and cowboy hats. One of the younger toughs said, "I always rope in tank tops and Hush Puppies."

"Not here you don't," said the man.

Finally, they announce the team that's up, the team that's on deck, and the team in the hole. When you get to the point where your name is on the loudspeaker, it's time to warm up the horse, forget the prickling palms, build and unbuild your loop, and pick your way horseback through the kids from the concession stand.

Then they called us. Someone swung open the big gate and we rode into the arena. At this point a cloud forms around you and you can't see anything but your steer.

I built my loop and rode into the box, swung Dan toward the steer, and backed him into the corner. Allen Ray rode in on the other side and I as thinking, Let this be an honest hard-running steer, and let me be winding up and standing in my stirrups when we clear the box.

Allen Ray looked over and I nodded that I was ready. Dan was pricking alternate ears waiting for the chute to bang.

Allen Ray reined his horse to look at the steer, and nodded.

The gate slammed open and the steer was running. Dan came on so hard I had to keep my left hand on the horn, gradually coming up in the stirrups against that acceleration. I hazed the steer in close to Allen Ray until his loop went out and I faded a little to make that corner when he set the steer.

The steer tried to fall, but Allen Ray spurred his horse to line him out. Dan swerved in and I pitched my loop, caught both hind feet, and dallied. I felt Dan suck down under me, and the steer stretched out as the flag went down. We won.

When we released the steer I galloped up the rail. I don't win that often. My son was smiling like the first sunrise, and when I rode by he said, "Hey, Dad!" just to show everybody we knew each other.

Then someone offered to buy a victory drink at the Two Bit Saloon. Everybody headed for town and I loaded my horse, stowed my saddle, and my girl and I piled into the truck ready for a celebration.

The truck wouldn't start. So we headed to town on foot. We tried hitchhiking, to no avail; then Allen Ray came along in his truck and drove us to the Two Bit.

Inside, everyone was getting loud and the kids were playing pinball. "Hey, Dad," said mine, hovering over the plunger, "you'd really like this one!" I felt, for the first time in a decade, that I could do without the ranch. The Midwest wasn't a bad place to grow up; and maybe pinball was as interesting as my boy thought it was. Things keep moving on.

THE
HEART
OF THE
GAME

HUNTING IN YOUR own back yard becomes with time, if you love hunting, less and less expeditionary. This year, when Montana's eager frosts knocked my garden on its butt, the hoe seemed more like the rifle than it ever had before, the vegetables more like game.

My son and I went scouting before the season and saw some antelope in the high plains foothills of the Absaroka Range, wary, hanging on the skyline; a few bands and no great heads. We crept around, looking into basins, and at dusk met a tired cowboy on a tired horse followed by a tired blue-heeler dog. The plains seemed bigger than anything, bigger than the mountains that seemed to sit in the middle of them, bigger than the ocean. The clouds made huge shadows that traveled on the grass slowly through the day.

Hunting season trickles on forever; if you don't go in on a cow with anybody, there is the dark argument of the empty deep-freeze against headhunting ("You can't eat horns!"). But nevertheless, in my mind, I've laid out the months like playing cards, knowing some decent whitetails could be down in the river bottom and, fairly reliably, the long windy shots at antelope. The big buck mule deer — the ridge-runners — stay up in the scree and rock walls until the snow drives them out; but they stay high long after the elk have quit and broken down the hay corrals on the ranches and farmsteads, which, when you're hunting the rocks from a saddle horse, look pathetic and housebroken with their yellow lights against the coming of winter.

Where I live, the Yellowstone River runs straight north, then takes an eastward turn at Livingston, Montana. This flowing north is supposed to be remarkable; and the river doesn't do it long. It runs mostly over sand and stones once it comes out of the rock slots near the Wyoming line. But all along, there are deviations of one sort or another: canals, backwaters, sloughs; the red willows grow in the sometime-flooded bottom, and at the first elevation, the cottonwoods. I hunt here for the white-tailed deer which, in recent years, have moved up these rivers in numbers never seen before.

The first morning, the sun came up hitting around me in arbitrary panels as the light moved through the jagged openings in the Absaroka Range. I was walking very slowly in the edge of the trees, the river invisible a few hundred yards to my right but sending a huge sigh through the willows. It was cold and the sloughs had crowns of ice thick enough to support me. As I crossed one great clear pane, trout raced around under my feet and a ten-foot bubble advanced slowly before my cautious steps. Then passing back into the trees, I found an active game trail, cut cross-lots to pick a better stand, sat in a good vantage place under a cottonwood with the aught-six across my knees. I thought, running my hands up into my sleeves, This is lovely but I'd rather be up in the hills; and I fell asleep.

I woke up a couple of hours later, the coffee and early-morning drill having done not one thing for my alertness. I had drooled on my rifle and it was time for my chores back at the ranch. My chores of late had consisted primarily of working on screenplays so that the bank didn't take the ranch. These days the primary ranch skill is making the payment; it comes before irrigation, feeding out, and calving. Some rancher friends find this so discouraging they get up and roll a number or have a slash of tanglefoot before they even think of the glories of the West. This is the New Rugged.

The next day, I reflected upon my lackadaisical hunting and left really too early in the morning. I drove around to Mission Creek in the dark and ended up sitting in the truck up some wash listening to a New Mexico radio station until my patience gave out and I started out cross-country in the dark, just able to make out the nose of the Absaroka Range as it faced across the river to the Crazy Mountains. It seemed maddeningly up and down slick banks, and a couple of times I had game clatter out in front of me in the dark. Then I turned up a long coulee that climbed endlessly south, and started in that direction, knowing the plateau on top should hold some antelope. After half an hour or so, I heard the mad laughing of coyotes, throwing their voices all around the inside of the coulee, trying to panic rabbits and making my hair stand on end despite my affection for them. The stars tracked overhead into the first pale light, and it was nearly dawn before I came up on the bench. I could hear cattle below me and I moved along an edge of thorn trees to break my outline, then sat down at the point to wait for shooting light.

I could see antelope on the skyline before I had that light; and by the time I did, there was a good big buck angling across from me, looking at everything. I thought I could see well enough, and I got up into a sitting position and into the sling. I had made my moves quietly, but when I looked through the scope the antelope was two hundred yards out, using up the country in bounds. I tracked with him, let him bounce up into the reticle, and touched off a shot. He was down and still, but I sat watching until I was sure.

Nobody who loves to hunt feels absolutely hunky-dory when the quarry goes down. The remorse spins out almost before anything and the balancing act ends on one declination or another. I decided that unless I become a vegetarian, I'll get my meat by hunting for it. I feel absolutely unabashed by the arguments of other carnivores who get their meat in plastic with blue numbers on it. I've seen slaughterhouses, and anyway, as Sitting Bull said, when the buffalo are gone, we will hunt mice, for we are hunters and we want our freedom.

The antelope had piled up in the sage, dead before he hit the ground. He was an old enough buck that the tips of his pronged horns were angled in toward each other. I turned him downhill to bleed him out. The bullet had mushroomed in the front of the lungs, so the job was already halfway done. With antelope, proper field dressing is critical because they can end up sour if they've been run or haphazardly hog-dressed. And they sour from their own body heat more than from external heat.

The sun was up and the big buteo hawks were lifting on the thermals. There was enough breeze that the grass began to have directional grain like the prairie, and the rim of the coulee wound up away from me toward the Absaroka. I felt peculiarly solitary, sitting on my heels next to the carcass in the sagebrush and greasewood, my rifle racked open on the ground. I made an incision around the metatarsal glands inside the back legs and carefully removed them and set them well aside; then I cleaned the blade of my hunting knife with handfuls of grass to keep from tainting the meat with those powerful glands. Next I detached the anus and testes from the outer walls and made a shallow puncture below the sternum, spread it with the thumb and forefinger of my left hand, and ran the knife upside down to the bone bridge between the hind legs. Inside, the diaphragm was like the taut lid of a drum and cut away cleanly, so that I could reach clear up to the back of the mouth and detach the windpipe. Once that was done I could draw the whole visceral package out onto the grass and separate out the heart, liver, and tongue before propping the carcass open with two whittled-up sage scantlings.

You could tell how cold the morning was, despite the exertion, just by watching the steam roar from the abdominal cavity. I stuck the knife in the ground and sat back against the slope, looking clear across to Convict Grade and the Crazy Mountains. I was blood from the elbows down and the antelope's eyes had skinned over. I thought, This is goddamned serious and you had better always remember that.

There was a big red enamel pot on the stove; and I ladled the antelope chili into two bowls for my son and me. He said, "It better not be too hot."

"It isn't."

"What's your news?" he asked.

"Grandpa's dead."

"Which grandpa?" he asked. I told him it was Big Grandpa, my father. He kept on eating. "He died last night."

He said, "I know what I want for Christmas."

"What's that?"

"I want Big Grandpa back."

It was 1950-something and I was small, under twelve say, and there were four of us: my father, two of his friends, and me. There was a good belton setter belonging to the one friend, a hearty bird hunter who taught dancing and fist-fought at any provocation. The other man was old and sick and had a green fatal look in his face. My father took me aside and said, "Jack and I are going to the head of this field" — and he pointed up a mile and a half of stalks to where it ended in the flat woods — "and we're going to take the dog and get what he can point. These are running birds. So you and Bill just block the field and you'll have some shooting."

"I'd like to hunt with the dog," I had a 20-gauge Winchester my grandfather had given me, which got hocked and lost years later when another of my family got into the bottle; and I could hit with it and wanted to hunt over the setter. With respect to blocking the field, I could smell a rat.

"You stay with Bill," said my father, "and try to cheer him up."

"What's the matter with Bill?"

"He's had one heart attack after another and he's going to die."

"When?"

"Pretty damn soon."

I blocked the field with Bill. My first thought was, I hope he doesn't die before they drive those birds onto us; but if he does, I'll have all the shooting.

There was a crazy cold autumn light on everything, magnified by the yellow silage all over the field. The dog found birds right away and they were shooting. Bill said he was sorry but he didn't feel so good. He had his hunting license safety-pinned to the back of his coat and fiddled with a handful of 12-gauge shells. "I've shot a shitpile of game," said Bill, "but I don't feel so good anymore." He took a knife out of his coat pocket. "I got this in the Marines," he said, "and I carried it for four years in the Pacific. The handle's drilled out and weighted so you can throw it. I want you to have it." I took it and thanked him, looking into his green face, and wondered why he had given it to me. "That's for blocking this field with me," he said. "Your dad and that dance teacher are going to shoot them all. When you're not feeling so good, they put you at the end of the field to block when there isn't shit-all going to fly by you. They'll get them all. They and the dog will."

We had an indestructible tree in the yard we had chopped on, nailed steps to, and initialed; and when I pitched that throwing knife at it, the knife broke in two. I picked it up and thought, *This thing is jinxed.* So I took it out into the crab-apple woods and put it in the can I had buried, along with a Roosevelt dime and an atomic-bomb ring I had sent away for. This was a small collection of things I buried over a period of years. I was sending them to God. All He had to do was open the can, but they were never collected. In any case, I have long known that if I could understand why I wanted to send a broken knife I believed to be jinxed to God, then I would be a long way toward what they call a personal philosophy as opposed to these hand-to-mouth metaphysics of who said what to whom in some cornfield twenty-five years ago.

We were in the bar at Chico Hot Springs near my home in Montana: me, a lout poet who had spent the day floating under the diving board while adolescent girls leapt overhead; and my brother John, who had glued himself to the pipe which poured warm water into the pool and announced over and over in a loud voice that every drop of water had been filtered through his bathing suit.

Now, covered with wrinkles, we were in the bar, talking to Alvin Close, an old government hunter. After half a century of predator control he called it "useless and half-assed."

Alvin Close killed the last major stock-killing wolf in Montana. He hunted the wolf so long he raised a litter of dogs to do it with. He hunted the wolf futilely with a pack that had fought the wolf a dozen times, until one day he gave up and let the dogs run the wolf out the back of a shallow canyon. He heard them yip their way into silence while he leaned up against a tree; and presently the wolf came tiptoeing down the front of the canyon into Alvin's lap. The wolf simply stopped because the game was up. Alvin raised the Winchester and shot it.

"How did you feel about that?" I asked.

"How do you think I felt?"

"I don't know."

"I felt like hell."

Alvin's evening was ruined and he went home. He was seventy-six years old and carried himself like an old-time army officer, setting his glass on the bar behind him without looking.

You stare through the plastic at the red smear of meat in the supermarket. What's this it says here? *Mighty Good? Tastee?*

Quality, Premium, and *Government Inspected?* Soon enough, the blood is on your hands. It's inescapable.

Aldo Leopold was a hunter who I am sure abjured freeze-dried vegetables and extrusion burgers. His conscience was clean because his hunting was part of a larger husbandry in which the life of the country was enhanced by his own work. He knew that game populations are not bothered by hunting until they are already precarious and that precarious game populations should not be hunted. Grizzlies should not be hunted, for instance. The enemy of game is clean farming and sinful chemicals; as well as the useless alteration of watersheds by promoter cretins and the insidious dizzards of land development, whose lobbyists teach us the venality of all governments.

A world in which a sacramental portion of food can be taken in an old way — hunting, fishing, farming, and gathering — has as much to do with societal sanity as a day's work for a day's pay.

For a long time, there was no tracking snow. I hunted on horseback for a couple of days in a complicated earthquake fault in the Gallatins. The fault made a maze of narrow canyons with flat floors. The sagebrush grew on woody trunks higher than my head and left sandy paths and game trails where the horse and I could travel.

There were Hungarian partridge that roared out in front of my horse, putting his head suddenly in my lap. And hawks tobogganed on the low air currents, astonished to find me there. One finger canyon ended in a vertical rock wall from which issued a spring of the kind elsewhere associated with the Virgin Mary, hung with ex-votos and the orthopedic supplications of satisfied miracle customers. Here, instead, were nine identical piles of bear shit, neatly adorned with undigested berries.

One canyon planed up and topped out on an endless grassy

rise. There were deer there, does and a young buck. A thousand yards away and staring at me with semaphore ears.

They assembled at a stiff trot from the haphazard array of feeding and strung out in a precise line against the far hill in a dogtrot. When I removed my hat, they went into their pogostick gait and that was that.

"What did a deer ever do to you?"
"Nothing."
"I'm serious. What do you have to go and kill them for?"
"I can't explain it talking like this."
"Why should they die for you? Would you die for deer?"
"If it came to that."

My boy and I went up the North Fork to look for grouse. We had my old pointer Molly, and Thomas's .22 pump. We flushed a number of birds climbing through the wild roses; but they roared away at knee level, leaving me little opportunity for my over-and-under, much less an opening for Thomas to ground-sluice one with his .22. We started out at the meteor hole above the last ranch and went all the way to the national forest. Thomas had his cap on the bridge of his nose and wobbled through the trees until we hit cross fences. We went out into the last open pasture before he got winded. So we sat down and looked across the valley at the Gallatin Range, furiously white and serrated, a bleak edge of the world. We sat in the sun and watched the chickadees make their way through the russet brush.

"Are you having a good time?"
"Sure," he said and curled a small hand around the octagonal barrel of the Winchester. I was not sure what I had meant by my question.

The rear quarters of the antelope came from the smoker so dense and finely grained it should have been sliced as prosciutto. We had edgy, crumbling cheddar from British Columbia and everybody kept an eye on the food and tried to pace themselves. The snow whirled in the window light and puffed the smoke down the chimney around the cedar flames. I had a stretch of enumerating things: my family, hayfields, saddle horses, friends, thirty-aught-six, French and Russian novels. I had a baby girl, colts coming, and a new roof on the barn. I finished a big corral made of railroad ties and two-by-sixes. I was within eighteen months of my father's death, my sister's death, and the collapse of my marriage. Still, the washouts were repairing; and when a few things had been set aside, not excluding paranoia, some features were left standing, not excluding lovers, children, friends, and saddle horses. In time, it would be clear as a bell. I did want venison again that winter and couldn't help but feel some old ridge-runner had my number on him.

I didn't want to read and I didn't want to write or acknowledge the phone with its tendrils into the zombie enclaves. I didn't want the New Rugged; I wanted the Old Rugged and a pot to piss in. Otherwise, it's deteriorata, with mice undermining the wiring in my frame house, sparks jumping in the insulation, the dog turning queer, and a horned owl staring at the baby through the nursery window.

It was pitch black in the bedroom and the windows radiated cold across the blankets. The top of my head felt this side of frost and the stars hung like ice crystals over the chimney. I scrambled out of bed and slipped into my long johns, put on a heavy shirt and my wool logger pants with the police suspenders. I carried the boots down to the kitchen so as not to wake the house and turned the percolator on. I put some cheese and chocolate in my coat, and when the coffee was done I filled a chili bowl and quaffed it against the winter.

When I hit the front steps I heard the hard squeaking of new snow under my boots and the wind moved against my face like a machine for refinishing hardwood floors. I backed the truck up to the horse trailer, the lights wheeling against the ghostly trunks of the bare cottonwoods. I connected the trailer and pulled it forward to a flat spot for loading the horse.

I had figured that when I got to the corral I could tell one horse from another by starlight; but the horses were in the shadow of the barn and I went in feeling my way among their shapes trying to find my hunting horse Rocky, and trying to get the front end of the big sorrel who kicks when surprised. Suddenly Rocky was looking in my face and I reached around his neck with the halter. A twelve-hundred-pound bay quarter horse, his withers angled up like a fighting bull, he wondered where we were going but ambled after me on a slack lead rope as we headed out of the darkened corral.

I have an old trailer made by a Texas horse vet years ago. It has none of the amenities of newer trailers. I wish it had a dome light for loading in the dark; but it doesn't. You ought to check and see if the cat's sleeping in it before you load; and I didn't do that either. Instead, I climbed inside the trailer and the horse followed me. I tied the horse down to a D-ring and started back out, when he blew up. The two of us were confined in the small space and he was ripping and bucking between the walls with such noise and violence that I had a brief disassociated moment of suspension from fear. I jumped up on the manger with my arms around my head while the horse shattered the inside of the trailer and rocked it furiously on its axles. Then he blew the steel rings out of the halter and fell over backward in the snow. The cat darted out and was gone. I slipped down off the manger and looked for the horse; he had gotten up and was sidling down past the granary in the star shadows.

I put two blankets on him, saddled him, played with his feet, and calmed him. I loaded him without incident and headed out.

I went through the aspen line at daybreak, still climbing.

The horse ascended steadily toward a high basin, creaking the saddle metronomically. It was getting colder as the sun came up, and the rifle scabbard held my left leg far enough from the horse that I was chilling on that side.

We touched the bottom of the basin and I could see the rock wall defined by a black stripe of evergreens on one side and the remains of an avalanche on the other. I thought how utterly desolate this country can look in winter and how one could hardly think of human travel in it at all, not white horsemen nor Indians dragging travois, just aerial raptors with their rending talons and heads like cameras slicing across the geometry of winter.

Then we stepped into a deep hole and the horse went to his chest in the powder, splashing the snow out before him as he floundered toward the other side. I got my feet out of the stirrups in case we went over. Then we were on wind-scoured rock and I hunted some lee for the two of us. I thought of my son's words after our last cold ride: "Dad, you know in 4-H? Well, I want to switch from Horsemanship to Aviation."

The spot was like this: a crest of snow crowned in a sculpted edge high enough to protect us. There was a tough little juniper to picket the horse to, and a good place to sit out of the cold and noise. Over my head, a long, curling plume of snow poured out, unchanging in shape against the pale blue sky. I ate some of the cheese and rewrapped it. I got the rifle down from the scabbard, loosened the cinch, and undid the flank cinch. I put the stirrup over the horn to remind me my saddle was loose, loaded two cartridges into the blind magazine, and slipped one in the chamber. Then I started toward the rock wall, staring at the patterned discolorations: old seeps, lichen, cracks, and the madhouse calligraphy of immemorial weather.

There were a lot of tracks where the snow had crusted out of the wind; all deer except for one well-used bobcat trail winding along the edges of a long rocky slot. I moved as carefully as I could, stretching my eyes as far out in front of my detectable movement as I could. I tried to work into the wind, but it turned erratically in the basin as the temperature of the new day changed.

The buck was studying me as soon as I came out on the open slope: he was a long way away and I stopped motionless to wait for him to feed again. He stared straight at me from five hundred yards. I waited until I could no longer feel my feet nor finally my legs. It was nearly an hour before he suddenly ducked his head and began to feed. Every time he fed I moved a few feet, but he was working away from me and I wasn't getting anywhere. Over the next half-hour he made his way to a little rim and, in the half-hour after that, moved the twenty feet that dropped him over the rim.

I went as fast as I could move quietly. I now had the rim to cover me and the buck should be less than a hundred yards from me when I looked over. It was all browse for a half-mile, wild roses, buck brush, and young quakies where there was any runoff.

When I reached the rim, I took off my hat and set it in the snow with my gloves inside. I wanted to be looking in the right direction when I cleared the rim, rise a half step and be looking straight at the buck, not scanning for the buck with him running sixty, a degree or two out of my periphery. And I didn't want to gum it up with thinking or trajectory guessing. People are always trajectory guessing their way into gut shots and clean misses. So, before I took the last step, all there was to do was lower the rim with my feet, lower the buck into my vision, and isolate the path of the bullet.

As I took that step, I knew he was running. He wasn't in the browse at all, but angling into invisibility at the rock wall, racing straight into the elevation, bounding toward zero gravity, taking his longest arc into the bullet and the finality and terror of all you have made of the world, the finality you know that you share even with your babies with their inherited and ambiguous dentition, the finality that any minute now you will meet as well.

He slid a hundred yards in a rush of snow. I dressed him

and skidded him by one antler to the horse. I made a slit behind the last ribs, pulled him over the saddle and put the horn through the slit, lashed the feet to the cinch dees, and led the horse downhill. The horse had bells of clear ice around his hoofs, and when he slipped, I chipped them out from under his feet with the point of a bullet.

I hung the buck in the open woodshed with a lariat over a rafter. He turned slowly against the cooling air. I could see the intermittent blue light of the television against the bedroom ceiling from where I stood. I stopped the twirling of the buck, my hands deep in the sage-scented fur, and thought: This is either the beginning or the end of everything.

FISHING
THE
BIG HOLE

I FISH all the time when I'm at home; so when I get a chance to go on a vacation, I make sure I get in plenty of fishing. I live in south central Montana, and because of the drought and fires, it resembles one of the man-made hells like the Los Angeles basin or America in general east of St. Louis. I make a trip every summer to fish the Big Hole River, and this year, because I knew that it was somewhat out of the range of smoke and ash and heat, I particularly looked forward to it. My friends Craig and Peggy Fellin have a small fishing lodge, with a capacity of eight, and I am perhaps their most regular annual guest.

Montana is so large and contains such a diversity of distinct regions that a trip from where I live to the southwesternmost corner, the Big Hole, provides a tremendous transition of environment, change of weather, change of terrain, change of culture. The Big Hole ranchers are different from the other ranchers in the state, and many of their farming and stock management practices are also different. The age of that district is seen in the old ranch headquarters, the hoary barns, the places founded by Frenchmen and fur traders, the stables that once held famous racehorses, and, one valley over in the Bitterroot, the old mission churches.

But to head across Montana this year is alarming. With

limited annual rainfall, much of Montana's appearance is desertic to begin with. But this year the yellow desiccation of midsummer crawled closer to the green shapes of mountains, until finally the wooded high country stood in a sort of ghastly attendance over what looked to be a dying landscape. Then all the fires began — first in Yellowstone, then in the Scapegoat and Bob Marshall areas. Inspired by this festivity, Missoula arsonists began to have at it until the feeling began to be that, generally speaking, the state of Montana was on fire.

Water had become fascinating. It was fascinating to water the lawn. It was fascinating to direct a fine mist at a flowerpot. It was fascinating to take a bucket and measure the flow of water that filled the tank that watered my cows. It was fascinating to watch the saddle horses dip their muzzles in a spring. Suddenly other things in the landscape were not interesting. Wind generators were not interesting. Electricity was not interesting. Power lines were not interesting. Telephones were not interesting, and all the wires and relays over the prairie that laced this largely empty region to the fervid nation were not so very interesting anymore. Water had become the only interesting thing. It had rained one-quarter of an inch in three months. I had watched water-laden clouds go overhead at terrific speed without losing a drop. Montana was getting less rain than the Mojave Desert. The little clouds that look like the clouds on a baby's crib were the sort of thing you wanted to shout at. Wind beat the ground on the rumor of water. Cowmen hauled water to battered, unusable pastures to feed cows and calves. Forest springs remembered by generations suddenly went away.

I drove west on the interstate along the Yellowstone River. A big Burlington Northern train came around a curve in the river in the dry air. It approached in silence, then was alongside me at once in a whirring rush of metal and movement. Astonishingly, the air was filled with a train smell, a sort of industrial odor that stood out sharply in the drought-stricken air. But the ash in the air was from the fires, and the smoke that poured out from the valley of the upper Yellowstone had the inappropriately sentimental tang of autumn leaf-burning. Still the train rolled on, and the first thing one wondered was whether it was a machine for starting fires or not.

As I climbed toward the Continental Divide, it did seem that things were a little greener. Some of the hay meadows actually looked like they might be producing hay instead of emergency pasture. Passing through the round red rocks of Homestake Pass, wadded together like enormous pencil erasers, I descended toward Butte and stopped to refill my tank. While the attendant cleaned the windshield, I stood inside the cool gas station and looked at pictures of Our Lady of the Rockies, being constructed. Great cranes brought workers and their equipment to her vast robes. A helicopter arrived with her head. No other town in Montana felt so strongly about the Virgin Mary, and it brought to her memory a mighty effort.

As I headed south toward Idaho and the Missouri headwaters that I love to fish, I had some nervous thoughts. I knew that sections of the Jefferson, the Red Rock, and the Big Hole itself had dried up because of irrigation. Montana has no provision for decreed instream use of water; in a bad year, agriculture can take it all without regard to fish or the fishermen who spend more than $100 million annually. Montana farmers and ranchers make thousands of new enemies each year over this issue, and those enemies are becoming a political force that would like to review not only the efficiency of their water use but other subjects as well, such as the constitutionality of their grazing-lease arrangements on public land. Vestigial rivers flowing out of the smoke only make the plight more emphatic.

I took the turnoff toward Divide and saw the Big Hole for the first time since last year. The extremely low water just kind of percolated through rubble rock. Nevertheless, the beauty of the river's narrow valley, the sage-covered walls, and the slit of railroad bed on the far bank seemed quite intact.

I turned up the Wise River from the town of that name. The river headed into the Pioneer Mountains, and as I started up its valley I eyed its floor with the same thing in mind: Any water? A short time later I unpacked in my wonderfully comfortable small cabin on the side of the river. Water raced by! Irrigation water went overhead on a trestlelike affair. Standing underneath it on my way to dinner, I could smell the cold runoff dripping down the timbers that held it up. I was starting to feel encouraged, starting to feel that my fly rod might not have been a purely comic utensil. There wasn't even any smoke in the air.

I had a beautifully prepared meal with the Fellins and their guests. This small lodge seems to attract fairly serious fishermen. So the gloomy enthusiasms, the bursts of ill-directed sexuality, the unwelcome appearance of the alter ego, the showdowns between couples, and the displays of minor violence that one associates with high-powered sporting lodges are absent here. One dines well and sleeps comfortably, storing maximum energy for the rivers.

I headed for my cabin early. The Fellins' big Labrador male accompanied me partway. He didn't stray far, because in the nearby bush there were moose, which chased him back to the house. It is a great pleasure for a family man to sleep in some building by himself once in a while; I slept the night away in a kind of mock-bachelor bliss, the windows wide open and the chilly mountain air pouring over my lofty comforter. My first home was made of logs, and the smell and solidity of those structures restored my highly eroded sense of well-being. I began to think of sallying forth with fly rod in hand to tune and sample the universe in the name of trout. This has been an issue of consequence since my bowlegged early childhood, and the feeling has grown stronger.

It was early in the morning of a beautiful summer day in

Montana. What more could be asked? Hawks threw their cries against tall red cliffs along the Big Hole, then soared into transparency against the brilliant blue sky. The peculiar sluicing movement of the dewatered but still-beautiful Big Hole at the base of the cliffs and railroad bed, the powerful sage smell, the bright yellow clusters of drought-resistant resinweed, and here and there the slowly opening rings of feeding trout brought me on point. I suddenly longed to see the loop of my line stretch over moving water. The float, the gulp: This way, please.

We went to a portion of the river that split into two channels, one of which slowed down considerably and presented an ideal place to ambush fish feeding on tricorythodes, better known as tricos. These are minute, clear-winged mayflies as beautiful as all the mayflies whose poetic forms have found their way into the imagination of sportsmen, certain of whom have taken pen to paper.

By the time we reached the stream the duns were hatching and the forms of rising trout, variously called "sipping," "slurping," and "gulping," opened upon the water. The duns are the immature forms of mayflies, recently transmuted from the nymphal stage, and they are reasonably easy targets for trout. The tricos are unlike other mayflies in that they complete their cycle in a matter of hours instead of days. To the angler this means that good fishing is to be had while the duns are on the water. A few hours later an even better stage, the spinner fall, commences. Duns that flew up above the riffles molt and achieve sexual maturity in a whirlwind of sparkling mayfly turbulence, and then return to the surface of the streams to lay their eggs. At this stage they are duck soup for feeding trout, and the alert angler may now slip up and catch a few.

During the emergence of the duns, I managed to catch a few small but handsome and always mythologically perfect and wonderful brown trout. Trico fishing is never easy, because the flies are so small, size 22, and they're hard to see, especially if one uses a truly imitative pattern. I ended up using a small Adams, which says "bug" to the trout in a general but friendly and duplicitous way. I was swept by the perfection of things, by the glorious shape of each trout, by the angelic miniature perfection of mayflies, and by the pure wild silk of the Big Hole River. It is for such things that we were placed on this careening mudball.

Overhead, the duns had accumulated in a glittering, transparent mass. We awaited the spinner fall. The duns gradually stopped emerging. The trout that had been feeding in the riffles tailed back into the slick water. We watched and waited for the thousands of sparkling creatures to fall to the hungry trout. Then the wind came up and blew them all away. End of episode.

We were able to float one section of the Big Hole, though the long riffles were shallow and noisy under the boat. Floating is a fine way to fish western rivers, where the slow and careful dissection of pools is less appropriate than it is in the trout streams of the East. It is also a terrific way to see the country while maintaining an air of purpose. As you float, the all-important bank unrolls before you through the course of the day like a variegated ribbon of earth and water.

It is also the fastest way to get the feel of a new river. On the Big Hole there are elbows and back eddies and turning pools of white foam. There are dropping chutes of long bubble trails that hold trout. I've always thought the Big Hole had more midstream trout lies than other rivers I know. Pockets behind boulders are favorite spots, as are places where bottom structures cause angular turns of current where trout can shelter yet watch a steady procession of foods.

The wind followed us to the Beaverhead River that evening. This river is unlike any other in the state. With its brushy banks and downed trees sweeping the undercut banks, it looks almost like a Michigan or Wisconsin trout river. It has the largest trout in the state, and when conditions are difficult, as they were that evening, it's easy to see how they got to be so big. Almost as soon as the fly is presented in one of the holes and notches along the bank, it's time to pick it up and look for another place to cast. It's equally easy to lose your fly in the brush in front of you on the Beaverhead or in the obstructions behind you. The wind really defeated us that evening. Craig rowed heroically, trying to keep the johnboat in position. Just at dusk we stopped to fish a small run. There was an intense hatch of caddis, and in the cloud of insects myriad bats seethed. It seemed impossible to cast through the swarm without catching a bat. I managed that evening to catch a few of what Craig called the smallest fish ever to be caught out of the Beaverhead. But it had been a sixteen-hour fishing day, and my thoughts lay entirely with the down pillow on my bed in the cabin on the gurgling bank of the Wise River.

The next day, another banquet breakfast: baked eggs with asparagus spears, oatmeal pancakes, sausages, honeydew melon, homemade cinnamon rolls, coffee, and the kind of sleepy, merry conversation I associate with the beginning of a day astream. Then we were off on a different sort of junket. This time we drove awhile and then parked the truck and took off on a cross-country hike. I noticed that many of the wildflowers that had disappeared in my drought-ridden part of the state still bloomed here. We had a leisurely walk along an abandoned railroad bed and along the pine-covered slopes of foothills. An old Confederate whose plantation had been burned during the War Between the States had first run cattle here. Then gold-mining ventures, real ones and swindles, found an agreeable setting in the little valley. Now it was ghost towns and trackless railroad bed, sagebrush reclaiming it all into marginal pasture. I picked up an ancient rail spike and slipped it in my vest to take home for a paperweight.

We traversed a high slope above a river too small and fragile to be named, and descended to begin fishing. The river looked plain and shoally, inconsequential and dimensionless from above, but like so many things in the West that seem flattened by distance and separation, this little river was a detailed paradise at close range. Rufous and calliope hummingbirds were feeding in the Indian paintbrush along the bank, and the thin-water stretches were separated by nice pools. One pool in particular lay at the bottom of a low cliff and held enough water to imply good-size fish. I approached it cautiously and found fish feeding on a hatch of midges. Beneath them were several good trout nymphing and flashing silver messages up through the clear water as they turned on their sides to feed. But the fish were difficult, feeding with extreme selectivity on the midges. I caught a couple of small ones before deciding the pool was spooked, then moved on. I vaguely acknowledged that I had not quite met the challenge of the midges, a challenge I've failed to meet more than once. When flies get much smaller than size 20 and the leader lies on the water's surface like the footprints of water spiders, my confidence begins to dwindle.

Then, at the bottom of a small chute, I caught a nice brook trout. This is not the most common trout in Montana and, while its introduction was long ago, its accustomed venue is elsewhere. It is a wonderful thing to be reminded of the variety of beauties displayed in the quarry of trout fishermen. You want to cry, as a local auctioneer does at the sight of a matched set of fattened yearlings, "My, oh my!" The brook trout has a silky sleekness in the hand that is different from the feel of any other trout. Browns always feel like you expect fish to feel; rainbows often feel blocky and muscular; but the brook trout exists within an envelope of perfect northerly sleekness. He is a great original, to be appreciated poetically, for he is not a demanding game fish. Some of the most appalling arias in angling literature are directed at this lovely creature, who was with us before the Ice Age.

I moved along the stream toward the end of my trip, thinking about my own part of the state. There the tawny hills had an almost glassy hardness from lack of water, so that the handfuls of cattle grazing on them cast hard and distinct shadows, as though they stood on tabletops and flooring. I intensely valued the stream-bred rainbows I caught, small-headed relative to their breadth and wonderfully marked with bands of stardust pink. This unpurposeful note of festivity is matched by their vital show when hooked, by their abandoned vaults for freedom. The great privilege is the moment one is released, when the small, strong fish moves from your hand to renew its hold upstream. Then it's time to go.

RUNOFF

T HE FISHING LIFE in Montana produces a particular apprehension that affects fishermen like a circadian rhythm: irrational dread of runoff. Early spring is capable of balmy days; and though the water is cold, the rivers are as benign as brooks in dreams, their pools and channels bright and perfect. But year-round experience shows that in short order they will be buried in snowmelt and irrigation waste, and their babied low-water contours will disappear under the hoggish brown rush. Once runoff begins, the weather is often wonderful. The canopies of cottonwood open like green umbrellas. But it can be a long wait before the rivers clear, a wait so long it seems possible to lose track of the whole idea.

In early spring, it is time to begin when friends say, "I know I should get out. I just haven't had the time." Here is the chance to steal a march, to exercise those fish whose memory has been dulled by the long winter. Crazy experiments can be undertaken at this time, such as photographing a trout held in your left hand with a camera held in your right hand. Before-the-runoff is time out of time; it is the opportunity to steal fishing from an impudent year.

You can tell when you have started early enough when the first landowner whose permission you ask stares at you with zenophobic eyes. His first thought is that you are there to pilfer or harm his family. Let him examine your rod and scrutinize your eyes. The eyes of a fisherman are not so good; so keep them moving. Spot a bit of natural history and describe it. Above all, don't say that your dad and your granddad before you fished this same stretch at their pleasure. The landowner of today does not like any surprising seniority just now. He's having hell holding onto the place. Turn and go to your vehicle. Don't back to it.

A sign of real desperation for me is when I begin to tie my own flies. I once made the simple accommodation that others do this better than I do, that they are meant to fill a fly need in others. They are professional fly tyers and their monkish solitude is rendered habitable by the knowledge that their creations are helping all-thumbs types like myself drag hogs onto the gravel. But this compact with an invisible support team was something I could no longer honor by March; and I began to fill fly box after fly box with my crude elk-hair caddises, Griffith's Gnats, and Gold-ribbed Hare's Ears.

I wandered around the various forks of my home river, separated by many miles of rolling hills: one would be running off, the other clear, depending upon the exact kind of country it drained. I clambered down slick or snowy rocks to dangle my thermometer in the water. But in the spring there was, even on a snowy day, a new quality of light, as if the light had acquired richness that you could feel, that trees, grass, and animals could feel, a nutritious light coming through falling snow. There had come a turning point and now spring was more inexorable than the blizzards. I knew the minute this snow quit there would be someplace I could fish.

The next morning was still and everything was melting. I went to a small river out in the foothills north of where I live. This early in the year when I drive down through a ranch yard or walk across a pasture toward the stream, my heart pounds as it has all my life for a glimpse of moving water. Moving water is the most constant passion I've had; it can be current or it can be tide; but it can't be a lake and it can't be midocean, where I have spent some baffled days and weeks more or less scratching my head. The river was in perfect shape, enough water that most of its braided channels were full. There were geese on the banks and they talked at me in a state of high alarm as they lifted and replaced their feet with weird deliberation.

As soon as I got in the river, I felt how very cold the water was. Nevertheless, a few caddises skittered on top of the water. An hour later, some big gray drakes came off like a heavenly message sent on coded insects, a message that there would indeed be dry-fly fishing on earth again. I am always saying, though it's hardly my idea, that the natural state of the universe is cold; but cold-blooded trout and cold-blooded mayflies are signs of the world's retained heat, as is the angler, wading upstream in a cold spring wind in search of delight. Nevertheless, the day had opened a few F-stops at the aperture of sky, a sign and a beginning. I caught one of the mayflies and had a long look: about a No. 12, olive, brown, and gray the operative colors, two-part tail. I had something pretty close in my fly box, having rejected the Red Quill and the Quill Gordon as close but no cigar.

A couple of brilliant male mergansers went overhead. They are hard on fish and despised, but their beauty is undisputed. In a short time, they would migrate out of here and I didn't know where they went. They were referred to in Lewis and Clark's journals as the red-headed fishing duck, a better name.

The river combined in a single channel, where the volume of water produced a steady riffle of two or three feet of depth. I started where it tailed out and worked my way up to where slick water fell off into the rapids. The mayflies were not in great numbers but they were carried down this slick and over the lip into the riffle. My staring magnified their plight into postcards of Niagara Falls, a bit of sympathetic fancy canceled by the sight of swirls in the first fast water. I cast my fly straight into this activity and instantly hooked a good rainbow. It must have been the long winter's wait or the knowledge that the day could end any minute; but I desperately wanted to land this fish. I backed down out of the fast water while the fish ran and jumped; then I sort of cruised him into the shallows and got a hand on him. He was a brilliant-looking fish and I thought I could detect distress in his eyes as he looked, gulping, out into midair. I slipped the barbless hook out and eased him back into the shallows. Two sharp angles and he was gone in deep green water.

It started to cloud up and grow blustery. The temperature plummeted. I went back to my truck, stripped off my waders, put up my gear, and started home, past the black old tires hung on the fenceposts with messages painted on them about cafés and no hunting. I kept thinking that the sort of sporadic hatch that had begun to occur was perfect for leisurely dry-fly fishing, if the weather had held. By the time I got to the house, it was winter again and I was trying to look up that dun, concluding for all the good it would do me that it was *Ephemerella compar*. Even as I write this, I visualize a trout scholar in pince-nez rising up out of the Henry's Fork to correct my findings.

When you have stopped work to go fishing and then gotten weathered out, your sense of idleness knows no bounds. You wander around the house and watch the weather from various windows. From my bedroom I could see great gusts of snow, big plumes and curtains marching across the pasture. Did I really catch a rainbow on a dry fly this morning?

The next day broke off still and sunny, and spring was sucking that snow up and taking it to Yucatan. I ran into a friend of mine at the post office who had seen a young male gyrfalcon — a gyrfalcon! — hunting partridges on my place. In an hour, I was standing with my fly rod in the middle of a bunch of loose horses, looking off a bank into a deep, green-black pool where swam a number of hog rainbows. I had been there before and you couldn't approach the spot except to stand below where the slow-moving pool tailed out rather rapidly. The trouble was you had to stay far enough away from the pool that it was hard to keep your line off the tailwater that produced instantaneous drag. You needed a seven-foot rod to make the cast and a twenty-foot rod to handle the slack. They hadn't built this rod yet. It would have been a two-piece rod with a spring-loaded hinge driven by a cartridge in the handle with a flash suppressor. Many of us had been to this pool to learn why the rainbows had grown to be hogs who would never be dragged onto a gravel bar. They were going to stay where they were, with their backs up and their bellies down, eating when they wanted to. I had to try it anyway and floated one up onto the pool. I got a drag-free drift of around three-eighths of an inch and went looking for another spot.

Geese and mallards flew up ahead of me as I waded, circling for altitude in the big bare tops of the cottonwoods. The air was so still and transparent you could hear everything. When the mallards circled over my head, their wingtips touched in a tense flutter and made a popping sound.

In a little back-eddy, caddises were being carried down a line of three feeding fish. I arranged for my fly to be among them, got a drift I couldn't begin to improve on, and a nice brown sucked it down. I moved up the edge of the bar to some more feeding fish. There were geese on the bar who had been ignoring me but now began to watch me and pace around. I noted one of the fish was of good size and it was feeding in a steady rhythm. I made a kind of measuring cast from my knees. The geese were getting more nervous. I made a final cast and it dropped right in the slot and started floating back to the good fish. I looked over to see what the geese were doing. The trout grabbed the fly. I looked back and missed the strike. I delivered an oath. The geese ran awkwardly into graceful flight and banked on around to the north.

This was a wonderful time to find yourself astream. You didn't bump into experts. You didn't bump into anybody. There were times when you could own this place in your thoughts as completely as a Hudson Bay trapper. The strangely human killdeer were all over the place. I considered them human because their breeding activities were accompanied by screaming fights and continuous loud bickering. When they came in for a landing, their wings set in a quiet glide while their legs ran frantically in midair. The trees in the slower bends were in a state of pickup-sticks destruction from the activity of beavers. A kingfisher flew over my head with a trout hanging from its bill. I came around a bend without alerting three more geese, floating in a backwater, sound asleep with their heads under their wings. I decided not to wake them. I ended my day right there. When I drove up out of the river bottom in my car, I looked back to see a blue heron fishing the back eddy where I'd caught a trout. On the radio were predictions of high temperatures coming and I knew what that low-country meltoff would mean to my days on the river.

Spring was here and it was hot. In one day it shot up to the eighties. I could feel the purling melt come out from under the snowbanks. Runoff was going to drop me in midstride.

I drove away from the places that I thought would get the first dirty water, away from the disturbed ground. It was daybreak, and out on the interstate I found myself in a formation of Montana Pioneers, driving Model-Ts. This piquancy didn't hold me up long and I soon made my way to a wonderful little district where various grasses, burgeoning brush, wildflowers, and blue-green strips of fragrant sage had all somehow got the news that spring had sprung. The cover was so deep in places that deer moving through it revealed only their ears, which flipped up and disappeared. An old pry bar lay lost in the grass, polished smooth by use. Ranchers never had the help they needed and they were all masters of prying; these bars had the poetry of any old tool, old dental instruments, old greasy hammers and screwdrivers around a man's workshop, especially when the tool owner is not in immediate evidence, or dead.

The river whispered past this spot in a kind of secretive hurry. I got in and waded upstream, and sat on a small logjam to tie on a fly. The logs under me groaned with the movement of current. I was suddenly so extremely happy, the sight of this water was throwing me into such a rapturous state of mind, that I began to wonder what it could mean. I sometimes wondered if there wasn't something misanthropic in this passion for solitude.

I put my thermometer into the river, knowing already it was going to come out in the 40s. Taking the temperature of the river is like taking your own temperature, the drama of the secret darkness of the interior of your mouth; you wait and wait and try to wait long enough. Is it 98.6 or am I right in thinking I don't feel too good? The water was 49 degrees, fairly acceptable for now.

Across from my seat on the logjam was an old cabin. These old buildings along Montana trout rivers were part of their provenance, part of what came back to you, like the wooded elevations that shaped, and bent, and pushed and pulled each river so that as you tried to re-create one in your mind that winter, there was always a point you got lost, always an oxbow or meander where a kind of memory whiteout occurred. I was always anxious to return to such a stretch and rescue it from amnesia.

To reach my pool, I had to wade across the riffle above the logjam and then work my way around a humongous, dead, bloated cow, inflated to a height of five feet at the ribcage. The smell was overpowering but I needed to get to that pool. There was a mule deer doe back in the trees watching me with her twin yearling fawns. One already was getting little velvet antlers.

For some reason, I was thinking how many angry people,

angry faces, you saw in these romantic landscapes. It was as though the dream had backfired in isolation. There were the enraged visages behind pickup truck windshields with rifles in the back window at all seasons of the year. I remembered an old rancher telling me about a rape that had just occurred in Gardiner, and in his eyes was the most extraordinary mixture of lust and rage I had ever seen. He lived off by himself in a beautiful canyon and this was the sort of thing he came up with. A friend of mine from the Midwest looked at the chairs in a restaurant covered with all the local cattle brands and cried out in despair, "Why are these people always *tooling* everything?" The pleasures of being seduced by the daily flux of the masses were not available. All the information about the world had failed to produce the feeling of the global village; the information had exaggerated the feeling of isolation. I had in my own heart the usual modicum of loneliness, annoyance, and desire for revenge; but it never seemed to make it to the river. Isolation always held out the opportunity of solitude: the rivers kept coming down from the hills.

Having reached my pool, having forded the vast stench of the cow, I was rewarded with a sparse hatch of sulfur mayflies with mottled gray wings. I caught three nice browns in a row before it shut off. I knew this would happen. A man once told me, when I asked him when you could assume a horse would ground-tie and you could go off and leave him, knowing he would be there when you get back: "The horse will tell you." When I asked an old man in Alabama how he knew a dog was staunch enough to break it to stand to shot, he said, "The dog will tell you." There are times for every angler when he catches fish because the fish told him he could; and times when the trout announce they are through for the day.

Two of the most interesting fish of the next little while were fish I couldn't catch. One was on the far side of a current that ran along the side of a log. The trout was making a slow porpoising rise. I managed to reach him and he managed to

rise; but drag got the fly at the instant he took and carried the
fly away. The next fish I saw, another steady feeder, rose to a
Light Cahill. The dinner bell at a nearby ranch house rang
sharply; I looked up, the fish struck and I missed it.

I caught a nice rainbow by accident, which is the river's way
of telling you that you've been misreading it. And then thunder and lightning commenced. I got out of the river. Bolting
rain foretold the flood. I went up and sat under the trunk lid
of my car, quite comfortably, and ate my lunch, setting a
Granny Smith apple on the spare tire. The thermos of coffee
seemed a boon almost to be compared to the oranges we kept
on ice during the hot early weeks of bird season. The rain
steadied down and I could watch two or three bends of the
river and eat in a state of deep contentment. I didn't know of
a better feeling than to be fishing and having enough time;
you weren't so pressured that if you got a bad bank you
couldn't wait until the good bank turned your way and the
riffles were in the right corners. And the meal next to a stream
was transforming, too, so that in addition to the magic apple
there was the magic peanut-butter-and-jelly sandwich.

The rain stopped and I went down to where an irrigation
ditch took out along a rip-rapped bank. I had a very nice
Honduran cigar to smoke while I watched a heron fish the
shallows. The air was still. I puffed a great cloud of smoke and
it drifted across the little river; I imagined it was the ghost of
my grandfather, who loved to fish. The ghost glided past the
heron, who ignored him politely.

I just knew something was going on. There was a readiness.
The rain had barely withdrawn. The sky looked so heavy you
felt if you scratched it you'd drown. This was the storm that
would loose the mountain snows, and the glistening fingers of
this small river system would turn brown as a farmer's hand.
Time, in its most famous configuration, was "running out." It
could be the storm that made runoff really get under way, my
last day on the stream for a good while. One had broken out

of the pattern of home life and work, and beaten inertia for the moment: might as well keep going.

I crawled down into a canyon made by the river. It was not far from where I had been fishing and the canyon was not that deep. But I needed both hands to make the descent, to lower myself from projecting roots and points of rock; and I had to throw the rod down in front of me because there was no good way to carry it. I found myself between tall cream-and-gray rock walls. The river flowed straight into dissolved chimneys, rock scours, solution holes, and fanciful stone bridges.

The sky overhead was reduced to a narrow band and the storm had reformed over that. More killdeer conducted their crazed, weeping, wing-dragging drama around my feet. The storm became ugly and I looked all around the bottom of the small canyon for a safe place to be. Lightning jumped close overhead with a roaring crack. The rain poured down, periodically lit up by the very close lightning. What little I knew about electricity made me think that bushes were a poor connection; so I burrowed into a thick clump of laurels and became mighty small, studied the laurel: round, serrated leaf, brownish yellow bark, a kind of silvery brightness from afar. It had become very gloomy. By looking at the dark mouths of the caves in the far canyon wall, I could monitor the heaviness of the rain while the steady rattle on the hood of my parka filled in the blanks. I spotted a lightning-killed tree at about my level on the far side. The river had seemed so cheerful and full of green-blue pools. Now it was all pounded white by rain and only the darker V's of current indicated that it was anything but standing water.

Then the air pressure could be felt to lift. The dark sky broke wide open in blue. An owl crossed the river, avoiding the return of light. The rain stopped and the surface of river was miraculously refinished as a trout stream. I looked at the drops of water hanging from my fly rod. I thought of the windows of the trout opening on a new world and how appropriate it would be if one of them could see my fly.

The standing water along roadsides in spring is a wonderful thing. On the way home, I saw a flight of northern shoveler ducks, eccentric creatures in mahogany and green; and off in a pasture stock pond, teal flew and circled like butterflies unable to decide whether to land. I wondered what it was about the edges of things that is so vital, the edges of habitat, the edges of seasons, always in the form of an advent. Spring in Montana was a kind of pandemonium of release. There were certainly more sophisticated ways of taking it in than mine. But going afield with my fishing rod seemed not so intrusive and the ceremony helped, quickened my memory back through an entire life spent fishing. Besides, like "military intelligence" and "airline cuisine," "sophisticated angler" is an oxymoron. And if it weren't, it would be nothing to strive for. Angling is where the child, not the infant, gets to go on living.

It was ten minutes to five. There was absolutely no wind. I could see the corners of a few irrigation dams sticking up out of the ditches. The cottonwoods were in a blush of green. I was ready for high water.

BUSTER

ALMOST A DECADE AGO, I was working in what is ponder-
ously known as the motion picture industry, which required my presence for a long spell in Los Angeles. I spent
my time in script conferences with a movie star who managed
to wake up in a different world each day. Sometimes our story
took place high in the mountains; other times the scene moved
to the desert or to a nonexistent little town that derived its
features from the star's days in movie houses, when he
dreamed of working on his draw instead of on his lines. Some
days the Indians won, some days the law. This was about to be
one of the last cowboy movies America would put up with.

But myth was something I was still interested in. And so, in
the evenings, my wife and I would drive out to Chino, where
our friend Joe Hcim trained cutting horses. His place was very
small, a couple of acres maybe, and the horses were penned
wherever space could be found. I particularly remember an
old oak tree where we used to hang the big festoon of bridles
and martingales. Joe lived in a trailer house, did his books on
a desk at one end and slept in the other. We worked cattle
under the lights, an absolute anomaly in a run-down suburb.
Joe is a first-rate hand whose succcess has since confirmed his
originality and independence. But on those warm nights when
cattle and horses did things that required decoding, Joe would

always begin, "What Buster would do here is . . ." I had never seen Buster Welch, but his attempts to understand an ideal relationship between horsemen and cattle sent ripples any- where that cows grazed, from Alberta to the Mexican border. It would be many years before I drove into his yard in West Texas.

Buster Welch was born and more or less raised north of Ster- ling City, Texas, on the divide between the Concho and Colo- rado rivers. His mother died shortly after he was born, and he was raised by his grandfather, a retired peace officer, and his grandmother on a stock farm in modest self-sufficiency. Buster came from a line of people who had been in Texas since before the Civil War, Tennesseans by origin. Growing up in the Roosevelt years in a part of Texas peculiarly isolated from modern times, Buster was ideally situated to understand and convey the practices of the cowboys of an earlier age to an era rapidly leaving its own mythology. The cutting horse is a sacred link to those times, and its use and performance are closer to the Japanese martial theater than to rodeo. Origi- nally, a cutting horse was used to separate individual cattle for branding or doctoring. From the "brag" horses of those early days has evolved the cutting horse, which refines the principles of stock handling and horsemanship for the purposes of com- petition.

When Buster was a young boy, his father remarried and moved his wife, her two children, and Buster to Midland, where the father worked as a tank boss for Atlantic Richfield. Buster's early life in Sterling City and the separation from his grandparents and their own linkage to the glorious past had the net result of turning Buster into a truant from the small poor school he attended, a boy whose dreams were triggered by the herds of cattle that were then trailed past the school- house to the stockyards. He became a youthful bronc buster at the stockyards and was befriended by people like Claude

"Big Boy" Whatley, a man so strong he could catch a horse by the tail, take hold of a post, and instruct Buster to let the other horses out of the corral. By the time Buster reached the sixth grade, he had run away a number of times, and at thirteen he had run away for keeps. In making his departure on a cold night, he led a foul old horse named Handsome Harry well away from the house so his family wouldn't hear the horse bawling when it bucked. From there he went to work for Foy and Leonard Proctor, upright and industrious cowmen who handled as many as thirty thousand head of cattle a year. Buster began by breaking broncs, grubbing prickly pear, chopping firewood, wrangling horses, and holding the cut when a big herd was being worked, a lowly job where much can be learned.

When you see Buster's old-time herd work under the lights in Will Rogers Coliseum or at the Astrodome in Houston, that is where it began. The Proctors are still alive, revered men in their nineties, descendants of trail drovers and Indian fighters. From them, Buster learned to shape large herds of cattle and began the perfection of his minimalist style of cutting horsemanship and cattle ranching in general. He was having to work with horses that "weren't the kind a man liked to get on." But as time went on in those early days, he was around some horses that "went on," including Jesse James, who became the world champion cutting horse. Nevertheless, he probably spent more time applying 62 Smear, a chloroform-based screwworm concoction, to afflicted cattle than to anything more obviously bound for glory.

Buster rode the rough string for the storied Four Sixes at and around Guthrie. One of the horses had been through the bronc pen two or three times and was so unrepentant that you had to ride him all day after you topped him off in the morning, relieving yourself down the horse's shoulder rather than getting off, and at the end of the day, buck down to the end of the reins, turn around, and scare the horse back before he could paw and strike you. But this was an opportunity to be around those good and important cowmen and to work cattle out with the chuck wagon or from the permanent camps on that big ranch. Buster is remembered for his white shirts and for being the only man able to ride the rough string and stay clean. Hands circulated from there to the Matador and the Pitchfork in what amounted to graduate schools for cowboys. Off and on in that period, Buster rode saddle broncs at the casual rodeos of the day, where the prospects for injury far outweighed the opportunity for remuneration. There was certainly in Buster's life a drive for individuality and authorship in his work that might have been realized earlier if someone had been good enough to leave him a ranch. Even by then ranches were in the hands of "sons, sons-in-law, and sons of bitches." To this day, he sees himself primarily as a rancher; though a balance sheet would certainly profile him fairly strictly as a cutting-horse trainer, and that at a time when genuine cutting horses are rarely used in ranch work. In many cases, they not only never see open country; they live the lives of caged birds, with an iron routine from box stall to training pen to hot walker to box stall, moving through the seasons of big-purse events to long retirement in breeding programs.

By the time Buster Welch began to establish himself as a horseman, beyond someone who could get the early saddlings on rough stock — that is, was able to bring a horse to some degree of finish and refinement — the cutting horse began to come into its own as a contest animal. The adversity of the Texas cattle business had a lot to do with Welch's career. His plan had always been to use his advantages in training the cutting horse to establish himself in the cow business. And he was well on his way to making that happen in the fifties, running eight hundred cows on leased land, when the drought struck. It ruined many a stouter operator than Buster Welch. In those tough times a horse called Marion's Girl came into Buster's life. The weather focused his options, and the mare focused his talent. Buster went on the road with Marion's Girl and made her the world champion cutting horse that year, 1954. If he ever looked back, he never said so.

Capitalizing on events, Buster began to train champion cutting horses at about the rate Westerners, and particularly Texans, were absorbing the concept of formal cutting-horse competitions. In those contests, a rider assesses a herd of cattle in order to select cows that will test his horse's ability and exhibit its virtues. Cattle separated from the herd are extremely resourceful in finding ways to get back. It takes a smart, fast, athletic horse to keep them from succeeding. A true cow horse moves only when the cow moves, matching the cow's attempts to return to the herd. This would be a standoff, except that the horse is smarter than the cow; the cow finally decides that the move-for-move tactics won't work anymore. It's a bad decision because they are the only tactics the cow has; when they fail, the horse has controlled the cow. That cow can now be abandoned by the horse and horseman in the contest situation so that another may be cut. Or in the situation of working a herd on the range, that cow may be sent out of the herd to the cowboys holding the cut.

The National Cutting Horse Association was founded. Many of the founders have departed the scene in various ways, drifted into an advisory capacity, quit, or died. But Buster Welch, with his unique capacity for refueling, continues to strike paranoia in the hearts of much younger trainers who have made a cottage industry out of wondering what he will do next.

I had been staying in Alabama and was getting ready to go home to Montana. I had managed to catch a ride for my horses from Hernando, Mississippi, to Amarillo, where I wanted to make a cutting, then go on home. This all seemed ideal for paying a visit to Buster at Merkel en route.

Buster greeted me from the screen door of the bunkhouse.

The ranch buildings were set among the steadily ascending hills that drew your mind forever outward into the distance. I began to understand how Buster has been able to refuel his imagination while the competition has burned out and fallen behind. There was a hum of purpose here. It was a horseman's experimental station right in the heart of the range cattle industry.

Buster and I rode the buckboard over the ranch, taking in Texas at this etiolated end of the Edwards Plateau. What is this we have here? The West? The South? The groves of oak trees and small springs, the sparse distribution of cattle on hillsides that seemed bounteous in a restrained sort of way, the deep wagon grooves in rock. We clattered through a dry wash.

"Nobody can ranch as cheap as I can," said Buster, leaning out over the team to scrutinize it for adjustment; the heavy latigo reins draped familiarly in his hands. "If I have to." But when we passed an old gouge in the ground, he stopped and said ruefully, "It took the old man that had this place first a lifetime to fill that trash hole up. We haul more than that away every week." Each year Buster and his wife, Sheila, win hundreds of thousands of dollars riding cutting horses.

Of the hands working on Buster's ranch, hailing from Texas, Washington, and Australia, there was an array of talent in general cow work. But so far as I could discern, nobody didn't want to be a cutting-horse trainer. There is considerable competition and activity for people interested in cutting horses in Australia, but the country is so vast, especially the cattle country, that well-educated hands go home and basically dry up for lack of seeing one another or for being unable to cope with the mileage necessary to get to cuttings. Nevertheless, such as the situation is, much of the talent in Australia grew up under Buster's tutelage. Buster is very fond of his Australians and thinks they are like the old-time Texans who took forever to fill the trash hole behind the house. One sees the cowboys at each meal; they have the well-known high spirits, but under Buster's guidance they are quiet and polite — they rise, introduce themselves, shake hands, and try to be helpful. The reticence and sarcasm of the ill-bred blue-collar horse moron is not found here. In their limited spare time these cowboys make the Saturday night run to town, or they attend Bible classes, or they hole up in the bunkhouse to listen to heavy metal on their ghetto blasters. Buster finds something to like in each of them: one is industrious, another is handy with machinery, another has light hands with a colt, and so on.

Buster has been blessed by continuity and by an enormous pride in his heritage. One of his forebears rode with Fitzhugh Lee and, refusing to surrender when the Confederacy fell, was never heard from again; another fought to defend Vicksburg. Buster's grandfather was a sheriff in West Texas, still remembered with respect. There are a lot of pictures of his ancestors around the place, weathered, unsmiling Scotch-Irish faces. Buster doesn't smile for pictures either, though he spends a lot of time smiling or grinning at the idea of it all, the peculiar, delightful purposefulness of life and horses, the rightness of cattle and West Texas, but above all, the perfection and opportunity of today, the very day we have right here.

By poking around and prying among the help, I was able to determine that the orderly world I perceived as Buster's camp was something of an illusion and that there were many days that began quite unpredictably. In fact, there was the usual disarray of any artist's mise-en-scène, though we had here, instead of a squalid Parisian atelier, a cattle ranch. But I never questioned that this was an artist's place.

For example, the round pen. Buster invented its present use. Heretofore, cutting horses not trained on the open range — and those had become exceedingly rare — were trained in square arenas. Buster trained that way. But one day a song insistently went through his head, a song about "a string with no end," and Buster realized that was what he was looking for, a place where the logic of a cow horse's motion and stops could go on in continuity as it once did on the open range, a place where walls and corners could never eat a horse and its rider and stop the flow. By moving from a square place of training to a circular one, a more accurate cross section of the range was achieved. A horse could be worked in a round place without getting mentally "burned" by annoying interruptions (corners); the same applied to the rider, and since horse and rider in cutting are almost the same thing, what applied to the goose applied to the gander. The round pen made the world of cutting better; even the cattle kept their vitality and inventiveness longer. But Buster's search for a place where the movement could be uninterrupted was something of a search for eternity, at least *his* eternity, which inevitably depends on a horseman tending stock. Just as the Plains Indians might memorialize the buffalo hunt in the beauty of their dancing, the rider on a cutting horse can celebrate the life of the open range forever.

Buster Welch's horses have a "look," and this matter of look, of style, is important. The National Cutting Horse Association book on judging cutting horses makes no mention of this; but it is a life-and-death factor. There are "plain" horses, or "vanilla" horses, and there are "good-moving horses," or "scorpions." Interestingly enough, if categorization were necessary, Buster's horses tend to be plain. It is said that it takes a lot of cow to make one of his horses win a big cutting. On the other hand, his cutting horses are plain in the way that Shaker furniture is plain. They are so direct and purposeful that their eloquence of motion can be missed. Furthermore, we may be in the age of the baroque horse, the spectacular, motion-wasteful products of training pens and indoor arenas. Almost no one has the open range background of Buster Welch anymore.

Those who worked cattle for a long time on the open range learned a number of things about the motion of cow horses. A herd of cattle is a tremulous, explosive thing, as anxious to change shapes as a school of fish is. Control is a delicate thing. A horse that runs straight and stops straight doesn't scare cattle. And a straight-stopping horse won't fall with you either. Buster Welch's horses run straight and stop straight. They're heads-up, alert horses, unlikely to splay out on the floor of the arena and do something meretricious for the tourists. They are horses inspired by the job to be done and not by the ambitions of the rider. Buster has remarked that he would like to win the world championship without ever getting his horse out of a trot. That would make a bleak day for the Fort Worth Chamber of Commerce but a bright one for the connoisseur.

There were three or four people hanging around the bunk-house when we got back. One was the daughter of a friend of mine in the Oklahoma panhandle, there with her new husband. They had all just been to a horse sale in Abilene, where they ran some young horses through. They were in shock. They just sprawled out on the benches in the dogtrot, which was a kind of breezeway, and took in what a rude surprise the price of horses had gotten to be. "Look at it this way," said Buster. "You don't have to feed those suckers anymore." He looked around at the faces. "You are the winners," he added for emphasis.

Buster is practical. He helped start the futurity for three-year-old horses because the good, broke, open horses lasted so long; the need for trainers was small and even shrinking. He thought it might be good to steal a notion from the automobile industry and build some planned obsolescence into the western cow horse.

It worked. The boom in cutting, the millions in prize money given away annually, is largely spent on the aged-event horses, especially three- and four-year-olds. Syndicates have prolifer-

ated, and certified public accountants lead shareholders past
the stalls of the assets. This year's horses spring up and vanish
like Cabbage Patch dolls, and the down-the-road open horse
is in danger of becoming a thing of the past, an object of
salvage. If the finished open horse doesn't regain its former
stature, the ironic effect of large purses for young horses and
the concentration of those events in Texas will be to deprive
cutting of its national character and to consign it to the minor
leagues.

One of the best horses Buster ever trained is a stud named
Haida's Little Pep. When Buster asked me if there was any
horse in particular I wanted to ride, I said Haida's Little Pep.
Buster sent a stock trailer over to Sterling City, where the
horse was consorting with seventy mostly accepting mares. I
couldn't wait to see the horse whose desire and ability, it had
been said, had forced Buster to change his training methods.
(He actually leaks some of these rumors himself.) Buster
watched the men unload the stallion, in his characteristic position: elbows back, hands slightly clenched, like a man preparing to jump into a swimming pool. Haida's Little Pep stepped
from the trailer and gazed coolly around at us.

We saddled him and went into the arena. "Go ahead and
cut you a cow," said Buster. Two cowboys held a small herd of
cattle at one end. My thought was What? No last-minute in-
structions?

I climbed aboard. Here I had a different view of this famous
beast: muscle, compact horse muscle; in particular a powerful
neck that developed from behind the ears, expanding back
toward the saddle to disappear between my knees. The stud
stood awaiting some request from me. I didn't know if, when
I touched him with a spur, he was going to squeal and run
through the cedar walls of the pen or just hump his back, put
his head between his legs, and send me back to Montana. But
he just moved off, broke but not broke to death; the cues
seemed to mean enough to get him where you were going but

none of the flat spins of the ride-'em-and-slide-'em school.
Haida's Little Pep, thus far, felt like a mannerly ranch horse.
I headed for the herd.

Once among the cattle, I had a pleasant sensation of the
horse moving as requested but not bobbing around trying to
pick cattle himself. His deferring to me made me wonder if
he was really cooperating in this enterprise at all. As I sorted a
last individual, he stood so flat-footed and quiet that I asked
myself if he had really mentally returned from the stallion
station. I put the reins down. The crossbred steer gazed back
at the herd, and when he turned to look at us, Haida's Little
Pep sank slowly on his hocks. When the steer bolted, the horse
moved at a speed slightly more rapid than the ability of cattle
to think and in four turns removed the steer's will power and
stopped him. The horse's movements were hard and sudden
but so unwasteful and accurate that he was easy to ride. Because of the way this horse was broke, I began thinking about
the problems of working these cattle. I immediately sensed
that the horse and I had the same purpose. I've been on many
other horses that produced no such feeling. There was too
much discrepancy between our intentions. We wanted to cut
different cattle. They didn't want to hold and handle cattle;
they wanted to chase them. They didn't want to stop straight;
they wanted to round their turns and throw me onto the
saddle horn. But this high-powered little stud was correct, flat
natural, and well intentioned.

We looked at some old films in Buster's living room. They
were of Marion's Girl, whom Buster had trained in the fifties,
the mare who had done a lot to change the rest of his life. I
had long heard about her, but I remember Buster describing
her to me for the first time at a cutting on Sweet Grass Creek
in Montana. The ranch there was surrounded by a tall, steep
bluff covered with bunchgrass and prickly pear; it was maybe
a thousand feet high and came down to the floor of the valley

ᴀᴛ a steep angle. Buster had said that Marion's Girl would run straight down something like that to head a cow, stop on her rear end, and slide halfway to the bottom before turning around to drive the cow. As all great trainers feel about all great horses, Buster felt that Marion's Girl had trained him; more explicitly, she had trained him to train the modern cutting horse. At that time most cutting horses kind of ran sideways and never stopped quite straight. Buster considered that a degraded period during which the proper practices of the open range were forgotten. Marion's Girl, like some avatar from the past, ran hard, stopped straight and hard, and turned through herself without losing ground to cattle.

As I watched the old film, I could see this energetic and passionate mare working in what looked like an old corral. Though she has been dead for many years, the essence of the modern cow horse was there, move after move. In the film Buster looked like a youngster, but he bustled familiarly around with his elbows cocked, ready to dive into the pool.

"Are horses smart or dumb?" I asked Buster.

"They are very smart," he said with conviction. "Very intelligent. And if you ask one to do something he was going to do anyway, you hurt his feelings, you insult his intelligence."

Everyone wants to know what Buster Welch's secret in training horses is; and that's it. Only it's not a secret. All you need to know is what the horse was going to do anyway. But to understand that, it may be necessary to go back forty years and sit next to your bedroll in front of the Scharbauer Hotel in Midland, waiting for some cowman to come pick you up. If you got a day's work, it might be on a horse that would just love to kill you. It was a far cry from the National Cutting Horse Futurity, but it was the sort of thing Buster began with and lies at the origins of his education as to what horses are going to do anyway.

*

I stayed in the living room to talk to Sheila Welch while, outside the picture window, horses warmed up in the cedar pen. Sheila is a cool beauty, a fine-boned blonde from Wolf Point, Montana, and a leading interpreter, through her refined horsemanship, of Buster's training. She is capable of looking better on Buster's horses than he does and certainly could train a horse herself. Cutting horses move hard and fast enough to make rag dolls of ordinary horsemen, but Sheila goes beyond poise to a kind of serenity. A little bit later, Sheila stood in the pen waiting for someone to give her the big sorrel horse she has used to dispirit the competition for years. When he was brought up, she slipped up into the saddle, eased into the herd, and imperceptibly isolated a single cow in front of her. The horse worked the cow with the signature speed and hard stops; Sheila seemed to float along cooperatively and forcefully at once. But I noticed that in the stops, those places where it is instinctive to grip with one's leg and where it is preferable not to touch the horse at all, there was a vague jingling sound. What was that vague jingling sound? It was the sound of iron stirrups rattling on Sheila's boots. Can't get lighter than that. My own riding came to seem hoggish wallowing, prize-repellent.

At its best, the poetry remains, not in the scared, melodramatic antics of the stunt horses but in the precision of that minority singled out as "cow horses," sometimes lost in the artificial atmosphere of the aged events but sooner or later restored to focus in the years of a good horse's lifetime.

In training horses, Buster's advantage is a broader base of information from which to draw. He frequently starts out under a tree at daybreak with a cup of coffee, reading history, fiction, politics, anything that seems to expand his sense of the world he lives in. This may be a compensatory habit from his abbreviated formal education, and it may be an echo of his revered grandfather's own love of books. In any event, Buster has made of himself far and away the most educated cutting-horse trainer there is. In any serious sense, he is vastly more learned than many of his clients, however exalted their stations in life. And apart from the intrinsic merits of his knowledge, there is a place for it in Buster's work; because an unbroke horse is original unmodeled clay that can be brought to a level of great beauty or else remain in its original muddy form, dully consuming protein with the great mass of living creatures on the planet.

But a cutting horse . . . well, a cutting horse is a work of art.

MIDSTREAM

IN OCTOBER, I looked off the wooden bridge and into the small river I had come to like so well. It was nearly covered with yellow cottonwood leaves; they diagramed its currents as they swept toward each other around the framework of the old boxcar out of which the bridge was made. A cold wind eddied down the river into my face, and I was ready to decide that to everything there is a season and that trout season was over. Fall gives us a vague feeling that the end of everything is at hand; here I felt that when the snow melted in the spring my wonderful little river would be gone.

I don't know if it was literally the first time I saw that river, but it is the first time I remember seeing it. I came down the side of the basin riding a young mare. I could see, first, the tree line of the small river, then, here and there, flashes of its runs and pools as it made its way through the pastureland of its own small valley. There were a few bright and geometric lines where irrigation ditches made diagonals from its more eloquent meanders, and a few small flooded areas where the water had stopped to reflect the clouds and the sky. It was a river with an indifferent fishing reputation.

Young anglers love new rivers the way they love the rest of their lives. Time doesn't seem to be of the essence and somewhere in the system is what they are looking for. Older anglers

set foot on streams the location of whose pools is as yet unknown with a trace of inertia. Like sentimental drunks, they
are interested in what they already know. Yet soon enough,
any river reminds us of others, and the logic of a new one is a
revelation. It's the pools and runs we have already seen that
help us uncode the holding water: the shallow riffle is a
buildup for the cobbled channel where the thick trout nymph
with mirror flashes; the slack back channel with the leafy bottom is not just frog water but a faithful reservoir for the joyous
brook beyond. An undisturbed river is as perfect a thing as we
will ever know, every refractive slide of cold water a glimpse
of eternity.

The first evening I fished the river, I walked through a
meadow that lay at the bottom of a curved red cliff, a swerving
curve with a close-grained mantle of sage and prairie grasses.
It could be that the river cut that curve, then wandered a
quarter-mile south; but there you have it, the narrow shining
band, the red curve, and the prairie. As I sauntered along
with my fly rod, hope began to build in the perceived glamour
of my condition: a deep breath.

"Ah."

There was a stand of mature aspens with hard white trunks
on the edge of meadow and next to the water. The grass was
knee deep. White summer clouds towered without motion.
Once I had crossed to that spot, I could make out the progress
of small animals, fanning away from my approach. I hurried
forward in an attempt to see what they were, and a young
raccoon shot up one of the slick aspens, then, losing traction,
made a slow, baffled descent back into the grass. By shuffling
around, I managed to have four of them either going up or
sliding down at once. They were about a foot tall, and something about their matching size and identical bandit masks,
coupled with their misjudgment of aspens as escape routes,
gave me a sense of real glee at the originality of things. The
new river gurgled in the bank.

I walked in and felt its pull against my legs. Current is a mysterious thing. It is the motion of the river leaving us, and it is as curious and thrilling a thing as a distant train at night. The waters of this new river, pouring from high in a Montana wilderness, are bound for the Gulf of Mexico. The idea that so much as a single molecule of the rushing chute before me was headed for Tampico was as eerie as the moon throwing a salty flood over the tidelands and then retrieving it. Things that pass us, go somewhere else, and don't come back seem to communicate directly with the soul. That the fisherman plies his craft on the surface of such a thing possibly accounts for his contemplative nature.

I once thought that this was somehow not true of aircraft, that they were too new and lacked mystery. But I lived for a time in the mountainous path of B-52 nighttime traffic. The faraway thunder that rose and fell to the west had the same quality of distance and departure that trains and rivers have. One pale summer night, I made out the darkened shape of one of these death ships against the stars, and shivered to think of the freshness of the high prairie where I was living beneath that great bird and its eggs of destruction.

The only bird today was a little water dipper, one of those ouzel-like nervous wrecks that seem not to differentiate between air and water, and stroll through both with aplomb. I associate them with some half-serious elfin twilight, a thing which, like the raccoons, suggests that there is a playful element in creation. I began to feel the animal focus that a river brings on as you unravel the current in search of holding water.

The learning of this river corresponded with the waning of runoff. My casting arm was still cold from winter, and I waded like a spavined donkey. I am always careful to go as light as possible early on, knowing that any little thing will throw me off; and the matter of getting over round, slick rocks, judging the depth and speed of current — things like these start out tough. One feels timid. Later in the year, you make the long, downstream pirouettes in deep fast water that you'd never chance when you're rusty.

It is a matter of ceremony to get rid of stuff. The winter has usually made me yield to some dubious gadgets, and you're at war with such things if the main idea of fishing is to be preserved. The net can go. It snags in brush and catches fly line. If it is properly out of the way, you can't get it at when you need it. Landing fish without a net adds to the trick and makes the whole thing better. Make it one box of flies. I tried to stick to this and ended up buying the king of Wheatlies, a double-sided brute that allows me to cheat on the single-box system. No monofilament clippers. Teeth work great. Trifles like leader sink, flyline cleaner, and geegaws that help you tie knots must go. You may bring the hemostat, because to pinch down barbs and make quick, clean releases of the fabled trout help everything else make sense. Bring a normal rod, with a five- or six-weight line, because in early season the handle you have on hatches is not yet sufficient and you must be prepared to range through maybe eight fly sizes. Weird rod weights reflect armchair fantasies and often produce chagrin on the water.

I began to have a look at the river. It went through hard ground but cut deep. It was like a scribe line at the base of sine and cosine curves of bank banded at the top with a thin layer of topsoil. The river bottom was entirely rocks, small rounded ones, and on either side were the plateaus of similar stones, representing the water levels of thousands of previous years. A few mayflies drifted past in insignificant numbers. I understand that mayflies bear a rather antique genetic code themselves, expressed in size and color, and my hope is that if things pick up, I have the right imitations in my box.

As I face new water, I always ask myself if I am going to fish with a nymph or not. Presumably, you do not walk straight into rising trout. Camus said that the only serious question is whether or not to commit suicide. This is rather like the nymph question. It takes weight, a weighted fly, split shot. Casting becomes a matter of spitting this mess out and being orderly about it. It requires a higher order of streamcraft than any other kind of fishing, because it truly calls upon the angler to see the river in all its dimensions. Gone are the joys of casting, the steady meter and adjustment of loop that compare to walking or rowing. The joys of casting are gone because this ignoble outfit has ruined the action of your fly rod.

Still, you must show purpose. American shame at leisure has produced the latest no-nonsense stance in sport, the "streamside entomologist" and the "headhunter" being the most appalling instances that come readily to mind. No longer sufficiently human to contemplate the relationship of life to eternity, the glandular modern sport worries whether or not he is wasting time. Small towns used to have a mock-notorious character who didn't feel this way, the mythical individual who hung the GONE FISHIN' sign in the window of his establishment. We often made him a barber or someone remote from life-and-death matters. Sometimes we let him be a country doctor, and it was very rakish to drift grubs in a farm pond against the possible background of breech birth or peritonitis. Finally, we took it as very American to stand up and be superfluous in the glaring light of Manifest Destiny.

In the shock and delight of new water, my thoughts were entirely ineffective. What is the relationship of the bottom to the water, to the landscape through which it flows, to the life of the air around it all and the vegetation that alters the wind and interferes with the light? In other words, should one fish that deep outer bank — shaded by a hedge of wild junipers — with a nymph, or would it be better to imitate the few pale morning duns that are drifting around but not yet inspiring any surface feeding? In the latter case, that glassy run below the pool is the spot. For a moment, I avoid the conundrum by turning into another river object, a manlike thing with the unmoving fly rod. Because time has stopped, I really don't concern myself with an eager companion who has already put three on the beach.

Mortality being what it is, any new river could be your last. This charmless notion runs very deep in us and does produce, besides the tightening around the mouth, a sweet and consoling inventory of all the previous rivers in your life. Finally, the fit is so perfect that it gives the illusion that there is but one river, a Platonic gem. There are more variations within any one good river than there are between a number of good rivers. I have been fortunate in that my life-river has a few steelhead in the lower reaches, as well as Oregon harvest trout and the sea-run browns of Ireland; there are Michigan brook trout in the deep bends, braided channels in hundred-mile sections from the Missouri headwaters trout theme park; and here and there are the see-through pools of New Zealand. Fire and water unlock the mind to a kind of mental zero gravity in which resemblances drift toward one another. The trout fisherman finishes his life with but one river.

All this is getting fairly far-fetched; still, like the trout, we must find a way of moving through water with the least amount of displacement. The more we fish, the more weightlessly and quietly we move through a river and among its fish, and the more we resemble our own minds in the bliss of angling.

I came to a pool where a tree with numerous branches had fallen. Its leaves were long gone, and the branches tugged lightly in the slight current that went through the pool. A remarkable thing was happening: a good-size brown was jumping among the lowest branches, clearly knocking insects loose to eat. Every three or four minutes, it vaulted into the brush over its window and fell back into the water. I knew if I could get any kind of a float, I would have a solid taker. I looked at all the angles, and the only idea I could come up with was that it was a good time to light a cigar. In a moment, the excellent smoke of Honduras rose through the cottonwoods. I waited for an idea to form, a solution, but it never happened. In the end, I reared back and fired a size 14 Henryville Caddis into the brush. It wound around a twig and hung in midair. The trout didn't jump at it suicidally. I didn't get the fly back.

Angling doesn't turn on stunts. The steady movements of the habituated gatherer produce the harvest. This of course must be in the service of some real stream knowledge. But some fishing, especially for sea-run fish, rewards a robotic capacity for replicating casts, piling up the repetitions until the strike is induced. The biggest things a steelheader or Atlantic salmon fisherman can have — not counting waders and a stipend — are a big arm and a room-temperature IQ.

The river made an angular move to the south into the faraway smoky hills. In the bend, there was some workmanlike dry-wall riprap that must have reflected the Scandinavian local heritage. The usual western approach would be to roll an old car into the river at the point of erosion. Instead of that, I found neatly laid cobbles that gave the impression that the river was slowly revealing an archaeological enigma or the foundations of a church. But for the next forty yards, the clear water trembled deep and steady over a mottled bottom, and I took three hearty browns that flung themselves upon the bright surface of the run. When I was young and in the thrall of religion, I used to imagine various bands of angels, which were differentiated principally by size. The smallest ones were under a foot in height, silvery and rapid, and able to move in any plane at will. The three trout in that run reminded me of those imaginary beings.

The river lay down at the bottom of a pencil-thin valley, and though I could see the wind in the tops of the trees, I could barely feel it where I fished. The casts stretched out and probed without unwarranted shepherd's crooks, blowbacks, or tippet puddles. I came to a favorite kind of stretch: twenty or thirty yards of very shallow riffle with a deep green slot on the outside curve. In this kind of conformation, you wade in thin, fast water easily and feel a bit of elevation to your quarry. The slot seemed to drain a large oxygenated area, and it was the only good holding water around. Where had I seen so much of this? The Trinity? The Little Deschutes? It had slipped in the telescoping of rivers.

I couldn't float the entire slot without lining part of it. So I covered the bottom of my first casts, doping out the drift as I did, and preparing for the long float in the heart of the spot, one I was sure would raise a fish. The slot was on the left-hand side of the river and contoured the bank, but the riffle drained at an angle to it. I saw that a long, straight cast would drag the fly in a hurry. When the first casts to the lower end failed to produce, I tried a reach cast to the right, got a much better drift, then covered the whole slot with a longer throw.

The Henryville Caddis had floated about two yards when a good brown appeared below it like a beam of butter-colored light. It tipped back, and we were tight. The fish held in the current even though my rod was bent into the cork, then shot out into the shallows for a wild aerial fight. I got it close three times but it managed to churn off through the shallow water. Finally, I had it and turned its cold form upside down in my hand, checked its length against my rod — eighteen inches — and removed the hook. I decided that these were the yellow-est, prettiest stream-bred browns I had ever seen. I turned it over and lowered it into the current. I love the feeling when they realize they are free. There seems to be an amazed pause. Then they shoot out of your hand as though you could easily change your mind.

The afternoon wore on without specific event. The middle of a bright day can be as dull as it is timeless. Visibility is so perfect you forget it is seldom a confidence builder for trout. The little imperfections of the leader, the adamant crinkles standing up from the surface, are clear to both parties.

No sale.

But the shadows of afternoon seem to give meaning to the angler's day on about the same scale that fall gives meaning to his year. As always, I could feel in the first hints of darkness a mutual alertness between me and the trout. This vague shadow the trout and I cross progresses from equinox to equinox. Our mutuality grows.

A ring opened on the surface. The first rise I had seen. The fish refused my all-purpose Adams, and I moved on. I reached an even-depth, even-speed stretch of slick water that deepened along the right-hand bank for no reason: there was no curve to it. The deep side was in shadow, a great, profound, detail-filled shadow that stood along the thin edge of brightness, the starry surface of moving water in late sun. At the head of this run, a plunge pool made a vertical curtain of bubbles in the right-hand corner. At that point, the turbulence narrowed away to a thread of current that could be seen for maybe twenty yards on the smooth run. Trout were working.

I cast to the lowest fish from my angle below and to the left. The evenness of the current gave me an ideal float free of drag. In a moment of hubris I threw the size 14 Adams, covered the fish nicely for about five minutes while it fed above and below. I worked my way to the head of the pool, covering six other fish. quickly, I tied on a Royal Wulff, hoping to shock them into submission. Not a single grab. The fish I covered retired until I went on, then resumed feeding. I was losing my light and had been casting in the middle of rising fish for the better part of an hour: head and tail rises with a slight slurp. There were no spinners in the air, and the thread of the current took whatever it was down through the center of the deep water beyond my vision. This was the first time that day the river had asked me to figure something out; and it was becoming clear that I was not going to catch a fish in this run unless I changed my ways.

I was dealing with the selective trout, that uncompromising

creature in whose spirit the angler attempts to read his own fortune.

I tucked my shirt deep inside the top of my waders and pulled the drawstring tight. I hooked my last unsuccessful fly in the keeper and reeled the line up. Then I waded into the cold, deep run, below the feeding fish. I felt my weight decreasing against the bottom as I inched toward the thread of current that carried whatever the fish were feeding on. By the time I reached it, I was within inches of taking on the river and barely weighed enough to keep myself from joining the other flotsam in the Missouri headwaters. But — and, as my mother used to say, "it's a big but" — I could see coming toward me, some like tiny sloops, some like minute life rafts unfurling, baetis duns: olive-bodied, clear-winged, and a tidy size 18.

I have such a thing, I thought, in my fly box.

By the time I had moon-walked back to a depth where my weight meant something, I had just enough time to test my failing eyes against the little olive-emergers and a 6X tippet viewed straight over my head in the final light. Finally, the thing was done and I was ready to cast. The fly seemed to float straight downward in the air and down the sucking hole the trout made. It was another short, thick, buttery brown, and it was the one that kept me from flunking my first day on that river. It's hard to know ahead of time which fish is giving the test.